The Union Sixth
Army Corps in the
Chancellorsville Campaign

The Union Sixth Army Corps in the Chancellorsville Campaign

A Study of the Engagements of Second Fredericksburg, Salem Church and Banks's Ford, May 3–4, 1863

PHILIP W. PARSONS

FOREWORD BY MAC WYCKOFF

McFarland & Company, Inc., Publishers

Jefferson, North Carolina, and London

The present work is a reprint of the illustrated case bound edition of
The Union Sixth Army Corps in the Chancellorsville Campaign:
A Study of the Engagements of Second Fredericksburg, Salem
Church and Banks's Ford, May 3–4, 1863, *first published in 2006
by McFarland.*

Map Sources: John Bigelow, *The Campaign of Chancellorsville;* Troop Movement Maps,
Chancellorsville, National Park Service; *Official Records Atlas;* Jedediah Hotchkiss and
William Allan, *Chancellorsville;* National Archives Washington, D.C., Civil War Map File, RG 77.

LIBRARY OF CONGRESS CATALOGUING-IN-PUBLICATION DATA

Parsons, Philip W., 1959–
The Union Sixth Army Corps in the Chancellorsville Campaign : a study
of the engagements of Second Fredericksburg, Salem Church and
Banks's Ford, May 3–4, 1863 / Philip W. Parsons ; foreword by Mac Wyckoff.
p.   cm.
Includes bibliographical references and index.

ISBN 978-0-7864-6112-7
softcover : 50# alkaline paper ∞

1. Chancellorsville, Battle of, Chancellorsville, Va., 1863.
2. United States. Army. Corps, 6th (1862–1865)
3. Sedgwick, John, 1813–1864 — Military leadership.
4. Command of troops — Case studies.
5. United States — History — Civil War, 1861–1865 — Regimental histories.
6. Battles — Virginia — Chancellorsville Region — History —19th century.
7. Battles — Virginia — Fredericksburg Region — History —19th century.
8. Virginia — History — Civil War, 1861–1865 — Campaigns.
9. United States — History — Civil War, 1861–1865 — Campaigns. I. Title.
E475.35.P28   2010   973.7'33 — dc22   2006019833

British Library cataloguing data are available

On the cover: *Vermont Division at the Battle of Chancellorsville,*
Julian Scott, oil on canvas 48" × 72", 1871–1872 (Sotheby's)

Manufactured in the United States of America

*McFarland & Company, Inc., Publishers
Box 611, Jefferson, North Carolina 28640
www.mcfarlandpub.com*

Acknowledgments

In the course of writing this book, I have compiled many debts. The endnotes in the text identify some but not all of the intellectual debts that I owe to the many historians of the American Civil War that have preceded me. I would not have been able to amass sufficient resource material without help from numerous institutions, repositories, and individuals. The assistance I received while researching this book is greatly appreciated and is a debt not easily repaid.

Libraries are the single most important mechanism historians have at their disposal. I would like to extend thanks to the Maine State Library System with a special thanks to the staffs of the Fogler Library at the University of Maine, Orono, and the Bangor Public Library in Bangor, Maine. Without the Special Collections and excellent Inter-Library Loan Departments of these institutions, this book would not have been possible.

A sincere thanks is in order for the archival staffs of numerous institutions: Bailey-Howe Library, University of Vermont; Maine State Archives, Augusta; Fifth Maine Community Center, Peaks Island, Maine; Fairbanks Museum and Planetarium, St. Johnsbury, Vermont; Fredericksburg and Spotsylvania National Military Park, Fredericksburg, Virginia; Georgia Archives, Atlanta; Maine Historical Society, Portland; Museum of the Confederacy, Richmond, Virginia; Shelburne Museum, Shelburne, Vermont; United Daughters of the Confederacy, Richmond, Virginia; United States Military History Institute, Carlisle, Pennsylvania; Wilson Library, University of North Carolina, Chapel Hill; Vermont Historical Society, Barre; Western Reserve Historical Society Library, Cleveland, Ohio.

It is impossible to thank every individual who helped me complete this work, but there are some meriting special commendation. The park historian at Fredericksburg and Spotsylvania National Military Park, Mac Wyckoff, provided valuable assistance on my visits to Fredericksburg. Noted Civil War author and historian Jeffry Wert analyzed my manuscript and offered valuable advice. Donald C. Pfanz, staff historian at Fredericksburg and Spotsylvania National Military Park, reviewed parts of my manuscript and remarked on several points. Charlotte Ray in Atlanta located research material on various Georgia regiments. Paul Carnahan's assistance proved valuable at the

Vermont Historical Society. Thanks to John Pingree, who graciously allowed access to the Pingree Papers, and librarian/historian Kelly A. Nolin who originally did transcription. Thanks to Joan Huguenin and fellow members of the Northeast Kingdom Civil War Roundtable. Tony Pare read my manuscript and made suggestions. Tom Ledoux, Webmaster of Vermont in the Civil War, proved a valuable resource. Thanks to Gordon McRea and friends of the Richardson Roundtable in Sandy Point, Maine. Peg Killian closely read my manuscript and helped me put my words into final draft form.

I deeply appreciate the help of my family. I especially want to thank my wife Mary and daughters Kate, Emma, and Beth for their unfaltering love and support during the writing of this book. My mother, Carol Parsons, was very helpful by volunteering to read drafts of my manuscript. My sister Gail Doherty, my brother Steve Parsons, and their families were continuously supportive.

Finally, I want to thank my father, George, for instilling in me a love and appreciation of history. Few students of the American Civil War know more about the soldiers who fought under the Old Greek Cross than my dad. His breadth of understanding relating to the American Civil War is truly remarkable. To this end, I affectionately dedicate this book to my dad, George W. Parsons.

Contents

Foreword
by Mac Wyckoff

By January 1863 the Confederate States of America had accomplished great gains in establishing itself as a sovereign nation. On the battlefield Confederate armies in the western theater of war had repulsed attempts by Union forces to control the Mississippi River and split the Confederacy. In the east the largest Union force, the Army of the Potomac, was still recoiling from the December 1862 defeat at Fredericksburg, Virginia. Overall, the war to reunite the states had progressed poorly.

In the aftermath of the Union debacle at Fredericksburg, President Abraham Lincoln accepted the resignation of General Ambrose Burnside as commander of the Army of the Potomac. The President appointed Major General Joseph Hooker, known as "Fighting Joe," to command the army on January 25, 1863. Up to this point in the war, Hooker had proven himself as an aggressive general officer. On the other hand, he was a controversial figure known to be outspoken and apt to criticize his superior officer's command decisions.

Upon being given command, Hooker found the Army of the Potomac in tough shape and still licking their wounds suffered during the Fredericksburg defeat. Sick rolls had swelled into the thousands, rations were poor, and discipline and high morale were nonexistent. Union encampments were in disrepair and soldiers were deserting at a rate of two hundred a day. Sanitary conditions in many of the smoldering camps along the Rappahannock River were horrible as regiments strived to exist in the dreary camps. Long periods of cold rain, sleet, and snow added insult to injury, making living conditions miserable for the Union infantrymen. The winter of 1862–63 was the snowiest winter in central Virginia recorded history.

Throughout the winter of 1862–63, the fighting man of the Army of the Potomac had much time to ponder on the past two years of war. Many soldiers felt betrayed by their government and believed Washington had conducted the war poorly up to this point. Many men were unsure and disgruntled over Lincoln's Emancipation Proclamation, which had just become law on the first day of January 1863. Northern volunteers had fought and died to save their Union, but now the administration in Washington had altered the objective of the war.

As the contending armies observed each other from across the Rappahannock, Hooker went to work on rebuilding the Army of the Potomac. To curb desertion, he established a generous furlough program and implemented a system of corps insignia to easily identify soldiers and determine if they were at their proper place of duty. The Union camps were cleaned while new sanitary standards were set. Rations were now prepared by trained cooks. Soft bread and vegetables upgraded the men's diets. Daily company and battalion drill was conducted along with periodic parades and reviews helping to instill an *espirit de corps* among units.

The administrative efforts of the new army commander were effective. Hooker revamped the entire army's supply system. He sanctioned the reorganization of medical personnel, who established a very efficient Ambulance Corps. The Grand Divisions established by Burnside were abolished as Hooker opted for seven infantry corps commanders who all dealt directly with the army commander. A Bureau of Intelligence was created to control the information flow in and out of the Army of the Potomac's massive encampment. Hooker's artillery was redistributed to the divisions of each corps, and individual batteries could only be transferred under the authority of the chief of artillery, Brigadier General Henry J. Hunt. To improve the combat effectiveness of the cavalry branch, Hooker merged his cavalry regiments into one combined corps under Major General George Stoneman. Overall, Hooker did an outstanding job of uplifting morale and reorganizing the Army of the Potomac into an efficient war machine.

The disastrous experience at the stone wall in the first battle of Fredericksburg had revealed the need for Civil War armies to entrench. While the Northern soldiers remained in their winter camps, the Confederates strengthened their position on the heights west and south of the city. This gave Hooker time to prepare an excellent and complex plan to deal with the Confederate stronghold behind Fredericksburg.

History will attest that Hooker's attempt to defeat Robert E. Lee during the Chancellorsville Campaign failed and the Army of Northern Virginia won an important victory for the Confederate States of America. Lee seized control of the battlefield and masterfully divided his smaller force to engage Union forces when and where he wanted. Hooker never fully committed his entire army to battle and even when the situation did favor his larger force, he remained passive and failed to initiate an assault on the Army of Northern Virginia. Hooker refused to accept responsibility for the Chancellorsville defeat. Although he personally issued orders for his army to withdraw, he sought individuals to blame for the Army of the Potomac's defeat including the commander of the Sixth Corps.

The Sixth Corps seemed an unlikely target as a scapegoat. They enjoyed the only victory in the campaign and suffered more casualties than any other Union corps engaged in the Chancellorsville Campaign. Major General John Sedgwick did not directly come to Hooker's aid, though he did draw off much of Lee's army. Hooker failed to capitalize on this opportunity to destroy Jackson's Corps to his front and never advanced to Sedgwick's aid. In the final analysis, blame for the Union loss in the Chancellorsville Campaign rests squarely on the shoulders of Joseph Hooker.

The Sixth Corps learned a valuable lesson at Second Fredericksburg. A well coordinated attack using the element of speed to quickly get upon the opponent was an effective offensive weapon. This tactic would be used again by the Sixth Corps in subsequent actions: at Rappahannock Station on November 9, 1863, in Emory Upton's Charge at Spotsylvania on May 10, 1864, at Cold Harbor on June 1, 1864, and most importantly in the final assault at Petersburg on April 2, 1865. The success at Second Fredericksburg led to high *espirit de corps* among Sedgwick's men. This high morale and confidence combined with the tactic first used at Second Fredericksburg would lead to important Sixth Corps successes in the final year of the war.

To many, the Chancellorsville Campaign consists simply of "Stonewall" Jackson's flank march, attack, wounding, and death. In reality, it was one of the larger campaigns of the Civil War in complexity and in terms of ground fought and maneuvered over. There is a conduit linking the lack of understanding of the whole campaign to lack of conservation of the battlefield. Lack of understanding of the campaign has led to lack of conservation of the battlefield, which in turn contributes to further lack of understanding. It is a classic catch-22.

The battlefields associated with the Chancellorsville campaign sprawl across the city of Fredericksburg and the county of Spotsylvania. By the late 1960s the city and county governments favored development over preservation. Today the area has become part of suburban Washington, D.C., with shopping malls and subdivisions sprawling across the hallowed ground where Robert E. Lee had won his masterpiece a century before. Preservation success has not come as easily for preservationists as it did for "Marse Robert" at Chancellorsville. In the last two decades several books, articles, and essays have helped tell the story. Philip Parsons's book makes a major contribution to our understanding of the Sixth Corps in the Chancellorsville Campaign.

Fredericksburg, Virginia
June 2006

Mac Wyckoff is the park historian at Fredericksburg and Spotsylvania National Military Park.

I respectfully request that the regiments and batteries of the corps be permitted to inscribe "Fredericksburg" and "Salem Heights" on their colors. It is an honor they have bravely earned.

I am general, very respectfully, your obedient servant,
John
Sedgwick
Major General Commanding Sixth Army Corps.

Brig. Gen. S. Williams
Assistant Adjutant-General, Army of the Potomac.

(*Official Records, May 15, 1863*)

Preface

In the eastern theater of war, a shift occurred in the primary military objective of the Union's Army of the Potomac. The frequently heralded campaign cry of "On to Richmond" ceased to be voiced by the Federal high command in Washington following Major General Ambrose E. Burnside's disastrous Fredericksburg Campaign. In the spring of 1863, the essential mission for the Army of the Potomac became the destruction of Robert E. Lee's Army of Northern Virginia. In order to accomplish this formidable task, the newly promoted Major General Joseph Hooker led the Army of the Potomac on a carefully fashioned campaign to bring battle to Lee's army.

General Lee's Army of Northern Virginia defended a strong line of entrenchments running along the hills behind the city of Fredericksburg, Virginia. In an effort to avoid directly assaulting these elaborate Confederate earthworks, Major General Joseph Hooker maneuvered his army to outflank the Army of Northern Virginia and fight on ground more favorable to the Army of the Potomac. Hooker's offensive operations resulted in fighting on three combat fronts cumulating into the famous Chancellorsville Campaign.

Hooker's well-planned offensive began by dispatching Major General George Stoneman and his 11,000 Union horse soldiers on a raid far to the rear of the Army of Northern Virginia. Stoneman's less than successful cavalry foray was an attempt by Hooker to sever Lee's communication with the Confederacy's capital of Richmond, Virginia. Simultaneously, two major combat fronts developed as Hooker infantry operations unfolded. Below Fredericksburg the commander of the Sixth Army Corps made a demonstration on Lee's front, while the remainder of the Army of the Potomac marched on a roundabout trek to turn the left flank of Lee's army. Initially successful, Hooker gained his opponent's flank and seriously threatened to turn Lee's entrenched position behind Fredericksburg. Heavy fighting occurred on both infantry fronts, but Hooker's plan to bring battle to the Army of Northern Virginia failed to be put into effect and Lee won an impressive victory for the Confederate States of America.

Although an integral part of Major General Joseph Hooker's overall strategic plan, the operations of the Sixth Army Corps during the Chancellorsville Campaign were isolated actions conducted independently from the combat experienced by the bulk of the Army of the Potomac. There have been numerous volumes written on the Chancellorsville Campaign, but many accounts are strangely short on their coverage of the Sixth Corps engagements at Second Fredericksburg, Salem Church, and Banks's Ford. The limited coverage given to Sixth Corps operations leaves these battlefields obscure and greatly diminishes their significance to Hooker's offensive.

The decision to write only about the Union Sixth Army Corps in the Chancellorsville Campaign came about due to recent campaign interpretations concerning the combat actions of the corps. For more than a century, historians hailed the Sixth Corps' efforts as extraordinary and comprised of the most admirable events of the campaign. For example, a *National Tribune* article dated January 27, 1910, claimed, "This assault and capture of Marye's Heights, and the successful withdrawal by Gen. Sedgwick, of the Sixth Corps, from its perilous position when Lee was hurling his whole army upon it, was the most brilliant thing in the Chancellorsville Campaign."[1]

There is recent suggestion that the operations of the Sixth Corps were inconsequential, or even more troubling, were a major cause of the Union defeat. Chancellorsville Campaign accounts that portrait the actions of the Sixth Corps in a negative fashion signified to me that the engagements fought by the corps during the Chancellorsville Campaign were being cast only a brief look and subsequently neglected by many present-day students of the American Civil War.

The tendency to glance over the battles of Second Fredericksburg, Salem Church, and Banks's Ford frequently comes about as authors endeavor to capture all facets of Hooker's eight-day offensive, while striving at the same time to keep their narrative moving. To prevent concurrent Chancellorsville Campaign happenings from overshadowing Sixth Corps operations, the focus of this military history remains on the Sixth Corps engagements of May 3 and 4, 1863. The aim of this work is not to portray Sixth Corps operations during the Chancellorsville campaign as paramount to the battles fought by the remainder of the Army of the Potomac. This careful study of the engagements of Second Fredericksburg, Salem Church, and Banks's Ford is presented to shed light on these often forgotten battlegrounds and to evaluate the impact these combat actions had on Major General Hooker's misfired offensive.

The battles of Second Fredericksburg, Salem Church, and Banks's Ford marked the first time soldiers under the Greek Cross banners (the corps insignia) of the Sixth Corps independently went into action. The fighting done during these engagements greatly strengthened confidence within the Sixth Corps by providing a valuable boost in *esprit de corps*. A staff officer with the Sixth Corps reflected on these combat actions and explained, "This was glory enough for our young hearts and we began to be eager for the time when we could meet the enemy again." The battles of Second Fredericksburg, Salem Church, and Banks's Ford helped forge the Sixth Corps into what one renowned military historian has termed "probably the best fighting corps in the Army of the Potomac."[2]

At the close of the Chancellorsville Campaign, the regiments and brigades belonging to the Army of the Potomac deservedly acknowledged their participation in Major General Hooker's offensive by adding the name Chancellorsville to their standards.

Chancellorsville is not one of the official recorded battle honors of the Army of the Potomac's Sixth Corps. Contemporary observers would not have eyed Chancellorsville inscribed on any Sixth Corps banner, but likely would have noticed the titles Second Fredericksburg and Salem Heights proudly displayed.[3]

Following the Chancellorsville Campaign, Major General Hooker found it difficult to accept the stark reality of battlefield defeat. The army commander made great efforts to shift blame for the loss away from himself, and openly cast aspersions on several subordinate officers. The Sixth Army Corps became one of Hooker's main targets of condemnation. Hooker's finger-pointing naturally brewed dissention within his army, which helped foster a lingering animosity among many participants. Disagreement concerning the conduct of Major General Hooker during the Chancellorsville Campaign continues to spark discussion as military historians flesh out new research materials to bolster their campaign interpretations. The significance Hooker placed on Sixth Corps actions and his ensuing criticism of their Chancellorsville Campaign performance provides grounds for an exclusive examination.

Roughly two years after the Chancellorsville Campaign, following Lee's surrender at Appomattox Courthouse, Major General William Tecumseh Sherman passed through Spotsylvania County, Virginia, as his army marched home toward Washington. While encamped near the war-torn city of Fredericksburg, many soldiers, including Sherman, toured the silent battlefields encompassing the Chancellorsville and Fredericksburg areas. Arriving at Salem Church, Sherman caught sight of the unburied skeletal remains of American soldiers who had lost their lives on this field and others collected from surrounding battlegrounds. Upon reaching the country's capital, Sherman recounted the sights he had seen at Salem Church to the War Department. Sherman's report prompted Congress, in July 1865, to establish a National Cemetery at Fredericksburg, Virginia, in honor of the Federal soldiers who sacrificed their lives to preserve the Union. Local residents and organizations paid homage to Confederate soldiers who paid the ultimate price for their cause by creating the Fredericksburg and Spotsylvania Confederate cemeteries.[4]

Today Fredericksburg National Cemetery is located on Marye's Heights within the borders of Fredericksburg and Spotsylvania National Military Park. Established in 1927, Fredericksburg and Spotsylvania National Military Park preserve portions of the ground associated with the campaigns of Fredericksburg, Chancellorsville, and the battles of the Wilderness and Spotsylvania Courthouse. Many of America's historical landscapes are outside the boundaries of National Parks and are in danger of being lost forever to urban sprawl. Please become involved and support the preservation of Civil War battle sites.

CHAPTER 1

"No Advance Beyond Chancellorsville..."

In an attempt to flank Robert E. Lee's Army of Northern Virginia, the commander of the Union's Army of the Potomac, Major General Joseph Hooker, initiated an intricate offensive operation. The morale of the Army of the Potomac was high as the spring offensive got under way. Hooker's earlier efforts to improve conditions within the Army of the Potomac had paid great dividends, as his army's level of optimism was clearly evident. The army commander boasted during an interview that he commanded "the finest army on the planet."[1]

Prior to the opening of the campaign, Hooker had kept his own council when it came to his upcoming plan of operation. Being one who never was at a loss for words, Major General Hooker was eager to let people know what he thought of his stratagem: "My plans are perfect, and when I start to carry them out, may God have mercy on General Lee, for I will have none!" On April 11, 1863, an outline of Hooker's plan of attack was hand carried to President Lincoln by the Army of the Potomac's chief of staff, Major General Daniel Butterfield.[2]

Hooker's proposal was skillfully devised. Orders for Major General George Stoneman's Union cavalry instructed they circle far behind the Army of Northern Virginia's position and sever Lee's communications with Richmond. Hooker's infantry operations were fashioned to give the impression that the main Union thrust across the Rappahannock River would come from just above Fredericksburg, at Banks's Ford and United States Mine Ford. In conjunction with Federal troops operating at these fords, a large Federal force under Major General John Sedgwick would demonstrate below the city of Fredericksburg to hold Lee's attention. As all this was developing, the Fifth, Eleventh, and Twelfth Corps, under temporary command of Major General Henry Slocum, were to cross unnoticed farther upriver at Kelly's Ford and outflank Lee's entrenched army.

After crossing the Rappahannock, Hooker's flanking Union column planned to move southeast, crossing the Rapidan River and proceed down the southern bank of the Rappahannock to uncover United States Mine Ford. This route would enable the Union Second Corps to cross the Rappahannock at United States Mine Ford and join Hooker's force advancing on Lee's left. Continuing on this line of march, the Union flanking force would pass through the wooded area surrounding Chancellorsville Crossroads and gain the heights west of Fredericksburg. If Lee was to move to the offensive against the Federal flanking force, Slocum was to take a defensive position near Chancellorsville to receive the attack. If not attacked, Slocum was to continue on this line of march, rendering Lee's impregnable entrenchments behind Fredericksburg untenable. The Army of Northern Virginia would find itself between Slocum's advancing troops and a solid Federal force under Sedgwick. Figuratively, Slocum was a large swinging sledgehammer and Sedgwick was an anvil. Lee would be forced to retreat or else fight Hooker's force on ground more favorable to the much larger Army of the Potomac.[3]

Maneuvering the 130,000 troops of the Army of the Potomac would be no small task for Major General Hooker. The territory surrounding Fredericksburg consisted mostly of wooded tracts of land broken by farmland and small homesteads. The majority of roads that laced the Fredericksburg and Chancellorsville Crossroads areas were small, unimproved wagon lanes, which could quickly become impassable due to mud. The chief topographical engineer for the Army of the Potomac, Major General Gouverneur K. Warren, later described this part of Virginia as "a region whose characteristics is a dense forest of oak or pine, with occasional clearings, rarely extensive enough to prevent the rifle-men concealed in one border from shooting across the other side; a forest which, but few exceptions, required the axmen to precede the artillery from the slashings in front of the fortifications of Washington to those of Richmond."[4]

Across the Rappahannock River, Robert E. Lee's Army of Northern Virginia was strongly entrenched along the hills overlooking the city of Fredericksburg, Virginia. Prior to the war Fredericksburg was an important railroad link between Washington and Richmond, but in 1863 the presence of warring armies had laid much of the area to waste. The great natural strength of the hills behind Fredericksburg was improved on by many months of pick and spade work performed by Confederate infantrymen.

Lee's earthworks stretched up river some twenty miles from Port Royal northwest behind the city of Fredericksburg to Banks's Ford. Lee's Second Corps, under Lieutenant General Thomas J. "Stonewall" Jackson, stretched from the far right of Lee's defensive position up to but not including the hills that rose directly to the rear of Fredericksburg, known as Marye's Heights. The sector of entrenchments extending along Marye's Heights toward Banks's Ford was occupied by First Corps troops under Lieutenant General James Longstreet.

Among these imposing entrenchments were gun emplacements that commanded the city of Fredericksburg and the adjacent open plain. Closer to the river, batteries guarded likely crossing points the Federals might attempt to use. Two hundred and thirty-two guns comprised Lee's twelve artillery battalions and were under the overall command of the Army of Northern Virginia's chief of artillery, Brigadier General William Pendleton. Detachments from Major General James E.B. Stuart's cavalry division actively patrolled both flanks of Lee's army.[5]

The muster rolls for Lee's seasoned force at the start of the Chancellorsville Campaign listed just over 60,000 men ready for action. Lee's First Corps commander, Lieutenant General James Longstreet, and three of his divisions were on detached duty at Southside, Virginia, to guard against Federal raids along the coast. General Lee would sorely miss Longstreet's 20,000 infantrymen and thirty-five cannon during the Chancellorsville Campaign. "Old Pete" Longstreet's other First Corps divisions, under Major General Lafayette McLaws and Major General Richard H. Anderson, remained with Lee in his winter camp behind Fredericksburg.[6]

Lee's hardened veterans acquired supplies by way of the Richmond, Fredericksburg, and Potomac Railroad (R.F. & P.) in conjunction with the Virginia Central Railroad. Adequate quantities of supplies were forwarded into Virginia to Hanover Junction and on to advanced depots at Chesterfield, Guiney's Station and Hamilton's Crossing. The local food supply in the surrounding Virginia countryside had been exhausted. Poor road conditions along with the South's limited rail system made it difficult for Jefferson Davis and his fledgling government to transport food and forage throughout the Confederacy.

Major General Joseph Hooker, commander of the army of the Potomac (Massachusetts MOLLUS Collection, U.S. Military History Instutue).

Memories of past triumphs remained strong in the minds and hearts of Lee's warriors. Although existing on short rations, the Army of Northern Virginia maintained great confidence in their commanders and wholeheartedly expected to whip the invading Yankees. Sergeant Reuben A. Pierson of the 7th Louisiana wrote, "I am in excellent health; in fact all of the troops in this department of the southern army are in most excellent condition every way, well armed — well clad — in high spirits — very sanguine of victory whenever the hour comes to meet our enemies."[7]

On April 12, 1863, Hooker's spring offensive had begun to unfold. Orders were sent out from the Army of the Potomac's headquarters at Falmouth, Virginia, for Major General Stoneman to be ready to move the next day at sunrise. Each well-equipped

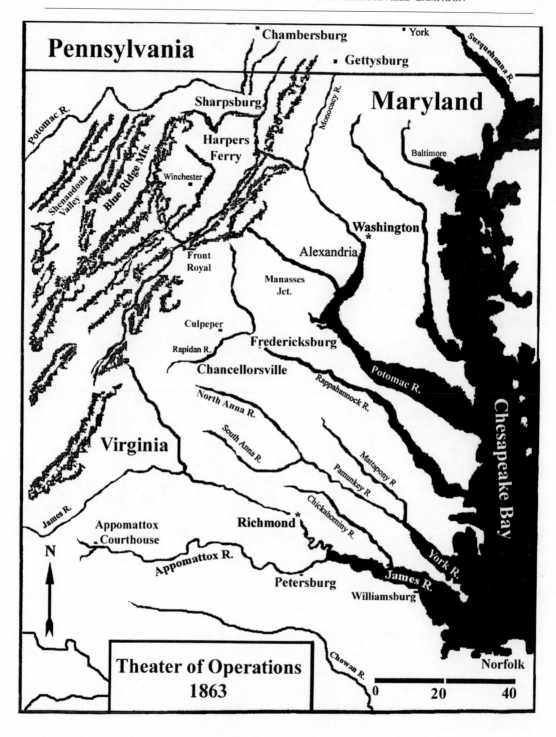

Theater of Operations, 1863.

Federal cavalryman would carry three days' rations and grain, with at least forty rounds of ammunition for his carbine and twenty for his revolver. Wagon trains would carry an additional eight days of food for the men and horses. One small cavalry brigade consisting of three regiments, under Brigadier General Alfred Pleasonton, would remain at Falmouth with Hooker to act as advance guards for Union infantry columns.

Stoneman's assignment was a rather large undertaking, especially for a new corps commander in charge of troopers who had never gone into action together as a combined cavalry force. Stoneman's mission statement, as explained by Hooker, read, "...for the purpose of turning the enemy's position on his left, and of throwing your command between him and Richmond, and isolating him from his supplies, checking his retreat, and inflicting on him every possible injury which would tend to his discomfiture and defeat." Hooker held great

General Robert E. Lee (C.S.A), commander of the Army of Northern Virginia (Massachusetts MOLLUS Collection, U.S. Military History Institute).

expectations for his newly reorganized cavalry and would rely heavily on their success.[8]

After a slow start Stoneman's two columns of 10,000 sabers and twelve guns crept along the muddy roads leading up the Rappahannock River, toward Beverly Ford. Before the main body arrived at the ford heavy rains fell, causing the waters of the Rappahannock to rise significantly. Stoneman chose to call a halt and wait out the rains north of the swollen Rappahannock. For two weeks the Federal cavalry commander remained encamped near Warrenton Junction on the Orange and Alexandria Railroad.[9]

Rainy weather and muddy roads also delayed Hooker from launching his infantry's advance. Hooker initiated some false moves, in an effort to keep Lee guessing. Bogus messages were intentionally wigwagged up and down the Rappahannock to be intercepted by Lee's signalmen. On April 19, a more elaborate ruse began as Hooker sent Brigadier General Abner Doubleday's Third Division, First Corps, twenty miles down the banks of Rappahannock to Port Conway, opposite Port Royal. These troops were to feign a river crossing at that point. Doubleday's skirmishers actually crossed the river in boats, but were quickly recalled as orders were received from Hooker to return to Falmouth. Doubleday's foot soldiers arrived back at Falmouth on April 22.[10]

On April 26, Hooker was ready to move and issued preemptory orders for his infantry advance. Before dawn of the following day, carrying eight days' rations, Major

General Oliver O. Howard's Eleventh Corps and Major General Henry W. Slocum's Twelfth Corps were put into motion in a northwesterly direction up the Rappahannock River. To prevent being observed by the Confederates, their journey took them away from the river on a twenty-seven-mile trek toward Kelly's Ford.

Each infantry corps would march with one battery and two ambulances to a division. A pack mule train of small arms ammunition would accompany the column in lieu of the standard ordnance wagons. A small number of wagons would accompany the column to camp with forage for horses and mules. Beef cattle and the balance of Hooker's trains remained out of sight of the enemy in the vicinity of Banks's Ford. To prevent detection by the enemy, strict orders were issued prohibiting the troops from approaching the river or lighting campfires. The Eleventh and Twelfth corps bivouacked for the night at Hartwood Church, fifteen miles shy of Kelly's Ford. Later that night, these troops were joined by Major General George G. Meade and his Fifth Corps.[11]

The weather was mild, and spirits were high as Hooker's infantry marched. Once out of earshot of their enemy, the long Federal columns periodically sounded-off with loud cheers or song. One popular verse occasionally cadenced out by Hooker's foot soldiers on this long march stated:

> The Union boys are moving on the left and on the right, the bugle call is sounding, our shelters we must strike; Joe Hooker is our leader, he takes his whiskey strong, so our knapsacks we will sling, and go marching along.[12]

As these troops wound their way up river, Union Second Corps commander Major General Darius N. Couch received orders to move at sunrise of the following day. On Tuesday the 28th of April, Private James Daniels of the 5th New Hampshire noted, "Orders came to march; broke camp and marched at 7:00 A.M. Camped at night in front of a man's house. Rained all day." Two of Couch's divisions moved from their camp at Falmouth up river to the vicinity of Banks's Ford. Lieutenant Colonel Charles E. Hapgood commanding the 5th New Hampshire recalled, "A detail was posted at every crossroad and at every house on our front, and all communication towards the enemy's line stopped." Within plain view of Confederate pickets, Second Corps troops established themselves along the Banks's Ford road leading along the slopes edging the river in this area.[13]

Second Corps' regimental commanders had their men commence corduroying the muddy roads in an effort to give the appearance of a Federal crossing. "We commenced at once making demonstrations to attract the attention of the enemy such as cutting down trees, opening roads to the bank of the river, measuring distances with a tape line, &c, in order that they might see us with their glasses and think the crossing was intended to take place there," recalled a member of the 50th New York Volunteer Engineers. One of Couch's brigades, accompanied by a battery, also advanced farther up river to the vicinity of United States Mine Ford. As all this developed, Brigadier General John Gibbon remained headquartered at James Horace Lacy's house, "Chatham," directly opposite the city of Fredericksburg. Gibbon's encamped soldiers lingered within easy eyesight of Confederate picket outposts across the river.[14]

Almost forty miles up the swollen Rappahannock River, near Warrenton Junction, Major General Stoneman received a supplemental order modifying his original instructions. Due to the weather delay, he was now to cross his Union cavalry somewhere between Kelly's Ford and Rappahannock Ford. The cavalry chief was to detach a portion of his command under Brigadier General William W. Averell to move in the direction of Louisa Court House and raid along the Orange and Alexandria Railroad. Stoneman would take the larger cavalry force and advance to destroy the Richmond, Fredericksburg, and Potomac (R.F. & P.) Railroad, crippling Lee's army by severing its supply line.[15]

General Lee received a message from his Confederate cavalry chief, Major General J.E.B. Stuart, on the evening of April 28. Stuart notified Lee of a Federal force of all arms moving up the Rappahannock in the direction of Kelly's Ford. Lee felt it would be very difficult to prevent the Federals from crossing the Rappahannock. He reported, "As in the first battle of Fredericksburg, it was thought best to select positions with the view to resist the advance of the enemy, rather than incur the heavy loss that would attend any attempt to prevent his crossing."[16]

Advanced Federal detachments from Slocum's flanking force arrived at Kelly's Ford just before dark on the 28th. At the crossing point the 73rd Pennsylvania opened a lively fire with the Confederate outposts on the far bank. Unobserved, a short distance below the ford at Marsh Run, Federal skirmishers of the Eleventh Corps rapidly crossed the Rappahannock in pontoon boats. The Confederate pickets guarding the crossing were outflanked and many could not avoid capture. Surviving Confederate pickets escaped with the news of the Federal crossing. Detachments of the 15th New York Engineers and an abutment party went to work positioning bridging material at the edge of the river. Support wagons were quickly unloaded as pontooniers prepared for the laying of a canvas pontoon bridge across the swollen Rappahannock River.

Brigadier General Henry Benham's Engineer Brigade consisted of the 15th New York, 50th New York, and a Regular Army battalion of U.S. Engineers. The volunteers of the 15th and 50th New York regiments consisted of Erie Canal boatmen and construction laborers recruited from upstate New York. Trained as miners, sappers, and pontooniers, these often forgotten construction workers performed vital duties, much of the time exposed to enemy fire.

Dirt roads made miserable by rain slowed the Federal infantry's progress. Leather knapsack straps bit into the men's shoulders as they tramped along in their wet, ankle-high peg shoes. The sides of the roads were strewn with accouterments the infantrymen had tossed aside to lessen their loads. Marching along or at short halts, troops lightened their backpacks by unloading overcoats, blankets, rations, and even some of the sixty rounds of ammunition issued to each man. Shortly after this campaign Chief Quartermaster Rufus Ingalls would attempt to reduce this waste by shortening the standard infantrymen's packing list. Future long marches and warmer weather would compel quartermasters to suggest infantrymen be allowed to stop wearing the cumbersome army issued knapsack in favor of the rubber blanket rolled and carried diagonally across the shoulder.[17]

By 7:45 P.M. on April 28, the head of Hooker's flanking force had moved north to Kelly's Ford. Engineers continued to work on the lengthy pontoon bridge. Benham's Engineer Brigade would use a total of nine pontoon bridges during the Chancellorsville Campaign. Two types of pontoon boats were available to Benham's engineers, the standard double-ended wooden pontoon boat and the state of the art Waterman Canvas Pontoon. The canvas pontoon or "flying pontoon" was chosen to accompany Hooker's flanking force due to its light weight. Weighing in at about half the weight of a standard wooden pontoon, the canvas pontoon tipped the scales at a mere 640 pounds. Throughout the campaign, five of Benham's bridges would be laid and then re-laid at different locations. Of the fourteen bridges built, the canvas pontoon bridge constructed at Kelly's Ford would stretch the longest, measuring nearly three hundred feet in length.[18]

Hooker had moved his headquarters from Falmouth to Morrisville, five miles east of Kelly's Ford. His chief of staff, Major General Butterfield, remained behind at Falmouth to coordinate between the Federals operating in the Fredericksburg area and Hooker's flanking forces. Around 10:00 P.M., the Federal flanking force commenced crossing the bobbing bridge over the Rappahannock. In a shroud of fog, Howard's 12,977-man Eleventh Corps, preceded by the 17th Pennsylvania Cavalry Regiment, crossed the canvas pontoon bridge. Completing their crossing by daylight, the Eleventh Corps established a perimeter enabling the Twelfth and Fifth Corps to cross unharmed.[19]

Skirmishers from Major General Stuart's cavalry observed from a safe distance in order to discover the Federals route of travel. Sporadic skirmishing erupted along the Federals' path. Following the Federals' crossing, Confederate cavalry commander Stuart reported, "We captured prisoners from three army corps — Eleventh [Howard's], Twelfth [Slocum's], and Fifth [Meade's], and soon after learned that the column had marched direct for Germanna Ford." This intelligence was telegraphed to the Army of Northern Virginia's commanding general. Lee wired his chief of artillery Brigadier General William N. Pendleton at Chesterfield Depot, and ordered forward all his artillery.[20]

Stoneman's troubled Federal cavalry finally arrived at Kelly's Ford, almost a day behind schedule. Instead of the cavalry raiding party preceding the infantry toward Chancellorsville and beyond, the blue-clad horsemen had to dismount and wait in the rain several hours as long columns of slow moving infantry crossed. Eventually Stoneman's troopers were able to cross in front of the trailing division of Meade's Fifth Corps. Even after crossing, poor road conditions combined with many horses pulling cannon, mules carrying small arms ammunition, and seemingly endless columns of infantry frustrated the advance of Stoneman's horse soldiers.[21]

With the troopers of the 17th Pennsylvania in the van, Slocum's 12,169-man column of the Twelfth Corps, followed by Howard's Eleventh Corps, advanced on the Germanna Ford Road toward the Rapidan River. Slocum's Union infantry column reached the Rapidan River at 3:00 P.M. on the 29th of April. A detachment of Federal cavalry forded the river and captured two persistent companies of Louisiana infantry. Two Federal infantry brigades from Slocum's corps waded the waist-deep river as Union engineers quickly built a bridge with timbers left there by the retiring Confederates.[22]

A short distance to the east, on Ely's Ford Road, Meade's 15,824-man Fifth Corps steadily marched toward the Rapidan and reached Ely's Ford at 5:00 P.M. on the 29th of April. A member of the 83rd Pennsylvania recalled, "The men plunged boldly into the cold, rapid river and, as the water took them up to the arm-pits, they were compelled to hold their cartridge boxes above their heads in the crossing." Once the bulk of Meade's corps had crossed, large bonfires were kindled on the far bank, allowing many Federals to dry their coarse wool clothing. During the crossing of the Rapidan, Slocum, Howard, and Meade's corps had only met light resistance from Confederates skirmishers. Hooker's grand flanking movement was proceeding just as the Federal army commander had planned.[23]

Stuart's cavalrymen had closely observed Hooker's progress over the Rapidan and steadily sent back reports to General Lee's headquarters. At 9:00 P.M., on April 29, Lee reacted to the Federal force moving on his left flank toward Chancellorsville Crossroads. The Southern commander ordered Stuart to have his cavalry continue to harass the Federal column, while moving to rejoin the left flank of the Army of Northern Virginia. Lee also directed Major General Richard H. Anderson to "draw in your brigade at United States Mine Ford, and throw your left back so as to cover the road leading from

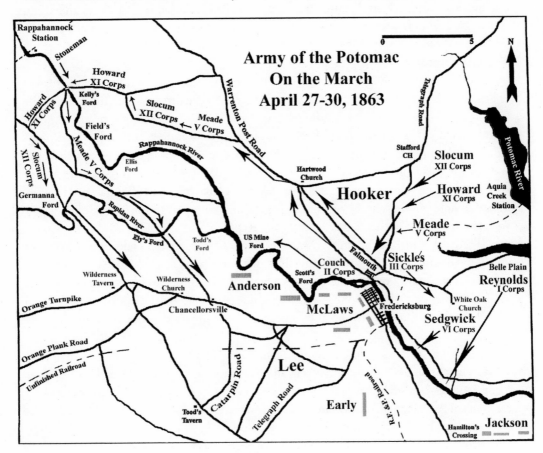

Army of the Potomac on the march: April 27–30, 1863.

Chancellorsville down the river, taking the strongest line you can, and holding it to the best advantage. I wish you to go forward yourself and attend to this matter."[24]

Anderson marched his five brigades south down the Mine Road to intersect with the Orange Turnpike, which lead to Chancellorsville Crossroads. One of Anderson's brigades, under the command of West Point graduate Cadmus M. Wilcox, was soon ordered to countermarch to its previously held position located four and a half miles below United States Mine Ford at Banks's Ford. Wilcox's mission was to guard against a possible Federal crossing at Banks's Ford, and prevent Hooker from easily reuniting his army. The shifting of Anderson's four brigades relinquished control of United States Mine Ford to Hooker's Federals.[25]

Later that evening, Lee wrote Jefferson Davis concerning the Army of the Potomac's flanking movement. Lee wanted any available troops along the Virginia and Carolina coasts to be put in motion in his direction. Lee explained the developing situation to Davis, "Stuart to cross Rapidan last night, to interrupt enemy's column at Germanna.... Union's object evidently to turn our left. If I had Longstreet's division, would feel safe."[26]

Anderson arrived east of Chancellorsville Crossroads just after midnight. Confederate line officers had their troops set all their spades to work, entrenching on a ridge-line between the Tabernacle and Zoan churches. Anderson advanced skirmishers into the tangled wilderness area to his front in the direction of Chancellorsville. Sporadic rifle fire pierced the night air as contact was quickly made with Federal skirmishers of Slocum's corps.[27]

At the Rapidan, long columns of Union troops continued to ford the swollen river as brigade commanders readied their men to march in the direction of Chancellorsville Crossroads. Around 4:30 A.M., under pressure from companies of Union cavalry, Anderson's Confederate skirmishers fell back just outside the wooded area to the junction of Mine Road and Orange Plank Road. If at all possible, Lee wanted to contain the Federals within the dense wilderness area, which would reduce the effectiveness of Hooker's larger force. Lee telegraphed his plan to the War Department in Richmond, "I determined to hold our lines in the rear of Fredericksburg with part of the force and endeavor with the rest to drive the enemy back to the Rapidan."[28]

Thursday April 30, at sunrise, Meade's Fifth Corps left the vicinity of Ely's Ford and moved southeast toward Chancellorsville Crossroads. To Meade's right flank, Slocum's column, followed by Howard's Eleventh Corps, departed Germanna Ford at 7:00 A.M. Meade's corps, having a shorter route and meeting less resistance, reached the Chancellorsville area around 11:00 A.M. Slocum's vanguard appeared near Chancellorsville Crossroads at 2:00 P.M. Within the next few hours Hooker's flanking force, 42,000 strong, took position around Chancellorsville. Meade immediately sent forward a detachment of cavalry and a brigade of infantry in the direction of United States Mine Ford. Skirmishing erupted as advanced Fifth Corps troops ran into the trailing elements of Anderson's Confederate division, en route to Chancellorsville. Meade's Federals secured the crossing, and construction of pontoon bridges commenced at United States Mine Ford. Major General Couch's two Second Corps divisions prepared to cross and to join Hooker's flanking force advancing toward Chancellorsville Crossroads.[29]

Meanwhile, Stoneman's Federal cavalry plodded south to raise havoc with Lee's line of communication. One of Stoneman's columns, under Brigadier General Averell, held up at Rapidan Station. Averell believed that the wooded nature of that area rendered cavalry work "impracticable." These 3,400 Union troopers remained idle north of the Rapidan River for the entire Chancellorsville Campaign. Accomplishing little, Hooker would later recall Averell's troopers on the 2nd of May. Hooker summarily relieved Averell of command, but Averell would later be reinstated. Brigadier General Pleasonton took command of Averell's Union horse soldiers.[30]

Farther south, Stoneman divided his larger cavalry column into several raiding parties and assigned them each specific targets to destroy. None of the parties met heavy Confederate resistance, but none managed to accomplish any major wreckage that actually added up to anything. Stoneman's raid sent great alarm throughout Richmond, but in effect this cavalry foray did little to help Hooker accomplish his mission of destroying Lee's Army of Northern Virginia.[31]

At Chancellorsville Crossroads, Northern troops of Hooker's flanking force converged on the small hamlet during the remainder of April 30. Having met only light resistance, Union corps commanders wanted to press on, putting the tangled wilderness area behind them. Here events took a turn, and the brake applied to the Union offensive. Hooker directed, "No advance beyond Chancellorsville until columns are concentrated [referring to the Fifth, Eleventh, Twelfth, and Second Corps]." The Army commander's instruction drastically altered the original order issued to Major General Slocum of advancing the Army of the Potomac's flanking force and halting only if Lee moved to the offensive and attacked. In the late afternoon, Major General Hooker was greeted with enthusiastic hazzahs as he rode toward Chancellorsville past long blue-clad columns of infantry.[32]

CHAPTER 2

"May God Help Us and Give Us Victory"

A main component of Hooker's operational plan involved a demonstration below the city of Fredericksburg, Virginia, to hold Lee's attention as the Army of the Potomac's flanking force maneuvered into attack position. Major General John Sedgwick orchestrated the operations below Fredericksburg and had temporary command of 59,000 Union troops. The infantry comprising Sedgwick's force were Major General John F. Reynolds's First Corps, Major General Daniel E. Sickles' Third Corps, and the largest corps in the Army of the Potomac, Sedgwick's own Sixth Corps.

The forwarding of extra clothing and camp equipment to the Union supply depot at Belle Plain was the first indication of an upcoming advance for Sedgwick's foot soldiers. From the Sixth Corps' encampment at White Oak Church, Frank Lemont of the 5th Maine wrote home, "...we are now under marching orders, with eight days' ration to be carried in our haversacks & knapsacks. We are ordered to be ready to move tomorrow morning." On the overcast morning of April 28, 1863, Union line officers barked out strict orders against straggling and the lighting of fires as the First and Sixth Corps assembled to march.[1]

At noon, Sedgwick's first operation as Sixth Corps commander got under way. The pace of the march was slow. There were many

April 28, 1863

Major General John Sedgwick, commander of the Sixth Army Corps (Massachusetts MOLLUS Collection, U.S. Military History Institute).

starts and stops as officers endeavored to maintain the correct route. Reynolds' First Corps moved west from their encampment at Belle Plain along muddy roads leading to Stafford Heights. At 3 P.M., the Sixth Corps followed, marching from their camps at White Oak Church. "It rained, of course, but not quite hard enough to prevent our marching or to dampen our spirits," recalled Private Wilbur Fisk of the 2nd Vermont.[2]

leave White Oak Church

Once on the heights overlooking the battle-scarred Rappahannock River Valley, Sedgwick's troops viewed Professor Thaddeus S. C. Lowe's balloon detachment organizing their rather strange-looking reconnaissance equipment. Tethered by long ropes, Union aeronauts would ascend at sunrise in their hydrogen-filled balloon and provide Union commanders with periodic "balloon in the air reports." Newly assigned to the Corps of Engineers, Professor Lowe's developing balloon department was struggling to establish itself as a viable intelligence-gathering service for the Union army.[3]

The Federal infantrymen's knapsacks were tightly packed. Along with personal items, each man carried eight days' rations, overcoat, rubber blanket, full canteen and sixty rounds of ammunition. After their sojourn in winter quarters, the men's 30- to 40-pound leather packs felt extra heavy. Rain made the dirt roads slippery and marching was difficult. Halting shy of the river to await darkness, Sedgwick's muddied troops went into bivouac in ravines that concealed them from their enemy across the Rappahannock River. Sedgwick's troops remained under arms and attempted to get comfortable; intermittent rain showers continued to fall into the night.

night of April 28, 1863

Sedgwick dispatched Major Thomas W. Hyde four miles upriver to Third Corps headquarters located near the town of Falmouth, Virginia. Major Hyde recalled, "I was sent at 11 P.M. with [Captain Charles A.] Whittier to put Sickles' Corps in position." From his winter encampment, Sickles began marching his 18,721-man Third Corps to a support position on Stafford Heights. Third Corps supply trains remained parked near Falmouth. Sickles was instructed to place his corps to the rear of the First and Sixth corps in order to provide reinforcement where Sedgwick might need it.[4]

At midnight the command to "fall-in" was heard as the First and Sixth corps were roused from their soggy respite. Sedgwick's long blue columns marched slowly down the slopes to assigned positions where they were to cross the Rappahannock and make their demonstration. By 3:30 A.M., Wednesday April 29, the Sixth Corps had descended the heights and settled into a position on the foggy plain, south of the city of Fredericksburg. Sedgwick's upper crossing point, known to Federals as Franklin's Crossing, was located at the same point that Major General William B. Franklin had used to cross his "Left Grand Division" in Major General Ambrose E. Burnside's failed Fredericksburg Campaign.[5]

April 29 1863

Two batteries from Brigadier General Henry Hunt's General Artillery Reserve covered Sedgwick's crossing point from the heights above. The 15th New York manned six twenty-pounder Parrott rifles and Company M of the 1st Connecticut Heavy Artillery, manned four 4.5-inch siege rifles capable of accurately launching thirty-two-pound projectiles. Twenty-four ten-pounder Parrott rifles of the Sixth Corps, under Colonel Charles H. Tompkins, were positioned on the plain below the heights to command Franklin's Crossing.[6]

Captain Andrew J. Russell, assigned to the U.S. Military Railroad, photographed the 1st Connecticut Heavy Artillery of the General Artillery Reserve manning their 4.5 inch siege rifles on Stafford Heights, May 3, 1863 (U.S. Military History Institute).

A mile and a half downstream, Major General Reynolds marched his First Corps into position. In the rainy darkness, battery drivers maneuvered their teams of horses into position as gun commanders readied their pieces. Twenty ten-pounder Parrott rifles of the Artillery Reserve were deployed on the high ground to Reynolds's rear. Fourteen additional light rifles and six twelve-pounder Napoleons were maneuvered into position closer to the bank of the river, commanded by the First Corps' chief of artillery, Colonel Charles S. Wainwright.[7]

One mile farther down river, Lieutenant Colonel Edward R. Warner, inspector of artillery for the Army of the Potomac, established sixteen guns near Travelers Rest. On property owned by Widow Gray, he positioned twelve ten-pounder Parrott rifles of the 15th and 32nd New York batteries along with a battery of four twenty-pounder Parrotts belonging to the 5th New York. Positioned on a knoll, these Federal batteries were assigned the dual duty of anchoring Reynolds' left flank while providing fire support across the river once the First Corps advanced. In support of these batteries, Reynolds sent over the 135th Pennsylvania Volunteers from Brigadier General Abner Doubleday's Third Division. The green-clad troops of the 1st Regiment United States Sharpshooters, assigned to the Third Brigade, First Division of Sickles' Third Corps, also arrived to anchor Reynolds's left.[8]

Upstream at Franklin's Crossing, under the independent command of Brigadier General Henry Benham, pontoon boats slowly began moving toward the dark riverbank. In an attempt to conceal the Federals' crossing, the commander of the Engineer Brigade ordered the boats hand-carried down the muddy slope to the river's edge. Members of the 15th New York Engineers were assisted by troops of Brigadier General Calvin E. Pratt's Light Division along with detachments from Colonel Alexander Shaler's brigade.

[handwritten marginal note: carry boats down muddy slope to river]

Pratt's Light Division consisted of five picked infantry regiments: the 6th Maine, 5th Wisconsin, 61st Pennsylvania, 43rd New York, and the 31st New York. Artillery support was provided by the six ten-pounder Parrott rifles of Lieutenant William A. Harn's 3rd New York Independent Light Battery. Formed February 3, 1863, on Hooker's order, this small fourth division, or brigade as Sedgwick termed it, wore the green Greek Cross of the Sixth Corps. Organized as special troops, these regiments were to make rapid forced marches and reconnaissance without large cumbersome baggage trains. For rapid deployment, all rations and ammunition of the Light Division would be carried by army pack mules.[9]

A little more than a year previous, Pratt had received a facial wound during the Peninsula Campaign and the rifle ball had remained lodged in his face. Pratt finally submitted his resignation to the War Department in early April 1863 but continued to serve until his resignation went through official channels. Unbeknownst to Pratt, his resignation had been accepted, dated April 25, 1863. Pratt continued on duty until the news authorizing his resignation reached him on April 27, 1863, one day prior to the Sixth Corps' advance. Colonel Hiram "Grizzly" Burnham of the 6th Maine replaced Pratt as the Light Division commander. At this time in the United States military the concept of rapid deployment was short-lived, as the Chancellorsville offensive would be the only campaign for the Light Division. On June 11, 1863, the War Department disbanded the Light Division. As for Pratt, the rifle ball remained lodged in his face for thirty years until it was finally surgically removed.[10]

Details of thirty-six men were assigned to carry each boat down to the bank of the Rappahannock. The men had great difficulty muscling the 1,250-pound wooden boats the required distance to the edge of the river. The operation became jumbled as an argument erupted between Brigadier General Benham, the engineer in charge of the pontoons, and the Sixth Corps' officers commanding the troops who would make the initial crossing. Expectedly, tempers were short, owing to the officers' lack of sleep. The cover of early morning darkness was passing quickly and Benham grew furious with several Sixth Corps officers who would not heed his instructions. In an attempt to fight off fatigue, the usually reliable Benham had been quenching his thirst with a canteen filled with sherry.[11]

In an intoxicated state, Benham loudly argued with several officers of Sedgwick's First Division as he attempted to issue instructions for the crossing. Lieutenant Stephen Minot Weld, a member of Benham's staff, wrote home mentioning the disgraceful behavior of his commander. Weld described one encounter: "He was yelling out in a loud tone of voice and Goddamning him. This, too, right on the bank of the river and when he had been cautioning everyone to keep quiet." The vociferous Benham attempted to have Brigadier General David A. Russell, commander of the Third Brigade of Sedgwick's First Division, placed under arrest for not following his orders.[12]

Benham's liquor-fueled anger came to a crescendo and then ceased after he had words with the commander of Sedgwick's First Division, Brigadier General William T. H. Brooks. Nicknamed "Bully" by his peers, Brooks was a hard-eyed Regular who wielded a coarse vernacular frequently accentuated with profanities. He was not the least bit inclined to be ordered about by a half-soused brigadier general, especially one not in his direct chain of command. Benham's threats to place Russell under arrest proved empty, and preparations for the crossing continued.[13]

Sedgwick's first boats arrived at the foggy riverbank just before daylight. Troops of Brigadier General Russell's Third Brigade were the occupants of the lead boats to push off through the murky fog. Four companies of Colonel Clinton G. Colgate's 15th New York Engineers acted as the oarsmen to propel the five-foot wide, thirty-one-foot-long vessels. The lead boats contained nearly 1,200 members of the 95th and 119th Pennsylvania. Soldiers were unable to see to their front and quickly became disoriented. Oarsmen in boats containing the 49th Pennsylvania and part of the 32nd New York also struggled to stay their course as they moved toward the blackness of the far shore.[14]

The relative quiet of the wee hours was abruptly shattered. Lieutenant Colonel Martin McMahon recalled, "Suddenly upon the damp night air there rang from the enemy one single clear word distinctly heard in all the boats and across upon our bank

An Alfred Waud sketch depicts Brigadier General Russell's Third Brigade, First Division, Sixth Corps at Franklin's Crossing (Deep Run) April 29, 1863 (Library of Congress).

and well understood. That word was fire!" Pickets of the 54th North Carolina squeezed off a volley, which lit up the fog. Sporadic firing continued to break the murkiness as Southern defenders shot in the direction of anything that moved or made a sound. Federal riflemen positioned along the river's edge were unable to see the opposite bank and could not safely return fire.[15]

The Federals huddled low in their boats as oarsmen rowed as fast as they could in the direction of the hazy muzzle flashes. Obscured by the fog and darkness, the first wave of twenty-three boats crossed the river nearly unscathed. A few luckless Federals waiting to embark on the far shore became victims of errant Confederate fire that whizzed over the heads of the occupants of the boats. Beaching their boats under the protection of the bank, Russell's Federals clamored up the incline, forcing the majority of Confederate defenders to abandon their riverfront position. Immediately, the wooden boats returned to cross more of Russell's infantry, while engineers and an abutment party went to work anchoring boats for a pontoon bridge. In the first gray light of dawn, outlines of the countryside began to appear as Federal skirmishers were thrown forward, provoking random rifle fire to their front. One squad of skirmishers rushed forward and surrounded a house, surprising several dozing Confederate pickets and an officer who were taken captive.[16]

Riders quickly to spread the alarm to the sleeping Confederate camps. Drums beat the long roll and in short time, line officers had their regiments assembled. Reacting quickly, Major General Jubal Early advanced his four brigades to the embankment supporting the rails of the R.F. & P. Railroad. Large Federal guns to the rear of Sedgwick's position opened on Early's troops as they deployed in the dawn's early light. Once positioned behind the railroad embankment, Early sent forward three regiments as skirmishers, who spread out amongst a row of large cedars edging the sunken roadbed of the Bowling Green Road. (The Bowling Green Road was also locally known as the Stage Road or Richmond Stage Road, but to reduce confusion will here be referred to as the Bowling Green Road.)[17]

After the Federals had secured the far bank, more of Benham's engineers were free to go to work and hastened the assembly of three pontoon bridges. Anchoring the double-ended boats, the men lashed them together with twenty-seven-foot-long wooden beams (balks) as squads of engineers rapidly lashed decking planks (chesses) to the beams. By 7:00 A.M., the first bridge was completed and immediately the remaining regiments of Brigadier General Brooks' First Division began crossing without incident. Remarkably, Sedgwick's losses during this river crossing amounted to only eleven casualties.[18]

As daylight grew and the morning fog rose, "Bully" Brooks recalled, "We found our picket line face to face with that of the enemy, separated only by 100 yards." Sedgwick crossed the six twelve-pounder Napoleons of Battery D, 2nd U.S., commanded by Lieutenant Edward B. Williston. Brooks' First Division troops took position in the vicinity of Alfred Bernard's home "The Bend." Spreading out down river, Brooks' men positioned themselves among numerous large shade trees and secured several outbuildings surrounding the stone ruins of Arthur Bernard's mansion, "Mannsfield."[19]

Members of the 15th New York Engineers (Engineer Brigade) overlooking Franklin's Crossing, May 1863 (The Western Reserve Historical Society, Cleveland, Ohio).

One of Early's men, Private Urbanus Dart Jr. of the 26th Georgia, recalled the Confederate reaction to the crossing of the Federal Sixth Corps:

> I never worked so hard in my life, every Co. and regiment looking to its own safety began strengthening our position by cutting heavy logs and piling them on the Railroad [R.F. & P.], also what crossties and iron we could get, and by nightfall we had made a splendid fortification and believe me there was not a handful of dirt thrown upon the work with hoe or shovel, but with coats off and sleeves rolled up we pitched in with bayonets etc for loosing the dirt, and our hands for throwing it on and you would be surprised to look upon the amount of work done and to think that it was done by our hands alone.[20]

A mile and a half downstream from the Sixth Corps' crossing point was the location where Major General Reynolds would cross his First Corps. This crossing was known as Fitzhugh's Crossing, named for the family who owned the surrounding acreage extending down to the edge of the Rappahannock River. Various accounts refer to this crossing point as Pollock's Mill Crossing. Pollock's Mill was located along White Oak Run, which flowed into the Rappahannock a short distance below Fitzhugh's Crossing. Directly across the river from Reynolds's assigned fording point sat the ruins of the plantation titled "Smithfield," owned by Thomas Pratt. Along the steep banks of the Rappahannock, Confederates had felled trees and dug rifle pits to command the area.

Brigadier General James S. Wadsworth's First Division of Reynolds' corps was ordered to make the crossing. Wadsworth selected Brigadier General Solomon Meredith's brigade to force the river crossing. Reaching the dark riverbank, Meredith's men quietly waited for the arrival of the pontoon boats. In order to move the boats to the riverbank, detachments had placed bridge-decking planks under the boats and heaved them onto their shoulders. Reynolds's timetable fell apart as troops encountered problems with hauling the heavy wooden boats to the muddy bank. Shortly after daybreak, Reynolds realized the futility of transporting the vessels in this manner and instructed the head teamster to order forward the pontoon trains. First Corps troops placed the boats on wagons to be hauled to the riverbank by teams of horses.[21]

Well after daylight the first boats neared the riverbank. Many horses soon fell victim to Confederate rifle fire, forcing the wagons to be rolled to the bank by detachments of volunteers. Deadly Confederate fire continued from the far shore as teamsters and engineers from the 50th New York attempted to unload the boats from the wagons. Fire from the 13th Georgia of Colonel John B. Gordon's brigade made it nearly impossible for the Federals to work on the exposed bank, as several men were killed before the remainder were driven off. Under an accurate Confederate fire as well as the verbal taunts from their foe, companies B, E, and D of the 2nd Wisconsin finally were able to position several pontoon boats at the river's edge.[22]

From within a slight depression near the river's edge, the 6th Wisconsin and the 24th Michigan responded to Confederate fire from the prone position. Good fortune shined on the 84th New York, or "Fourteenth Brooklyn," as they were able to fire from behind a small stone wall that ran close to the river. Reynolds instructed batteries A, 1st New Hampshire; C, 4th Pennsylvania; and F, 1st Pennsylvania, to open a converging fire from their elevated position overlooking the ford.

Shortly before 9:00 A.M., Brigadier General Benham arrived at Fitzhugh's Crossing. Earlier that morning, the inebriated Benham had fallen from his horse and bloodied his face. The wobbly engineer was unhorsed as he attempted to shake the hand of Brigadier General Pratt, who had just received the news of the acceptance of his resignation from the army. Obviously still far gone to drink, Benham galloped up to Major General Reynolds' headquarters and exclaimed to his former Mexican War comrade, "Hurrah Josh! [a nickname of Major General Reynolds] Hurrah for here and Buena Vista!"[23]

After exchanging fire with the enemy for an hour, Brigadier General Solomon Meredith sent the 24th Michigan and 6th Wisconsin of his "Black Hat Brigade" rushing at the double-quick toward the river. Accompanied by their white-haired division commander, Brigadier General James S. Wadsworth, these Westerners of the First Brigade, First Division, First Corps, better known as members of the "Iron Brigade," piled into their boats on the run with fixed bayonets. Private Elon Brown of the 6th Wisconsin recorded seeing his commanding officers leading the way: "They both crossed in nearly the first boats that went over — Meredith swinging his hat and hurrahing, and Wadsworth leading his horse which was swimming behind the boat."[24]

Along the opposite bank, members of the 13th Georgia held fast to their entrenchments as they expended the majority of their ammunition. Ordered to retire, the

Georgians were relieved by Colonel William Monaghan and his 6th Louisiana of Brigadier General Harry T. Hays' brigade. The Confederate fire was soon bolstered by the arrival of Colonel Henry Forno's 5th Louisiana. Henry Walker of the 13th Georgia noted, "...we never lost but one man while we was in the rifle pits but when we went to leave they swept our boys down like they was chaff."[25]

For protection, members of the Iron Brigade hugged the gunnels of their boats as oarsmen pulled with all their strength. Wounded Federals struggled to regain the shore as the current carried off several blue-clad corpses. Union sharpshooters positioned along the shoreline continued a lively cover fire from behind improvised firing positions. Wadsworth's men reached the far shore, jumped from their boats, and scrambled through the mud up the sloping bank. A number of Confederates were shot; others were captured as the Federals advanced inland rapidly, cutting off their retreat. The remaining companies of Monaghan and Forno's Louisiana skirmishers fell back from their outpost with some parting shots.

Federal company commanders assembled their men and advanced up the bluff onto an open plain. To their right front, Confederate skirmishers had taken position in and around the ruins of Thomas Pratt's red brick mansion, "Smithfield." The 6th Wisconsin met with light resistance as they advanced through an orchard to secure the dwelling and surrounding area. The 24th Michigan moved forward and deployed in a large ravine, protecting the 6th Wisconsin's flank and expanding the Federals' perimeter. Losses to the Iron Brigade amounted to fifty-seven men killed or wounded. Following closely, a second wave of boats containing more troops of Wadsworth's division made their way across the Rappahannock. Quickly these units strengthened and extended the Iron Brigade's skirmish line as construction of a pontoon bridge began. Rough estimates place Confederate losses at thirty killed and ninety captured.[26]

Telegraph lines were stretched from Sedgwick's temporary headquarters near Franklin's Crossing three miles up river to Hooker's headquarters at Falmouth. A telegraph wire extended between Sedgwick and Reynolds's transitory headquarters, replacing the three-man flag stations at Smith's house and Fitzhugh's farmhouse. Miles of telegraph wire would eventually be strung up and down the Rappahannock River. Due to breaks on the line caused by unobservant Federal artillery drivers and wagoneers, the magneto electric signal telegraph proved inconstant. A Federal signal officer recalled, "Great deal of trouble was occasioned by careless teamsters and soldiers breaking the line, and, although a guard was placed along the whole line from headquarters to the United States [Mine] Ford, the line was frequently broken."[27]

Behind Hooker's schedule, Brigadier General Benham's Engineer Brigade went to work laying the first of two pontoon bridges at Fitzhugh's Crossing. Shortly after 10:00 A.M., Wadsworth's remaining regiments began marching across the completed bridge spanning the fast flowing Rappahannock River. Wadsworth's Federal skirmishers slowly felt their way out in a large semicircle, while Confederate skirmishers offered light resistance and slowly withdrew to positions along the Bowling Green Road. Once Wadsworth's infantry crossed, they extended downriver, establishing outposts and occupying some high ground abutting the Alsop's property.

Major General Hooker wanted some explanation for the delay in the laying of the pontoon bridges below Fredericksburg. However, at the time there was much in the works for the army commander, and in spite of Benham's antics Sedgwick's demonstration below the city had continued to move forward. The commander of the Engineer Brigade would redeem himself by performing solidly throughout the remainder of the campaign. Hooker never censured his former West Point classmate for his performance on the banks of the Rappahannock. Benham later attempted to escape responsibility for the delay by stating that Brooks had assumed command of the crossing. He claims to have told Brooks, "The responsibility for the crossing now rests with you, but I will aid you in any way that you wish, and all my men are at your orders...." Brigadier General Russell of the Sixth Corps explained without adornment that, at the upper crossing, "The arrangements for the crossing were not perfected til 4:20 o'clock." Reynolds reported the delay downstream was incurred because of the long distance his men had to carry the boats in order to reach the riverbank.[28]

At a farmhouse near Hamilton's Crossing, Lieutenant General Thomas J. Jackson's Second Corps' headquarters was astir upon hearing of the Federal crossing. Jackson immediately instructed his three remaining division commanders to prepare for action. From across the river, at Travelers Rest, Federal artillery opened with a roar. Through the drifting morning fog Lieutenant Colonel Edward R. Warner observed faint outlines of Jackson's troops maneuvering west toward Hamilton's Crossing. Warner's accurate shelling prevented Jackson's divisions from passing over a bridge spanning Massaponax Creek. To safely deploy his troops, Jackson was forced to detour some distance to his rear around a large marshy area surrounding Massaponax Creek.[29]

Jackson's three divisions eventually marched into position behind the embankment of the R.F. & P. Railroad, to the right of Early's division. Jackson's aide-de-camp, Lieutenant James Power Smith, galloped up the Mine Road to army headquarters and informed General Lee of developments. Smith wrote:

> Finding Lee still slumbering, quietly, at the suggestion of Colonel Charles S. Venable, who I found stirring, I entered the general's tent and awoke him. Turning his feet out of his cot he sat upon its side as I gave Lee the tidings from the front. Expressing no surprise, Lee playfully said: "Well, I thought I heard firing, and was beginning to think it was time some of you young fellows were coming to tell me what it was all about. Tell your good general that I am sure he knows what to do. I will meet him at the front very soon."[30]

Jackson's blood was up and he wanted to attack the invading Yankees to his front. General Lee arrived at Jackson's position and after surveying the situation decided not to send forward his infantry. Lee felt the numerous Federal batteries in position across the river would command the open field, making an attack impracticable. Respecting his commander's wishes, the combative Jackson suspended his eagerness to engage his much hated enemy.[31]

The few remaining citizens in the city of Fredericksburg were awakened early that morning by peals of bells originating from the Episcopal church. The news of the Federal crossing below the war-torn city spread quickly. Many women, children, and elderly citizens had long evacuated the city, seeking safety beyond the Confederate lines to the rear of Fredericksburg. In defiance of the invading Northerners, other Confederate loyalists refused to be displaced from their Old Dominion homes and remained in cellars within the city. A handful of Unionists also remained, anxiously awaiting the Federals' crossing. Brigadier General William Barksdale's Mississippi Brigade patrolled the city as Confederate pickets, along the waterfront, observed the blue-clad army on the far shore.[32]

To the rear of the Sixth and First corps, Major General Sickles maneuvered his Union Third Corps down into the ravines on Stafford Heights. Closer to the river, Sixth and First corps troops marched about, deployed as if on a parade field. Sixth Corps regimental bands blared *Dixie* and *Hail Columbia* as Sedgwick's Federal troops staged their performance under the watchful eye of their Rebel hosts. Confederate regimental bands responded by playing *Yankee Doodle* and *The Bonnie Blue Flag*. Federal officers had their men sound off with bellowing huzzahs, which echoed across the open plain and over the heights. Surgeon George T. Stevens of the 77th New York recorded, "The contest seemed for a time to depend on strength of lung, and our boys certainly beat them at shouting."[33]

Across the river, the remainder of the 29th proved uneventful for Sedgwick as his First Division held fast along the edge of their perimeter protecting their bridgehead. Downstream, Wadsworth's First Corps division sat snug behind natural cover, firmly establishing Sedgwick's command on Rebel soil. The openness of the country forced the Federals who had crossed to remain close to the riverbank for cover. The sun burnt off the river fog, revealing a memorable sight: "Our magnificent batteries going into position as if by clockwork, and all the banners of the Greek Cross flaunting in the breeze, made a picture that has survived many years," recalled the Sixth Corps' provost marshal, Major Thomas Hyde.[34]

To the front of Sedgwick's upper crossing, Brigadier General Russell extended his picket line toward some high ground on Alfred Bernard's estate. Alfred's property bordered his brother Arthur's estate, "Mannsfield." Sedgwick gave instructions for a trench line to be dug to the front of the bridgeheads at Franklin's Crossing. From the far shore, twenty-one-year-old First Lieutenant Elisha Hunt Rhodes wrote on the evening of April 29, "May God help us and give us victory. The Rebel lines are in plain sight, and the hills are covered with forts and rifle pits, but with God's help we can and will take them."[35]

Sedgwick's demonstration proceeded smoothly until late in the afternoon, when the sixteen guns of Lieutenant Colonel Richard S. Andrews' battalion began shelling the Federals on the open plain. Things became a little hot as Union batteries boomed in response to the Confederate artillery barrage. That evening on picket duty Private John L. G. Wood of the 53rd Georgia recalled, "When the Yanks had crossed the river on their pontoon bridges we were in full view of the Yanks. I could hear them crossing all night. I went out on scout to see and walked from 125 to 150 yards of them. They were a savage looking set of bluebirds."[36]

CHAPTER 3

Make a Demonstration

Daybreak April 30 found the First and Sixth corps settled into assigned positions as Sedgwick awaited orders from Hooker. Picket lines were established. Shovels were distributed and makeshift rifle pits were dug by the Federal infantry. To strengthen their entrenchments near Fitzhugh's Crossing, Wadsworth's First Corps troops confiscated local farm equipment to improvise hasty barricades. Several units tore down nearby barns and outbuildings in the area to provide lumber for their entrenchments. Lieutenant James Stewart's Battery B, 4th Regulars, and Captain R. Ransom's Battery C, 5th Regulars, rumbled over a pontoon bridge at Fitzhugh's Crossing, and were positioned by Colonel Wainwright amongst Wadsworth's idle division.[1]

Upriver, Sixth Corps' troops also dug entrenchments to protect their bridgehead at Franklin's Crossing. Once established, Sedgwick's troops had the chance to light their pipes, boil coffee, or write letters, as the Confederate pickets to their front awaited action. From the far bank Samuel Pingree wrote, "Have not gone over yet — Brooks still holds the plantation. It rains hard — P.M. Fighting on our left by artillery." Opposing picket lines were close enough to one another that conversations between the two could easily be carried on. The close proximity of the picket lines enabled a brisk trade in coffee and tobacco to be conducted covertly amongst the contending soldiers.[2]

While the Sixth Corps prepared defenses, a letter originating from Major General Butterfield's headquarters arrived at Sedgwick's position. The chief of staff described a private conversation he had had with Hooker prior to the army commander's departure from Falmouth. Butterfield's correspondence plainly spelled out Hooker's intentions. The chief of staff wrote, "He [Hooker] expected, when he left here, if he met with no serious opposition, to be on the heights west of Fredericksburg to-morrow [May 1] or shortly after, and if opposed strongly, to-morrow night." Butterfield closed with, "Please consider this confidential, and written privately for your information. Communicate as much of it as you think proper, confidentially, to Reynolds."[3]

At 8:30 A.M., Sedgwick received instructions from Hooker's headquarters. Sent by Hooker's adjutant general, Brigadier General Seth Williams, the dispatch read:

I am directed by the Major-General commanding to instruct you to make a demonstration on the enemy's line in the direction of Hamilton's Crossing at 1 o'clock, the object being to

On May 3, 1863, south of Fredericksburg, Captain A.J. Russell photographed members of the New Jersey Brigade of Brooks' First Division awaiting action behind the embankment of the R.F. & P. Railroad. (The Western Reserve Historical Society, Cleveland, Ohio).

ascertain whether or not the enemy continues to hug his defenses in full force, and if he should have abandoned them, to take possession of his works and the commanding ground in the vicinity.... The demonstration will be made for no other purpose than that stated. The enemy must not be attacked behind his defenses, if held in force.... If you are certain that the enemy is in full force in your front, I am instructed by the commanding general to say the demonstration herein directed will not be made.... The enemy has a pontoon train at Hamilton's. The general expects that you will not permit them to cross the river....[4]

First Corps troops were made ready, but before Reynolds could initiate the demonstration Hooker placed the maneuver on hold. Butterfield notified Sedgwick at 11:30 A.M., "Let demonstration be suspended until further orders." Reynolds and Sedgwick were left speculating. Reynolds reported the sighting of enemy troop movements, possibly Confederate reinforcements from Richmond. Butterfield's headquarters had obtained false information from Confederate deserters concerning the arrival of Major General John Bell Hood's division from Richmond. This information was forwarded to Hooker's headquarters. Butterfield received back a cocksure response from the army's commander, which was relayed to Sedgwick: "General Hooker hopes they are from Richmond, as the greater will be our success."[5]

A little after noon, orders from Hooker reached Major General Sickles directing him to march his Third Corps upriver to United States Mine Ford. Sickles was to cross the Rappahannock River by 7:00 A.M. of May 1 and connect with Hooker's force at Chancellorsville. Two hours after receiving his orders, Sickles' three divisions stepped off on a roundabout trek detouring to the rear of their position on Stafford Heights. This line of march was chosen in an effort to avoid detection by Lee's army across the river.[6]

Just after sunset on April 30, Lowe sent up a balloon to observe the number of enemy campfires across the river. Lowe wrote to Sedgwick, "I find them [fires] most numerous in a ravine about one mile beyond heights opposite General Sedgwick's forces, extending from opposite lower crossing to a little above upper crossing. There are also many additional fires in rear of Fredericksburg. From appearances I should judge that full three quarters of the enemy's force is immediately back below Fredericksburg."[7]

From his headquarters at Chancellorsville, Hooker dispatched his chief of artillery, Brigadier General Henry J. Hunt, to oversee the Federal force protecting the approaches to Banks's Ford. Upon his arrival, Hunt found the force positioned at this crossing point insufficient and immediately wired Butterfield at Falmouth requesting reinforcements be sent to him. Brigadier General John Gibbon, positioned near Falmouth, was instructed to send one brigade of infantry to Banks's Ford. Butterfield sent up ten light rifles of the horse artillery, from their park near Falmouth. Twelve three-inch ordnance rifles and four 12-pounder Napoleons, from the Artillery Reserve, would soon join the artillery guarding the approaches to Banks' and Scott's fords. Hunt also directed Battery B of the 1st Connecticut Heavy Artillery to report to Banks's Ford, which boosted the number of guns under Hunt to thirty. Hunt placed Brigadier General Robert O. Tyler in overall command of this reserve artillery dug in on the slopes overlooking Banks's and Scott's fords.[8]

Providing observations for Tyler's artillery at Banks's Ford was Union aeronaut E. S. Allen, in his balloon "Eagle." Allen conducted his balloon operations in the vicinity of Banks's Ford for an extended period of time, but surprisingly his dispatches recording his birds-eye view of the Rappahannock River Valley are few in the official reports of this campaign. Once Banks's Ford was sufficiently reinforced, Butterfield deployed the remainder of the Artillery Reserve. Twelve light 12-pounder Napoleons were positioned on Stafford Heights to command the Falmouth Road, and sweep the streets of Fredericksburg. A battery of four twenty-pounder Parrotts moved from Falmouth downriver and joined batteries positioned on the high ground overlooking Fitzhugh's Crossing.[9]

Back in command shape, Brigadier General Benham received orders to have his engineers, secretly under the cover of darkness, take up two bridges. One bridge each from Franklin's Crossing and Fitzhugh's Crossing were to be moved up river to Banks's Ford. This would leave Sedgwick with three ten-foot-wide wooden pontoon bridges spanning the Rappahannock below Fredericksburg. Shortly before 8:00 P.M., Benham's men went to work. The 136th Pennsylvania Volunteers began disassembling a pontoon bridge at Fitzhugh's Crossing. The cumbersome bridging material was dragged ashore under the supervision of Lieutenant Colonel William H. Pettes, of the 50th New York Engineers, and was moved by teams north up the Riverside Road.[10]

[handwritten in left margin: 4/30 — More Pontoon Bridge]

Upriver at Franklin's Crossing, the 26th New Jersey was ordered to fall in without arms or equipment. The troops were instructed to remove a pontoon bridge from Franklin's Crossing and haul it seven miles upriver to Banks's Ford. Under the direction of Colonel Clinton G. Colgate of the 15th New York Engineers, the bridging material was pulled out of the water and with great effort placed on wagons. Mule teams pulled the pontoon trains, and the men of the 26th would assist by pulling or pushing when necessary. Many sections of the roadway held standing water as recent rains had turned the low spots into gooey quagmires. Sergeant-Major Cummings remembered, "The mudholes became deeper, team after team was stuck, some were overturned, some were unladen, and two mules broke from their traces and skedaddled." Well into their journey, exhausted and covered with mud, about half the detail fell to the side of the road and slept. In the foggy darkness the remaining troops continued on this mini mud-march until daylight, finally being relieved by Second Corps troops of Brigadier General Joshua Owens's Philadelphia Brigade.[11]

Unknown to Sedgwick, his role as Hooker's stalking-horse had been fully identified by the commander of the Army of Northern Virginia. Hooker's attempts at deception, such as the shifting troops, false river crossings, and even the use of bogus flag messages, had failed to have much of an effect on Lee. By midnight of April 30th, Lee had figured out that Sedgwick's crossing was merely a demonstration and he reacted by ordering Major General Lafayette McLaws' division, minus one brigade, to march to Major General Anderson's support on Tabernacle Church Ridge. Confederate regimental commanders were instructed to march in the rear of their columns with a strong guard and fixed bayonets to prevent straggling.[12]

To conceal his departure, Lee temporarily detained Lieutenant General Jackson's command until after dark. A possible advance by Sedgwick's Federals in the direction of Hamilton's Crossing also concerned Lee. The commander of the Army of Northern Virginia clearly understood Hooker's aim was to flank his army. Well before daylight of the first of May, Jackson's Corps, minus Early's division, was on its way toward Anderson's position. Lee later reported, "The enemy to our front [Sedgwick] near Fredericksburg,

Major General Jubal A. Early (C.S.A.) (Massachusetts MOLLUS Collection, U.S. Military History Institute).

continued inactive; and it was now apparent that the main attack would be made upon our flank and rear."[13]

Jackson's departure left Sedgwick's former West Point classmate Major General Jubal Early defending the Confederate position to the rear of Fredericksburg. Promoted in January of 1863, "Jube" Early held the least amount of time-in-grade among major generals in Lee's army. Known for his irritable disposition and biting commentary, Early often made fellow officers' blood boil with his sharp, penetrating remarks. A captain in Stuart's cavalry, John Esten Cooke, would later write of Early, "Every one who ventured upon word-combats with Lieutenant-General Early sustained a palpable hit.... Sarcastic and critical, he was criticized in return, as a man of rough address, irascible temperament, and as wholly careless whom he offended." The forty-seven-year-old Early had also earned the reputation as a brave and capable combat infantry officer. Confederate staff officer Captain Henry Kyd Douglas venerably remarked after the war, "There was none of General Lee's subordinates, after the death of General Jackson, who possessed the essential qualities of a military commander to a greater extent than Early."[14]

Commanding Early's brigades were Brigadier Generals Harry T. Hays, William "Extra Billy" Smith, and Robert F. Hoke. Colonel John B. Gordon commanded Early's remaining brigade. Earlier in April, Gordon had been placed in charge of Alexander R. Lawton's brigade as Lawton had suffered a severe wound at the battle of Sharpsburg. Gordon himself was also wounded at the battle along Antietam Creek and was still recovering from four flesh wounds and a head wound that had left him face down in his hat, unconscious. Only a bullet hole in the Georgian's hat allowed blood to drain away, preventing Gordon from drowning. Colonel Gordon's appointment to brigadier general was originally forwarded on November 1, 1862, but his confirmation was postponed, as his recovery from wounds was questionable. After rejoining Lee's army, his reappointment to brigadier general came on May 11, 1863, with rank to date from May 7, 1863.[15]

The Confederate earthworks Early was to defend had come a long way since the Confederate States Army first occupied these commanding heights with one regiment and a battery in the fall of 1862. A letter written home by Major Alexander S. "Sandie" Pendleton of Jackson's staff described the entrenchments in the spring of 1863:

> The greatest destruction and change in appearance of the country, is from the long lines of trenches and redoubts which crown every hillside from ten miles above Fredericksburg to twenty miles below. The world has never seen such a fortified position. The famous lines at Torres Verdras could not compare to them. As I go to Mossbeck I follow the lines, and have to ride in the trenches. These are five feet wide and two and a half feet deep, having the earth thrown towards the enemy, making a bank still higher. They follow the contour of the ground and hug the bases of the hills as they wind to and from the river, thus giving natural flanking arrangements; and from the tops of the hills frown the redoubts for the sunken batteries and barbette batteries ad libitum, far exceeding the number of guns; while occasionally, where the trenches take straight across the flats, a readout stands out defiantly in the open plain to receive our howitzers, and deal destruction broadcast to the Yankees, should their curiosity tempt them to an investigation.[16]

The left of Early's long line of entrenchments began atop the high ground of Dr. Taylor's property overlooking the Falmouth Rapids on the Rappahannock River. From the Taylor property, locally known as Taylor Hill, two miles of entrenchments stretched south along Stansbury Ridge to the Orange Plank Road. Since Lee's departure for Chancellorsville these rifle pits were vacant of Confederate troops. The only unit in this vicinity was a small picket contingent from Wilcox's brigade, posted at Dr. Taylor's red brick house, "Fall Hill."

Barksdale's Mississippi brigade, detached from Major General Lafayette McLaws' division, controlled the Confederate entrenchments that extended south from the Orange Plank Road across Marye's Heights and Telegraph Hill. Following the first battle of Fredericksburg, Telegraph Hill would become known as Lee's Hill, in honor of the Confederate commander. (The title Lee's Hill will be used throughout this story.) Twelve companies of Barksdale's men were positioned well to the front of Marye's Heights and Lee's Hill within the city of Fredericksburg. South of Barksdale's sector, beginning near Deep Run, Major General Early had positioned his four brigades along the base of the ridgeline stretching toward Hamilton's Crossing.[17]

On the heights to the rear of Fredericksburg, forty-eight pieces of artillery supported Early's infantry. The Army of Northern Virginia's Chief of Artillery Brigadier General "Reverend" William N. Pendleton remained on the heights with Early and commanded the artillery. The Confederate guns were selectively placed amongst the entrenchments covering likely enemy approaches.[18]

Early's 12,700-man combined force was not a large number of defenders to hold the long line of entrenchments behind Fredericksburg. Several sections of entrenchments were unmanned. His occupied entrenchments stretched nearly seven miles and held approximately one man per every three yards, but the distinctive geography of the Fredericksburg area favored the defense. The elaborate earthworks combined with open fields of fire strengthened the defenders' belief that their elevated position would make up for their inferiority in numbers. The nearest sizable infantry support for Early was Wilcox's brigade, positioned two miles upriver near Banks's Ford.

In the predawn darkness of May 1, Benham's Federal engineers, assisted by soldiers from Owens' Philadelphia Brigade, delivered two wooden pontoon bridges to the vicinity of Banks's Ford and awaited orders. An exchange of rifle fire broke out between Owens' Federals and Confederate pickets posted across the river. A half-mile downstream from Banks's Ford sat Scott's Mill and another crossing spot known as Scott's Ford. Due to the close proximity of the two fords, Scott's Ford most often was misidentified as Banks's Ford in both Confederate and Federal reports. The actual site of the laying of these pontoon bridges was at the lesser known crossing called Scott's Ford.[19]

Farther upriver, Sickles' Third Corps steadily marched toward United States Mine Ford. Having to march twenty miles while afforded only one four-hour rest, Sickles' lead regiments arrived shortly after daylight at their assigned crossing point. Around 7:30 A.M., Sickles crossed one of the existing pontoon bridges and rode ahead toward Chancellorsville in order to coordinate with the commander of the Army of the Potomac.[20]

Friday morning, May Day, found Sedgwick still awaiting instructions from Hooker.

The informal truce on his front continued as opposing pickets held their assigned positions. Closer to the river behind Sedgwick's picketed perimeter, Union troops stood down and tried to relax. The situation was so calm that several regiments even took the time to muster for pay. Some ingenious troops stretched their wet blankets between lines of muskets that were stuck in the ground by their bayonets, allowing the men to dig entrenchments out of view of enemy pickets. Adjutant of the 5th Maine, Lieutenant George W. Bicknell, wrote, "Our blankets did us good service then; and had we been attacked, we might have had occasion to be very thankful that the fog wet our blankets, and that the opportunity was offered to dry them, accomplishing what otherwise might have been impossible."[21]

On the opposite side of the river, atop Stafford Heights, Professor Lowe ascended at 9:15 A.M. in his balloon "Washington." Lowe sent a dispatch to Sedgwick chronicling the first departure of Confederate troops from the heights behind Fredericksburg. Lowe's message read, "General: Heavy columns of the enemy's infantry and artillery are now moving up river accompanied by many army wagons, the foremost column being about opposite Falmouth and three miles from the river. There is also a heavy reserve on the heights opposite the upper crossing [Franklin's crossing], and all the rifle-pits are well filled."[22]

At 11:00 A.M., Lowe notified Sedgwick, "The largest column of enemy is moving on the road to Chancellorsville. The enemy on the opposite heights I judge considerably diminished. Can see no change under the heights and in the rifle-pits. I can see no diminution in the enemy tents." Again at 12:30 P.M., Lowe wrote Sedgwick, "A large force of the enemy are now digging rifle-pits extending from Deep Run to down beyond the lower crossing [Fitzhugh's Crossing] just by the edge of the woods at the foot of the opposite heights. There are but few troops in sight now except those manning batteries and in the rifle-pits. There appears to be a strong force in the rifle-pits."[23]

At Chancellorsville, the morning of May 1 witnessed Hooker initiating plans for an advance. After sparring with advanced skirmishers of Anderson's command, the Federals established their lines on slightly higher ground more favorable to Union artillery and infantry. Surprisingly, Hooker stopped his army's movement and ordered his advanced troops back to positions around Chancellorsville Crossroads. Hooker issued instructions to his corps commanders to have their men fortify positions around Chancellorsville. The often-cantankerous Major General George Meade, whose troops were in contact with Anderson's Confederates, angrily remarked, "My God! If we can't hold the top of the hill, we certainly can't hold the bottom of it."[24]

Hooker assumed his army's arrival at Chancellorsville would pressure the Southern commander into either vacating his formidable entrenchments or force him to attack the flanking Federal column. Hooker's halt at Chancellorsville was inopportune, as Lee's army would only feel pressured if Hooker advanced his infantry and applied it. The Army of Northern Virginia maintained its interior line and was free to maneuver at will. Lee would only withdraw if he were forced to do so and attack only if it was on his own terms. Reluctantly, Union corps commanders ordered their men to pull back to Chancellorsville Crossroads and entrench. A Union officer recalled, "The soldiers were as discomfited as if they had been checked by a serious repulse...." John Esten Cooke, a Confederate staff officer, remarked, "That this was a grave military error there can be no doubt, as, by this retrograde movement, General Hooker not only discouraged his troops ... but lost the great advantage of the open country, where his larger force could be successfully manuevered."[25]

On May 1 at 2:00 P.M. Hooker notified Butterfield, "From character of information have suspended attack. The enemy may attack me — I will try it. Tell Sedgwick to keep a sharp look out, and attack if can succeed." Hooker's idea of digging in and awaiting an attack was not poor military strategy, but this sudden change of tactics was a drastic deviation from Hooker's original intention of advancing his flanking force and bringing battle to Lee's army. This too after making it clear, prior to his departure from Falmouth, his designs were to advance and gain the heights west of Fredericksburg no matter how strongly he was opposed. Hooker's decision to change his objective relinquished control of the battlefield to his opponent.[26]

Sedgwick was oblivious to Hooker's halt. His mission was radically altered as the effort of Hooker's flanking force to attack and destroy Lee's army virtually ceased. The Sixth Corps commander remained anxious as he waited to see signs of Hooker's vanguard appear on the heights west of Fredericksburg. As the day wore on, Sedgwick became troubled by the slow-developing situation on his front. Sixth Corps casualties to this point were small, totaling only twenty men. Sedgwick awaited orders as occasional rumbles of battle reached his ears from the direction slightly east of Chancellorsville.

The telegraph line between Hooker and Sedgwick was found to be down, complicating the situation for Union commanders. Professor Lowe managed to make an observation and sent a cipher to Sedgwick. At 3:45 P.M., Lowe informed Sedgwick, "Everything opposite here remains the same."[27]

News of Hooker's halt eventually reached Sedgwick shortly before 4:00 P.M. Butterfield notified Hooker:

> Your dispatch received. A copy announcing suspension of your attack sent to Sedgwick. He and Reynolds remain quiet. They consider that to attack before you have accomplished some success, in view of the strong position and numbers in their front might fail to dislodge the enemy and render them unserviceable at the proper time. They are anxious to hear from you.[28]

Hooker's abrupt halt near Chancellorsville had greatly diminished the offensive zeal of the soldiers of the Army of the Potomac. The Federal soldiers' confidence in "Fighting Joe" Hooker began to wane. Neither Sedgwick or Reynolds could fathom why Hooker had halted his flanking column's advance and altered his plan to bring battle to Lee's army. At this juncture, the First and Sixth corps' commanders were more than anxious to hear from Major General Hooker.

Just after 5:00 P.M., Sedgwick received a glimmer of encouraging news in an order headed 1:00 P.M. Hooker's dispatch instructed him to make a demonstration as severe as possible without it being an attack. Sedgwick must have interpreted these instructions as a positive sign Hooker was going to resume the offensive. Why else would the army commander desire a demonstration below Fredericksburg?[29]

Sedgwick immediately issued orders for a display of force. On the far side of the river the two divisions of Wadsworth and Brooks were positioned as if they were readying to advance. Reynolds's Second and Third divisions did not cross, but were made visible by marching and countermarching along the River Road. At Franklin's Crossing, Brigadier General Newton's Third Division was sent across the Rappahannock by Sedgwick. Newton was instructed to move downriver toward Fitzhugh's Crossing to strengthen Wadsworth's First Corps division. Sedgwick also crossed the five regiments of Burnham's Light Division to support Brooks' division, deployed to the front of Franklin's Crossing. Shortly after the deployment of these troops, Sedgwick's expectations were again dashed and his confidence in Hooker fell another notch as a message was received canceling the order for a demonstration below Fredericksburg. Butterfield to Sedgwick, "General Hooker countermands the demonstration as too late, and orders it in. Acknowledge."[30]

Later that evening in a note to Hooker, Sedgwick described the situation on his front:

> General Reynolds has Wadsworth's division over the river occupying the rifle-pits. General Newton, with Brooks' division, occupies the upper crossing with the Light Brigade, 9,600 men. Inexpedient to cross a larger force unless they remain exposed to fire without protection or capacity for a reply. To make a good demonstration it would be necessary to take the Bowling Green Road, which would lead to an engagement and possibly a check. The road could not be held only as a picket line, it being enfiladed opposite the two crossings. The railroad line has been strengthened by rifle-pits both along the front of it. The object of the demonstration was to expose their lines of battle.[31]

Concern for defending his bridgeheads prevented Sedgwick from ascertaining accurate Confederate troop dispositions on his front. Federal intelligence reports arrived regularly at Sedgwick's headquarters, but most were inconclusive. Several reports told of large Confederate troop movements above the heights in the direction of Chancellorsville, while others reported no change in enemy troop strength in the rifle pits on or below the heights to Sedgwick's front. From a short distance downriver, Reynolds cautioned Sedgwick not to be drawn into an engagement. Reynolds interpreted the situation as, "They have been keeping up appearances, showing weakness, with the view of delaying Hooker, in tempting us to make an attack on their fortified position, and hoping to destroy us and strike for our depot over our bridges."[32]

CHAPTER 4

"The Enemy Is Fleeing..."

As Saturday, May 2, dawned, Sedgwick was awakened and instructed to put Reynolds' corps in motion toward Chancellorsville Crossroads. A rider was sent at the gallop to Reynolds' headquarters. Colonel Charles S. Wainwright of Reynolds' First Corps recorded the scene: "Before seven o'clock this morning an aide from General Sedgwick came to us, with his horse all in a foam, with orders for the First Corps to proceed at once to United States Mine Ford and join General Hooker."[1]

Reynolds assembled his First Corps and had his columns on the move by 7:00 A.M. Ten- and twenty-pounder Confederate Parrott rifles of Andrews' battalion began shelling Reynolds's blue columns as they marched back across the Rappahannock. Confederate cannoneers fired from their entrenched positions on Prospect Hill as well as from the gun emplacements on the Howison property. Sixth Corps batteries and Union reserve artillery on the opposite side of the river attempted to silence the Rebel gunners' fire. A lively artillery duel continued for almost an hour until Confederate cannonfire slackened. Southern fire proved accurate as one pontoon boat was hit, killing two Federals and wounding ten. Eight horses also fell victim, and three Federal limbers were destroyed. During their demonstration at Fitzhugh's Crossing, April 29 through May 2nd, the total casualty count for Reynolds' First Corps would amount to 172 officers and men.[2]

Having crossed the pontoon bridge, Reynolds' men marched up the Riverside Road past the Sixth Corps' crossing point, north toward Falmouth. Hundreds of Sixth Corps soldiers laid quietly on either side of the roadway as the First Corps marched north in the direction of United States Mine Ford. A member of the 6th Wisconsin noted, "The 'Light' or 'Flying Division' of the 6th Corps was then over the river, not having evacuated their portion of the line when we did ours. As we passed, the pickets of that division and those of the enemy were exchanging shots as rapidly as possible."[3]

Included in Reynolds' orders were instructions for Sedgwick to take up all bridges at Franklin's Crossing and below before daylight. These orders were delayed in getting to Sedgwick, and by the time he had received the instructions, the sun was well up. To attempt the removal of the bridges in broad daylight was inviting disaster. Sedgwick was under the impression a large percentage of Lee's force remained on the heights to his front. The Sixth Corps commander reported, "This order was received after daylight, and could not, of course, be executed without attracting the observation of the enemy, and leaving him free to proceed against the forces under General Hooker."[4]

Sedgwick extended Newton and Brooks's troops downriver as Reynolds completed his withdrawal. The day's first intelligence observations concerning enemy troops dispositions arrived at Sedgwick's headquarters. "There is no visible change since last evening.... No change as to numbers in the rifle-pits nor in range of our vision." Sedgwick immediately wired Hooker informing him of the situation on his front. Once Reynolds had recrossed the Rappahannock, the remaining pontoon bridge at Fitzhugh's Crossing was pulled out of the water and piled on the riverbank.[5]

Sedgwick's two bridges at Franklin's Crossing were left intact, while the Sixth Corps commander attempted to coordinate with Hooker. Sedgwick wired Butterfield, "I have not dared to take up the bridge at Franklin's Crossing. Reynolds's bridge ought not to be taken away until after dark; it may cost the loss of many boats. Will pontoon wagons be sent to take them at dusk? Shall the bridges at Franklin's Crossing be taken up at dark without further orders? Please communicate (answer)." Four hours later Sedgwick received this wire from headquarters, "The bridges can be taken up at such a time as General Sedgwick thinks best." The idea of removing all the bridges while his corps remained on the enemy's side of the river did not sit well with Sedgwick.[6]

At 8:15 A.M., Butterfield inquired of Lowe, "Has enemy's force decreased any?" Lowe responded, "I cannot say that the enemy have decreased, but they do not show themselves quite as much this morning, and I can see no reserves on opposite heights."[7]

Sedgwick crossed his remaining division, under Brigadier General Albion P. Howe, and all guns of the Sixth Corps' artillery. The bulk of Sedgwick's four divisions were positioned close to the riverbank under the bluff. Explosions increased as Confederate cannoneers reacted to the extension of Sedgwick's picket line to the rear of the Bernard mansion, "Mannsfield." Rolling into battery on the open plain, Sixth Corps cannon responded to the Confederate shelling. Sporadic rifle fire on Sedgwick's front broke out as perimeter skirmishers clashed. Union reserve batteries positioned across the river added additional response to Confederate battery fire.

A small insurrection arose near Franklin's Crossing as one hundred men from the 20th New York of Brigadier General Thomas H. Neill's brigade refused to cross the Rappahannock. The volunteers from Howe's Second Division believed their term of enlistment had expired according to the date they were mustered into service by a representative of the state of New York. The Federal government claimed their service started several weeks later, when a Federal representative issued the oath of allegiance. After threats of arrest or execution the majority of protestors were persuaded to fall in. Holdouts who refused to cross the river earned a court-martial and a sentence of hard labor for the duration of the war without pay or allowance due them.[8]

Hooker's headquarters at Chancellorsville sent off instructions to Butterfield regarding Sedgwick's mission. The dispatch stated, "The General commanding desires you to instruct General Sedgwick, if the opportunity presents itself with reasonable expectation of success, to attack the enemy in his front.... It is impossible for General Hooker to determine here whether it is expedient for him to attack or not. It must be left to his discretion."[9]

The suggestion of an attack came as a bit of a shock to Sedgwick, especially after having two of the three corps under his command drawn away by Hooker. Sedgwick was well aware there were only a few infantry reinforcements and no Union cavalry in his vicinity. Hooker's headquarters earlier had cautioned Sedgwick to safeguard against an enemy river crossing below Fredericksburg. The Army of the Potomac would surely be in grave danger if Lee were to lunge across the Rappahannock below Fredericksburg.

The responsibility of preventing an enemy river crossing concerned the Sixth Corps commander greatly. Sedgwick's apprehension was well founded, considering Lee could sever Hooker's line of communication with Washington and have unfettered access to the Army of the Potomac's massive supply depot at Aquia Creek. Two weeks earlier, Hooker received intelligence regarding just such a move by Lee. Hooker had written the President, "Deserters inform me that the talk in the rebel camp is that when we cross the river it is their intention to fall on our rear and attack our depots at Aquia. Recent reports of the arrival of a Confederate pontoon train at Hamilton's Crossing, immediately opposite Sedgwick's position, lent credence to Sedgwick's concerns."[10]

Having been issued the previous day, May 1, Major General Hooker's General Order No. 47 reached Sedgwick's corps. Hooker's congratulatory order proclaimed:

> It is with heartfelt satisfaction the Commanding General announces to the army that the operations of the last three days have determined that our enemy must either ingloriously fly or come out from behind his entrenchments and give us battle on our own ground, where certain destruction awaits him. The operations of the Fifth, Eleventh, and Twelfth Corps have been a succession of splendid achievements.[11]

To Sedgwick's immediate front the situation remained static. Although Confederate troop movements were reported, Federal intelligence reports indicated no substantial change in enemy troop strengths opposite Sedgwick. Stiff winds hindered Professor Lowe's balloon operation, but one ascension and observation was managed at 1:05 P.M. Butterfield forwarded the findings to Hooker. "The enemy remains the same opposite this point, and no movement is visible on any of the roads." The wind continued to gust, and for the next two hours Lowe's aeronauts were prevented from obtaining the needed altitude to observe enemy troop dispositions on Sedgwick's front.[12]

Sedgwick continued to establish his Sixth Corps close to the river, while amongst the Confederates on heights new developments had arisen. As Early was meeting with Pendleton on Stansbury Ridge, Colonel Robert H. Chilton, Lee's chief of staff, arrived with orders from the Confederate commander. Chilton, Early's former West Point classmate, explained Lee's intentions. Early was instructed to leave one infantry brigade with artillery support at Fredericksburg and to send the rest of his force to Lee's support at Chancellorsville. These orders appeared odd to both Early and Pendleton. After questioning the orders, Early reluctantly complied with Chilton's instructions and made arrangements for his command to evacuate the heights.

Early understood the importance of holding the heights behind Fredericksburg, especially with a sizable Federal force to his front. Joined by Pendleton and Hays, he continued querying Chilton about the illogical instructions to join Lee at Chancellorsville. Early understood the final decision to hold the heights was not his to make. Amazingly, unbeknownst to Early, the instructions given him by Colonel Chilton were incorrect. Chilton had misconstrued Lee's verbal instructions, and the directions given him were not what Lee had wanted. Lee's intentions were for Early to send any available troops to Chancellorsville only if the entire Federal force near Fredericksburg had withdrawn back across the Rappahannock.[13]

After over an hour of shifting troops and batteries, Early's men were formed for their march to Chancellorsville. The withdrawal was made using great caution so to attract as little attention as possible. Confederate infantry began moving off first. Pendleton's artillery followed. The gray infantry filed toward Hamilton's Crossing and turned west, up the Mine Road toward the Telegraph Road in order to intersect with the Orange Plank Road, which would lead them to Chancellorsville. Conforming to orders, the bulk of Pendleton's artillery had been limbered up and waited in column along the Telegraph Road as the infantry passed. Andrews' battalion and Graham's battery, along with a Whitworth six-pounder and various cannon of the Reserve Artillery, followed Early's column. Remaining behind on the heights was a small force consisting of Hays' brigade and fifteen guns under Pendleton. The 18th Mississippi of Barksdale's brigade also remained positioned in the city of Fredericksburg. Hays' combined force numbered approximately 2,600 men.[14]

Early employed deceptive measures in an attempt to conceal the troop withdrawal. Confederate battery commanders were instructed to shift positions giving the appearance that more guns were arriving on the heights. Smaller guns were brought up to replace larger, more valuable guns that were to depart with Early. Brigadier General Pendleton reported, "I had quite a display made of artillery horses and carriages conspicuously moving forward, as if bringing up instead of taking away guns, while those leaving were to be withdrawn as much under cover as possible." Federal signal stations had observed much Confederate activity along the heights, but reports remained indecisive.[15]

Shortly after 3:00 P.M., positive reports of Confederate troop withdrawals began to filter into Butterfield's headquarters at Falmouth. Professor Lowe managed to launch a balloon. He reported, "A brigade of the enemy left from opposite our upper crossing fifteen minutes since, and crossed Deep Run, and is now moving to the right towards Banks' Ford." Another report told of four regiments retiring from Sedgwick's front. Several Union observations of enemy troop movements on Sedgwick's front were received by Butterfield and quickly passed on to Hooker's headquarters. The reports were also forwarded to Sedgwick, but the Sixth Corps commander saw little change on his immediate front and was convinced a sizable enemy force remained behind Fredericksburg.[16]

At 4:15 P.M. a balloon in the air reported, "The enemy have entirely withdrawn their advanced line, with the exception of a small picket force." Shortly after, Lowe again informed Sedgwick, "Nearly all of the enemy's force have withdrawn from the opposite side.... Cannot at this time get sufficient elevation to tell what roads they take, but should judge by the appearance of the army wagons moving to the right that the troops are moving that way too." The Sixth Corps commander had not personally witnessed any change on his front and remained unconvinced of any large enemy troop withdrawls.[17]

Sedgwick continued to side with caution. His reluctance stemmed from a concern that a substantial enemy force was laying low in an attempt to lure him in to attacking. The nature of the terrain and long sections of entrenchments afforded the possibility of Confederate troops concealing their presence by sitting or lying down. The swift flowing Rappahannock to Sedgwick's rear was also of concern as it restricted his corps' maneuverability. If Sedgwick's isolated corps met with stiff resistance or was attacked, the river could become a major obstacle and prevent a rapid withdrawal out of a perilous situation.

Sedgwick understood his corps' situation better than anyone. He knew his command was operating within a large river basin, which meant any forward movement would entail an uphill fight over unknown terrain. The fortified range of hills to the rear of Fredericksburg was a substantial geographical obstacle. Hooker himself illustrated the significance of the high ground surrounding the Fredericksburg area in a letter written prior to the campaign. To a friend Hooker wrote, "You must be patient with me.... Remember that my army is at the bottom of a well and the enemy holds the top."[18]

At 5:00 P.M., Butterfield notified Sedgwick, "Signal at Phillips's house [F. Signal Station] reports enemy evacuated your front." From the very "bottom of the well," where Sedgwick was operating, Confederate activity could be seen to his left front on Prospect Hill. Through his field glass Sedgwick could still clearly see Confederate artillery to his right front, atop Lee's Hill. The countryside was in full bloom, and several large stands of trees prevented the Sixth Corps commander from observing Confederate troop dispositions between these two points. Below the heights, to Sedgwick's immediate front, Brooks' skirmishers remained in contact with a Confederate force. Brigadier General Harry T. Hays' 1,400-man brigade continued to hold their position behind the fortified R.F. & P. railroad embankment.[19]

Sedgwick may have appeared to be dragging his feet, but Hooker had earlier given him the authority to act as he deemed appropriate. The instructions for Sedgwick stressed he was to attack only if there was reasonable chance of success. A failed attack by Sedgwick could spell disaster and would allow Lee to strike for the Army of the Potomac's depot across the Rappahannock. Little daylight remained and Sedgwick did not believe an opportunity to attack had presented itself. Cautiously adhering to his instructions, Sedgwick exercised his discretion, and the Sixth Corps remained on the plain below Fredericksburg as a grand opportunity for the Army of the Potomac dwindled away.

Throughout the day of May 2, the Federals fortified their Chancellorsville position with earth and logs as Lee probed the invaders' earthworks for weaknesses. The previous night important news from Brigadier General Fitzhugh Lee, commanding a cavalry brigade on the Army of Northern Virginia's left, arrived at Major General J.E.B.

Stuart's cavalry headquarters. The information gathered by Lee's nephew located the Union's right flank and uncovered the fact that Hooker's flank was "in the air." Major General Stuart carried this vital intelligence personally to Lee's headquarters. The following morning, Lee again boldly split his force and dispatched Jackson's corps on a sixteen mile flanking march designed to turn Hooker's exposed right flank. While en route, fierce fighting erupted as the tail end of Jackson's column was attacked by elements of Sickles's Third Corps. Only after some hard fighting by Jackson's rearguard and a brigade from Anderson's division were the Federals checked and the Confederate Second Corps able to continue their march.[20]

Close to 5:15 P.M., from the Chancellorsville vicinity rolled a thundering clamor of battle that could clearly be heard by Sedgwick's troops positioned below Fredericksburg. Unbeknownst to the Sixth Corps, the uproar was Stonewall Jackson and six of his brigades smashing into Hooker's right flank. Unprepared and totally surprised, Major General Oliver O. Howard's Union Eleventh Corps was stampeded. Luckily for Hooker, Jackson's assault was launched with little daylight remaining, which prevented the gray attackers from coordinating further assaults on Hooker's disarranged force. Under a full moon, Hooker scrambled to shore up his forces and managed to prevent a complete disaster. Jackson's flank attack, combined with Anderson and McLaws' persistent fighting on Hooker's front, left many Yankees badly rattled. But Hooker's force was far from whipped. The Union artillery, along with some hard fighting by Slocum and Sickles' corps, enabled the Federals to establish new lines and check the Confederate onslaught.[21]

Major General Early, still operating under the verbal instructions delivered by Colonel Chilton, continued to move his division up the Orange Plank Road in the direction of Chancellorsville Crossroads. Down the Orange Plank Road galloped a courier from Lee's headquarters. The rider reported to Early and explained that Lee did not order the evacuation of the heights behind Fredericksburg. About this time a rider arrived from the rear of Early's column with news from Hays and Pendleton on Marye's Heights. The message from Hays explained that Sedgwick had advanced, and that the entire Confederate force on Marye's Heights was in jeopardy of being captured unless reinforcements were sent. The latter rider went on to explain that Brigadier General Barksdale was marching his three regiments back to support the 18th Mississippi and assist Hays' brigade on the heights behind Fredericksburg.[22]

Early was livid over the apparent foul-up in orders. He had to act quickly. Did he have enough time to return to the entrenchments behind Fredericksburg? Early assumed the Federals were about to force the evacuation of Hays' small contingent holding Marye's Heights. In the dark, the angered Early again pondered his predicament, wanting only to position his troops where they would be most effective. If Sedgwick had already captured the heights, then returning to his old position would be a waste of time and very possibly could leave his division vulnerable to attack.

As Early deliberated, Colonel John B. Gordon volunteered to return to the heights with his brigade to reinforce Hays and Barksdale. Early recognized that he could not further disperse his force and remain an effective fighting unit. His division had to be kept together and orders were given instructing his entire column to turn about in order to return to the heights behind Fredericksburg. The officer responsible for Early's misguided withdrawal, Colonel Chilton, was a longtime friend of General Lee and was never officially brought to account for his error. The Confederate Senate had shelved Chilton's original appointment to brigadier general advanced in October 1862. After nearly two more years of mediocre performance, Chilton's appointment to brigadier general would be granted in February 1864.[23]

On the plain below Fredericksburg, Sedgwick received a dispatch at 6:30 P.M. Written prior to Stonewall Jackson's attack, the instructions directed Sedgwick to cross the river as soon as indications would permit, capture Fredericksburg with everything in it, and vigorously pursue the enemy. The dispatch somewhat puzzled the Sixth Corps commander. Sedgwick was certain headquarters was aware that his command had already crossed the river and had been established there for the previous two days. Hooker's message went on to explain, "...the enemy is fleeing, trying to save his trains. Two of Sickles's divisions are among them."[24]

Hooker earlier had hastily come to the conclusion that the Confederate troops passing his front, toward his right flank, were retreating. Hooker's wishful thinking never came to fruition. His failure to properly investigate reports concerning enemy troop movements near Chancellorsville, combined with his blind assumption regarding Lee's intentions, placed his entire army in jeopardy. Unaware of Hooker's plight, Sedgwick's troops below Fredericksburg could hear the rolling crash of musketry and thundering rumble of cannon well into the night.

Most notably, the latest dispatch received by Sedgwick removed the Sixth Corps commander's authority to use his own discretion in determining when to advance. Sedgwick was now instructed to capture Fredericksburg and pursue the enemy. Immediately following the last dispatch, another reached Sedgwick's position. This message directed him to pursue the retreating enemy by the Bowling Green Road. There were no Confederate troop movements along the Bowling Green Road, and in reality Lee's army was not retreating. Sedgwick's own observations, along with intelligence information sent to him, confirmed Confederate movements along the Telegraph Road and toward the Orange Plank Road. Sedgwick understood that if he proceeded by the Bowling Green Road his corps would be moving away from Hooker's force at Chancellorsville as well as away from Lee's army.[25]

By this time darkness had fallen, and it was evident to Sedgwick that an enemy force of undetermined size remained entrenched to his front. Hays' brigade held their position, and sporadically skirmished with perimeter pickets of the Sixth Corps. After the campaign Sedgwick stated, "I had been informed repeatedly by Major General Butterfield, Chief of Staff, that the force in front of me was very small, and the whole tenor of his many dispatches would have created the impression that the enemy had abandoned my front and retired from the city and its defenses, had there not been more tangible evidence than the dispatches in question that the Chief of Staff was misinformed."[26]

The Confederate troops that remained below the heights were soon joined by

Barksdale's returning brigade. In the night, the glow from fires began illuminating the Confederate position on the heights. As Barksdale's troops marched along the heights, detachments were instructed to light many campfires in an attempt to magnify the size of the defending force.[27]

The Sixth Corps commander obviously was not comfortable with the situation on his front. He remained uneasy about the idea of distancing his corps from his bridgeheads, the only route out of enemy territory if disaster struck. After some deliberation, Sedgwick complied with his instructions by advancing the skirmishers of his First and Third divisions. By 8:00 P.M., Brooks advanced Bartlett's brigade to engage Confederate skirmishers to his front, and "after a brief but spirited engagement they were driven off." Bartlett gained control of a portion of the Bowling Green Road as Hays' Louisiana skirmishers fell back to the railroad embankment.[28]

In the dark, Newton's Third Division skirmishers had also crept forward in the direction of Hamilton's Crossing. Newton forced the 7th Louisiana back into the wood line on the far side of the Bowling Green Road. From Sedgwick's dispatch, headed 8:00 P.M., it appeared he had settled on the idea that his command could not advance farther that night. Sedgwick wrote, "General Brooks has taken the Bowling Green Road, in front of him; is still skirmishing, and will advance as long as he can see, and will then take position for the night...." Butterfield immediately forwarded this disturbing news to Hooker, and also fired back a dispatch to the Sixth Corps commander, "Can't you take Fredericksburg tonight!"[29]

Not long after, from the dark heights above the Sixth Corps came a great reverberating cheer. Thousands of voices jubilantly hollered from the darkness. This uproar was the vanguard of Early's brigades and batteries returning to their old positions on the heights behind Fredericksburg. In response, Sedgwick's soldiers of the Sixth Corps bellowed a tremendous howl in an attempt to drown out the boisterous Johnnies.

Sporadic skirmishing continued during the night of May 2 as Sedgwick's 24,000-man corps sustained their position between the Rappahannock and the Bowling Green Road. The ridgeline to Sedgwick's front came alive with many kindled fires, shooting flames into the night. Much activity could be heard coming from the heights as Early's troops reestablished themselves in their old positions. Sedgwick's Federals were not certain what to make of the enemy activity as great clouds of dark black smoke wafted into the clear night sky. Chaplain Alanson A. Haines of the 15th New Jersey recalled the commotion, "We supposed it to be the firing of the enemy's wagon trains to betoken their retreat toward Richmond, and that they had begun their inglorious flight. It was however, only the burning of the old winter camps."[30]

CHAPTER 5

"Between Us We Will Use Him Up"

At 10:00 P.M., May 2, Reynolds's weary First Corps, which had left Sedgwick's front earlier that morning, went into bivouac two miles shy of the United States Mine Ford. Before daylight of the next day, the First Corps crossed United States Mine Ford and marched toward Hooker's position. Reynolds's columns met panicked squads of Howard's routed Eleventh Corps trying to escape across the Rappahannock River. In the dark the going was slow for Reynolds's Federals as the roadway was obstructed with men and equipment. By sunrise Reynolds's men had completed their long trek and taken position near Chancellorsville Crossroads on Hooker's right.[1]

At 11:00 P.M., Sedgwick received instructions from Hooker's headquarters. The dispatch read:

> The Major-General commanding directs that General Sedgwick crosses the Rappahannock at Fredericksburg on receipt of this order, and at once take up your line of march on the Chancellorsville Road until you connect with us, and he will attack and destroy any force he may fall in with on the road. He will leave his trains behind except the pack train of small ammunition, and march to be in the vicinity of the general by daylight. He [Sedgwick] will probably fall on the rear of General Lee's forces and between us we will use him up. Send word to General Gibbon to take possession of Fredericksburg, and be sure not to fail.[2]

The wording of this last dispatch was again troubling for Sedgwick and his staff. Could it be possible for Hooker to have forgotten that the Sixth Corps had long crossed the Rappahannock? Did Hooker intend for the Sixth Corps to cross back over the Rappahannock, march to Fredericksburg, build bridges, and recross the river in order to capture Fredericksburg? The suggestion must have seemed absurd, but this sloppily dictated order left Sedgwick and his staff under a mist of uncertainty. Hooker and his staff apparently were extremely discomposed during this juncture, and were so worried about their own state of affairs at Chancellorsville that they could not recollect Sedgwick's situation. The stress levels at Hooker's headquarters were obviously high as they also failed to inform Sedgwick that the Union's situation at Chancellorsville had worsened significantly after being hit by Stonewall Jackson's flank attack.[3]

Night operations while in enemy territory were risky undertakings. Most army commanders suspended operations at dark due to the difficulty of coordinating troop movements. Interpreting his instructions, Sedgwick cautiously advanced Newton's Third Division skirmishers, and began moving by the right flank up the Bowling Green Road toward the city of Fredericksburg.

Fog had covered much of the river along with adjacent low areas as lead units of the Sixth Corps marched north toward the city. The sky was clear and the moon shone full. Stubborn Confederate skirmishers would fire and disappear, making Sedgwick's lead elements cautious. The flash of musket fire forecasted the Federals' progress to Early and his entrenched men on the heights.[4]

Colonel Joseph E. Hamblin's 65th New York, or "1st U.S. Chasseurs," of Alexander Shaler's brigade, skirmished to Sedgwick's front. About one hundred yards to the left of his column, Hamblin deployed three companies as flankers to engage enemy skirmishers situated along the base of the heights. To his front, one company acted as advance guards as another company was deployed to the right of the dirt road. Along the roadway, to the rear of the advance guard, Hamblin led his main reserve consisting of five companies numbering about two hundred and thirty men.[5]

Following the 65th New York were the three brigades of Newton's Third Division, in column. Lieutenant Charles Brewster of the 10th Massachusetts remembered the scene: "The long dark columns of troops moved off with the moon light flashing from the bright barrels and bayonets of the guns it was magnificent." The five regiments of Colonel Hiram Burnham's Light Division, who had been temporarily attached to the Third Division, brought up the rear of Newton's column.[6]

Stops were frequent as Colonel Hamblin's First Brigade skirmishers felt their way forward. From the dark, Confederate riflemen continued their deadly game of hide and seek. "Nothing broke the deep silence of the night except an occasional shot followed by the never-to-be-forgotten ping of the minie-ball," recalled a member of the Sixth Corps. Lieutenant Colonel H. W. Jackson described the advance:

> Major General Newton, who was riding with the third or fourth regiment from the advance, called out: is anyone of my staff here? Those present promptly responded, and I was directed to ride ahead and tell Colonel Shaler to brush away the enemy's pickets. The road was filled with soldiers, some lying down, others resting on their guns, but a passage was quickly cleared. At Hazel Run Colonel Shaler and Colonel Hamblin were found standing together. Here the enemy made a determined resistance. Their pickets were but a few yards distance. On the other side of the creek the road made a sharp ascent and curved to the right. In a subdued tone Colonel Shaler said: Colonel Hamblin, you have heard the order from General Newton? At once Colonel Hamblin left. In a moment there was a noise of hurrying feet, the troops quickly disappeared in the dark: a shout, a bright sudden flash, a roll of musketry followed, and the road was open.

Hamblin's losses in killed and wounded amounted to fifteen. The major of the 65th New York, Thomas Healy, received a mortal wound while advancing his skirmishers.[7]

Captain Valarian Razderichin of Hooker's staff arrived at Sedgwick's position with news of Stonewall Jackson's flank assault at Chancellorsville. Razderichin reemphasized the orders earlier sent to Sedgwick and explained that the Sixth Corps' mission was to fall upon Lee's rear at daylight. "It seems to be of vital importance that you should fall on Lee's rear with crushing force," explained Razderichin. Sedgwick acknowledged his instructions, and Razderichin returned to Butterfield's headquarters.[8]

Sedgwick knew it would be all but impossible to reach Chancellorsville by daybreak. Hooker's proposed timetable for Sedgwick's arrival at Chancellorsville was only achievable if there remained no Confederate resistance on the Sixth Corps' front. Considering Early's Confederate force and the twelve-mile distance to Chancellorsville Crossroads, Hooker's instructions for Sedgwick were unrealistic. Brigadier General Gibbon also recognized this fact and would later state that Hooker's order to Sedgwick was not a practicable one.[9]

At midnight, Brigadier General Albion P. Howe ordered Sedgwick's Second Division to follow the advance up the Bowling Green Road. While waiting for the tail end of Newton's division to move, Brigadier General Thomas H. Neill's Third Brigade perimeter pickets were attacked. The assault fell on the outpost of Colonel Daniel B. Bidwell's 49th New York, who stood their ground, repulsing the Confederate incursion. Shortly after 1:00 A.M., Howe's Second Division was able to advance their white Greek Cross up the Bowling Green Road toward the city of Fredericksburg.[10]

Close to 2:00 A.M. on Sunday, May 3, Newton's Third Division vanguard reached the outskirts of Fredericksburg. Federal regiments were halted in the dark streets, while skirmishers slowly advanced, pushing Brigadier General Barksdale's Confederate skirmishers through the city. More than a mile below the city, Brigadier General W.T.H. Brooks's First Division was still deployed to protect the bridges at Franklin's Crossing. Clashing with Confederate skirmishers and artillery, Brooks was readying to receive an attack. Brooks reported, "The enemy kept a large force continually in our front while in this position, and appeared to be receiving reinforcements from our left...."[11]

A Negro entered the Sixth Corps's lines and was brought to Sedgwick's headquarters. The man reported that Confederates occupied the heights, and they were planning to cut the canal to flood the roads to the rear of Fredericksburg. This bit of intelligence worried several of Sedgwick's staff and the ensuing discussion caused a slight delay.[12]

Shortly before 3:00 A.M., as Howe's rear units began disappearing in the darkness up the Bowling Green Road, line officers of Brooks' Second Brigade began advancing their lead columns towards Fredericksburg. To protect Sedgwick's bridgeheads, Brigadier General David A. Russell's Third Brigade would remain behind on the plain between the river and the Bowling Green Road. In support of Russell's infantry, Captain William Hexamer's six ten-pounder Parrott rifles, commanded by Lieutenant Augustus N. Parsons, remained deployed around the ruins of the Bernard mansion "Mannsfield" along with six twelve-pounder Napoleons under the charge of Lieutenant E.B. Williston.[13]

Major General Gouverneur K. Warren, accompanied by Lieutenant James, arrived via Franklin's Crossing in order to assist in guiding Sedgwick's advance. Warren informed Sedgwick of developments at Chancellorsville Crossroads, while he observed Sedgwick's progress for Hooker's headquarters. Warren informed Sedgwick that any force to his front must be a small one, but the Sixth Corps commander was far from convinced.

Sedgwick refused to be pressured into reckless action, especially by a headquarters that he believed was operating on conjecture regarding the situation on his corps' front.[14]

Sedgwick appears to have held no confidence in Hooker at this time. Such lack of confidence is obviously a major obstacle in any offensive operation and may explain why Sedgwick's primary responsibility as a field commander became the protection of his corps. Sedgwick's command was isolated and in a precarious situation. His four divisions were stretched out in column for well over a mile, with an enemy force of undetermined size immediately on its left flank. In the darkness, the Sixth Corps continued marching and skirmishing up the Bowling Green Road toward Fredericksburg.

As the lead elements of Brooks' column approached the stream known as Deep Run, heavy skirmishing to his left and rear forced a halt. Brooks sent out support for his First Division skirmishers in an effort to secure a position behind the line of enemy entrenchments. A section of Napoleons, under Major J. W. Latimer of Andrews's Confederate battalion, opened fire on the Federals. Seeing that the Federal skirmishers were not being dislodged by the artillery fire, Brigadier General William "Extra Billy" Smith, commanding Early's old Virginia Brigade, sent out three regiments to push Brooks' skirmishers back. Andrews shifted the batteries of Graham and Brown in order to bolster the fire of Latimer's guns. Andrews also directed the fire of a rifled section under Carpenter, toward the Yankees near Deep Run.[15]

To check the Confederate thrust, Brigadier General Joseph J. Bartlett's Second Brigade formed in the small valley containing Deep Run. Bartlett's men clashed with Smith's Confederate skirmishers, who were soon joined on their left by skirmishers sent forward by Brigadier General Robert F. Hoke. Lieutenant James H. Rigby and Captain William H. McCartney's Federal batteries, under the overall command of Major John Tompkins, went into action, firing shell and case shot into the gray skirmishers. As daylight grew, Bartlett and Brown's brigades of Brooks' division were compelled by Confederate artillery fire to abandon their advanced position and seek protection with the remainder of their division in a line of abandoned Confederate entrenchments.[16]

While falling back, several regiments of Bartlett's brigade were forced to cross a ravine traversed by Deep Run. Confederate gunners had aligned several cannon's fields of fire to sweep the ravine. In order to gain the safety of the opposite embankment, Bartlett's Federals had to run a deadly gauntlet. With little choice, Bartlett's men took off sprinting across the exposed area, suffering numerous artillery casualties. An observer noted, "General Bartlett, sitting on his horse near by amidst bursting shells, watched the movement, and could only exclaim, as he saw these men rushing into the very jaws of death.... Noble men, noble men."[17]

Troop disbursements of the Sixth Corps kept Confederate Major General Jubal Early off balance. Early was uncertain as to the direction of Sedgwick's main thrust, which slowed him in concentrating his much smaller force. The Federals had met with such disaster on the high ground directly behind Fredericksburg the previous December that Early felt the enemy would only demonstrate toward the fortified Marye's Heights and strongly assault his center. During Burnside's Fredericksburg campaign, the Federals had found a small measure of success assaulting this center sector of the

Confederate defensive line. Early wrote, "I was very apprehensive that the enemy would attempt to cut my line in two by moving up Deep Run, which would have been the most dangerous move to us he could have made."[18]

As Sedgwick advanced, two pontoon bridges, arranged four abreast, one behind the other, were slowly rafted up river from Franklin's Crossing to a spot just below Fredericksburg. Sedgwick sent word to Hooker, "There is still a force in Fredericksburg; marching as rapidly as possible, but can not reach you by daylight." Sedgwick's arrival in Fredericksburg enabled Major Walter L. Cassin of the 15th New York Engineers to tow his pontoons farther up the Rappahannock River and position them just above J. Horace Lacy's house, "Chatham." Squads of engineers, assisted by members of Brigadier General John Gibbon's Second Corps division, went to work anchoring the boats in the early morning darkness. Moving upriver just behind Cassin was Captain Chauncey B. Reese and members of his battalion of U.S. Engineers, "Reese's Regulars." Reese floated his pontoons into position downstream, just below the destroyed trestle of the Richmond, Fredericksburg, and Potomac Railroad.[19]

Newton's troops slowly crept through the dark, deserted streets advancing toward the rear of Fredericksburg. Sporadic shots rang out as the 18th Mississippi withdrew from the city to forts on the hills behind the war-ravaged city. The last of Barksdale's stubborn skirmishers had evacuated the city by 4:00 A.M. Barksdale later remarked that his skirmishes retired "because it had felt that resistance was futile."[20]

Confederate artillery opened on the Federals, sending shot and shell crashing through buildings. Federal artillery unlimbered to the rear of the city and responded to the shelling with ear-pounding salvoes. The plunging fire of the Confederate guns proved more effective as several Sixth Corps guns were forced to reposition. One three-inch ordnance rifle of Captain Andrew Cowan's battery, First Lieutenant Theodore Atkins's section, had its carriage damaged by the intense Confederate fire. In the early morning darkness, siege rifles and other large rifled cannon of the Union Artillery Reserve became active on Stafford Heights. Union battery commanders fired shells toward the flashing signatures of Confederate guns entrenched on the heights to their distant front.[21]

Sedgwick's Third Division troops had advanced through Fredericksburg by 5:00 A.M. and controlled the city. Before dawn broke, signal officers had perched themselves in the cupola atop Fredericksburg's courthouse and in the spire of St. George's Church. Below in the streets, mounted orderlies waited anxiously for dawn and the forthcoming observations that were to be carried to Butterfield's headquarters at Falmouth. Sedgwick sent orders advancing his supply and hospital trains up the muddy River Road on the right bank, or Falmouth bank, of the Rappahannock River. Surgeon Henry Janes of the 3rd Vermont was one who struggled while the long trains of the Sixth Corps advanced. Janes was in charge of Sedgwick's Second Division tent hospital. He later wrote of the ordeal, "Owing to the changes of the position of the contending forces, it was necessary to move the hospital of the second division five times; the Rappahannock being twice crossed."[22]

Accompanying the Sixth Corps' trains were the pontoon boats and bridging material that had made up the last of Sedgwick's bridges positioned below the city of Fredericksburg. En route from Fitzhugh's Crossing, Major Edmund O. Beers of the 50th New York Engineers received instructions to place his bridge between the two bridges under construction to the rear of Fredericksburg. Beers' New Yorkers eventually placed this third bridge just below the nearly completed bridge, positioned in the vicinity of the Lacy house.[23]

No one with the Sixth Corps had a working knowledge of the roadways between Fredericksburg and Chancellorsville. Sedgwick attempted but failed to find guides who would detail the fastest route to Chancellorsville Crossroads. Sedgwick sought assistance from headquarters at Falmouth. Butterfield located and sent over to Sedgwick a contraband who was familiar with the Fredericksburg area. "Little Dan" Butterfield followed up by wiring Sedgwick, "Seize the mayor [Montgomery Slaughter], or any citizen. Put them ahead as guides on pain of death for false information." Sedgwick disregarded Butterfield's suggestion as he turned his attention to the Confederate force entrenched on his front.[24]

The first balloon to ascend on Sunday, May 3, drifted aloft at 5:15 A.M. Professor Lowe reported to Sedgwick and Butterfield, "The enemy have apparently increased their force during the night, and appear again at the foot of the opposite heights. There does not appear to be as many, however as yesterday morning."[25]

At Falmouth, Butterfield's headquarters was astir as Federal brass-pounders (telegraph operators) rapidly transmitted telegraph messages to Hooker at Chancellorsville. The overall tenor of Butterfield's dispatches clearly attest to the uncertainty Sedgwick's corps faced:

5:45 A.M.—Heavy cannonading in Sedgwick's front for the last twenty minutes, apparently in front of Fredericksburg.

6:08 A.M.—Balloon reports enemy reappearing on heights in front of Sedgwick's crossing. Sedgwick, judging from the sound is meeting with heavy resistance.

6:20 A.M.—Sedgwick reports himself at Sumner's old battleground at 5:30A.M., hotly engaged, and not sanguine of the result.

6:45 A.M.—Sedgwick's prospect here look unfavorable, from reports. He is not out of Fredericksburg.

7:05 A.M.—Sedgwick still in front of Fredericksburg, as far as I can judge. Trains were running up all night to the vicinity of Hamilton's Crossing. It may be that the enemy were reinforced.[26]

CHAPTER 6

Forward Into Battery

Up to this point, the campaign had been a case of hurry ups and waits for the Second Corps' troops under Brigadier General John Gibbon. Positioned directly across the river from Fredericksburg, his Second Division regiments had remained under arms for several days as they awaited orders. His troops' idleness proved detrimental as trouble arose on May 1, when a small insurrection occurred within the ranks. Six companies of the 34th New York refused to fall in on the belief that their two-year term of enlistment had expired.[1]

The New Yorkers' brigade commander, Brigadier General Alfred Sully and the colonel of the 34th New York, Byron Laflin, were unable to remedy the situation. Brigadier General Gibbon was a hard-bitten regular and would not tolerate any uprising in his Second Corps division. Sully was immediately relieved from brigade command for his inability to enforce discipline within his ranks. To quell the mutiny, Gibbon led the 15th Massachusetts to the 34th New York's camp and instructed the six companies to return to duty. Gibbon warned, "if they did not at once respond to this appeal and rejoin their regiment he would order the regiment in front to fire and kill every man it could, adding at once, "Every man willing to do duty, step to the front." The New Yorkers quickly realized that Gibbon meant business. All expeditiously stepped forward, ending the protest. Gibbon replaced Sully with Colonel Henry W. Hudson of the 82nd New York.[2]

On the evening of May 2 the newly appointed brigade commander, Colonel Hudson, reported to Gibbon well-besotted and reeking of distilled spirits. Gibbon instantly recognized his intoxication and placed Colonel Hudson under arrest. The command of Gibbon's First Brigade was given to Colonel Byron Laflin of the 34th New York. Laflin had gone to great lengths and worked hard throughout the ordeal in order to maintain discipline within his disgruntled regiment. Immediately following the protest, Laflin remarkably produced eighteen of twenty-five volunteers from among his ranks of malcontents for a proposed forced river crossing. Four regiments in his brigade were required to produce twenty-five volunteers each for the crossing. Sedgwick's advance into Fredericksburg in the early morning of May 3 rendered the forced river crossing unnecessary. Throughout the campaign, Colonel Laflin demonstrated an ability to instill a sense of duty within his regiment. In a year's time, Laflin's continued solid perform-ance would earn him a brevet to brigadier general of volunteers.[3]

The last planks of the first pontoon bridge into Fredericksburg were laid at 6:30 A.M., May 3. Gibbon crossed and galloped to Sedgwick's position as his Third Brigade, under Colonel Norman J. Hall, began marching over the Rappahannock. Closely fol-lowing Hall's brigade were the twelve rifled cannon of batteries B and G, 1st Rhode Island Light Artillery. Hall's foot soldiers halted on Princess Anne Street, stacked arms, and awaited instructions.

Gibbon's trailing First Brigade experienced a slight delay in crossing as Colonel Laflin was detained while deploying the 19th Maine in patrols to protect the military telegraph line running from Falmouth to Banks's Ford. The Fifth Corps' 20th Maine were also ordered to guard the telegraph line. Just prior to the start of the campaign, an outbreak of smallpox forced the 20th Maine out of action and into isolation on Quar-antine Hill. Orders were issued to put to death anyone caught tampering with the tele-graph line. The remainder of Laflin's Second Corps brigade eventually crossed and formed to the right of Hall's men at rest along Princess Anne Street. Gibbon's Second Brigade, under Brigadier General Joshua T. Owens, had previously been sent upriver to reinforce Brigadier General Tyler, whose guns were protecting the approaches to Banks's and Scott's fords.[4]

Trotting up the cobblestone streets, Gibbon and his staff arrived at Sedgwick's position to the rear of Fredericksburg. Sedgwick directed Gibbon to deploy his two brigades north of Fredericksburg and attempt to carry the heights opposite that point. The Sixth Corps commander's design was to diffuse Confederate troop strength to his immediate front by forcing his opponent to counter Gibbon's maneuvers. If the Con-federates defenders on Marye's Heights failed to react, their fortified position would be vulnerable to a Federal turning movement.

Some three miles upriver, Confederate Brigadier General Cadmus M. Wilcox's brigade was still positioned on the cliffs overlooking Banks's Ford. The previous day, May 2, Wilcox had witnessed large bodies of Union infantry and artillery (Reynolds' First Corps) marching up river. At dawn on May 3, Wilcox viewed only a small num-ber of Yankee sentinels across the river carrying just their haversacks. The Yankees' rel-ative inactivity convinced Wilcox that the majority of Federals seen the day before had moved upriver to cross at another ford. Wilcox had been earlier instructed by Lee to protect the approaches to Banks's Ford and to "hold at all hazards." He was also directed to leave a small contingent to watch the ford if, in his judgment, the enemy did not appear to be readying to cross the Rappahannock at that point. Responding to devel-opments, Wilcox detached the fifty troopers belonging to Major Charles R. Collins' 15th Virginia Cavalry to guard the approaches to Banks's Ford. Accompanying Collins were two guns, under Lieutenant James S. Cobbs of John W. Lewis's Pittsylvania (Vir-ginia) Battery. Lewis's Virginia Battery was under the command of Lieutenant Nathan Penick. Wilcox formed his Alabama regiments and prepared to march his 1,700 men to Lee's position at Chancellorsville.[5]

On Marye's Heights, directly to the rear of Fredericksburg, Brigadier General

Barksdale had deployed his Mississippi brigade among the earthworks. There was an obvious deficiency in the number of Confederate troops positioned to hold the elaborate entrenchments covering the heights. Remarkably, the defenders remained resolute in their belief that the natural strength of Marye's Heights would compensate for their sparse numbers. The 18th Mississippi and three companies of the 21st Mississippi held the sunken road behind the stone wall at the base of Marye's Heights. The remaining seven companies of the 21st Mississippi were positioned between the Marye house, "Brompton," and the Orange Plank Road. The 17th and 13th Mississippi regiments manned entrenchments running south, between Marye's Heights and Lee's Hill.[6]

The previous day, in an effort to strengthen his defenses near Deep Run, Major General Early had divided Brigadier General Harry T. Hays' brigade of Louisiana Tigers. The 6th and 9th Louisiana regiments, under Colonel William Monaghan, were sent up the trench line toward Barksdale's position. Monaghan placed his men in entrenchments to the right of Barksdale's Mississippians, along the base of Lee's Hill and the Howison property.[7]

With an attack imminent, the early hours of May 3 proved a trying time for Barksdale. His concern heightened over the small number of defenders positioned in his sector. The commander of the 21st Mississippi, Colonel Benjamin Humphreys, found Barksdale propped up against the base of a large tree trying to get some rest. As Humphreys approached, the colonel asked, "Are you asleep, General?" From underneath his blanket Barksdale spoke sharply, "No sir, who could sleep with a million of armed Yankees all around him." In the morning darkness, Barksdale sent a rider down the entrenchments to notify Early of the Federal buildup within Fredericksburg and to request reinforcements. Early responded by ordering Brigadier General Hays, near Hamilton's Crossing, to double-quick his 5th, 7th, and 8th Louisiana regiments up the trench line to strengthen Barksdale's force positioned to the rear of Fredericksburg.[8]

Prior to sunrise, Brigadier General William N. Pendleton replaced the majority of Confederate artillery that mistakenly had been pulled off the heights the day before. Colonel James B. Walton of the Washington Artillery commanded six guns entrenched along the ridgeline of Marye's Heights. Near the Willis family cemetery, Captain Charles W. Squires positioned his 1st Company's two three-inch ordnance rifles. Captain Merritt B. Miller commanded two twelve-pounder Napoleons, positioned in gun pits alongside the Orange Plank Road. Accompanying Miller's two pieces were two twelve-pounder howitzers of Captain B.F. Eshleman's 4th Company, under the command of Lieutenant Joseph Norcom. Two guns of the Washington Artillery belonging to Captain J. B. Richardson's 2nd Company were absent, under repair at Chesterfield depot.[9]

A pair of ten-pounder Parrott rifles under the charge of Captain Andrew Burnet Rhett brought the total number of guns on Marye's Heights to eight. Two days prior, on May 1, an unusual transfer of gun crews occurred involving Rhett's gun section, as both crews were replaced by cannoneers under Lieutenant John Thompson Brown of Captain William Parker's Richmond (Virginia) Battery. On General Lee's order, Colonel Edward P. Alexander dispatched Brown's men, who arrived at Marye's Heights on the morning of May 1. Dejectedly, Rhett's South Carolinians went to the rear and did not participate further in this campaign. Rhett's removal had long been in the works due to the captain's frequent absences from his company. Brown's Virginians took control of Rhett's ten-pounders dug in on Willis Hill. The Virginians' commanding position on Willis Hill made up the southern portion of the fortified heights collectively known as Marye's Heights.[10]

Colonel Henry C. Cabell commanded the artillery positioned on Lee's Hill and the Howison property. Atop the commanding position of Lee's Hill, Captain John C. Fraser prepared two ten-pounder Parrotts and one three-inch rifle of his Pulaski (Georgia) Battery. Accompanying Fraser's guns was a twelve-pounder Howitzer belonging to Captain George M. Patterson's Sumter (Georgia) Battery. To Fraser's right, positioned on the Howison property, were a Parrott rifle and a twelve-pounder Howitzer of Captain Henry H. Carlton's Troup (Georgia) Battery. The

Brigadier General William Barksdale (C.S.A.) (Massachusetts MOLLUS Collection, U.S. Military History Institute).

remaining two ten-pounder Parrotts of Carlton's battery were positioned in gun pits to the front of the Howison house, "Breahead." Above, on the ridge to the rear of Breahead, the remaining three twelve-pounder guns of Patterson's Sumter (Georgia) Battery were positioned.[11]

As Sedgwick deployed his Sixth Corps infantry in and around Fredericksburg, his artillery opened a spirited barrage onto Marye's Heights. Guns of the Federal reserve artillery, which included siege rifles and other guns of position, were in battery across the river at Falmouth and on Stafford Heights. Union reserve artillery kept up an almost constant cannonade since first light, and with the addition of Sedgwick's batteries, the air was thick with deadly exploding projectiles. A member of the 33rd New York observed the bombardment:

> One of the shells exploded a rebel caisson at the redoubt near the stone-wall, and killed ten horses. After blowing up the caisson struck two horses directly behind, and hurled eight others down the steep precipice in the rear into a yawning chasm beneath. They presented a hideous spectacle as they lay at the bottom, dead and dying.[12]

Colonel Cabell recalled a heroic deed performed by one of his Confederate gunners, Private Richard W. Saye. Cabell recorded, "A shell, with the fuse still burning, had fallen near; it was pointed out to Saye; he unhesitatingly seized it and threw it over the parapet, probably saving lives thereby, as the shell exploded a moment after." Holding tight to their entrenchments, much of the Confederate artillery did not respond to this shelling in order to preserve ammunition for the Federal infantry assault that was sure to be launched on their position.[13]

At 7:00 A.M., Gibbon began advancing his 3,400 Federals toward the northern edge of Fredericksburg. Gibbon intended to deploy his Second Corps troops via the River Road and attack the Confederate left, which was believed to be lightly held. In advance of this Federal force, Major General Warren had ridden forward to reconnoiter the ground. Warren crossed a small bridge, spanning a millrace, and galloped to the vicinity of the partially constructed monument honoring George Washington's mother, Mary Ball Washington. From this advanced position, Warren observed a large canal carrying water into the city of Fredericksburg. Retiring Confederates had earlier dismantled a bridge crossing the thirty-foot-wide, six-foot-deep canal. The planks covering the bridge had been removed, leaving only the large wooden supports spanning the waterway. Warren put heels to his horse and galloped back to Gibbon's advancing columns. Warren instructed squads of pioneers to pull planks from nearby barns for material to lay as decking planks for the bridge.

To Sedgwick's distant front, the majority of Brigadier General Hays' three Louisiana regiments arrived at the base of Marye's Heights. In an effort to counter Gibbon's line extension to the north of Fredericksburg, the 5th, 7th, and 8th Louisiana were directed to continue their trek toward the far left of the Confederate defensive line. Hays' men eventually arrived and collapsed from exhaustion in the rifle pits along the lower portion of Stansbury Ridge. While en route, fatigue had forced some of Hays' men to fall out and take position among the defenders on Marye's Heights. Running almost eight miles of Confederate trench line, while dodging Union artillery fire, Hays' men had little time to rest as three regiments of Gibbon's Federal infantry advanced toward the disassembled canal bridge.[14]

Confederate pickets atop Taylor Hill earlier viewed Gibbon's appearance at the northern edge of Fredericksburg. Riders raced to the vicinity of Banks's Ford to inform Wilcox of developments. Wilcox immediately put his brigade in motion toward Fredericksburg, and rode ahead to Taylor Hill to investigate. Glassing toward the Stansbury house, "Snowden," Wilcox observed Hays' Confederate troops establishing themselves amongst entrenchments along Stansbury Ridge. He rode down to the rifle pits to meet with Hays. Barksdale joined them, and the three discussed the developing situation regarding the Federal build-up in Fredericksburg. Wilcox quickly dispatched riders with orders to reposition his brigade into the earthworks on Dr. Taylor's property, overlooking Fredericksburg.[15]

Once established on Taylor Hill, Wilcox's men observed Gibbon's Union troops advancing through the early morning fog. Wilcox directed Lieutenant Nathan Penick to position two rifled guns into gun pits near Dr. Taylor's house, "Fall Hill." Penick's entrenched guns rapidly attempted to get the range of Gibbon's men advancing toward the canal. The barking reports of Penick's Confederate artillery immediately drew response from Federal reserve batteries positioned across the river at Falmouth. Penick adjusted and lobbed shells at the Federal batteries on the other side of the Falmouth Rapids. Wilcox's remaining guns were hauled down to Stansbury Ridge and took position in gun pits. Four rifled guns of Captain J. D. Moore's Norfolk (Virginia) Battery opened on Gibbon's force, advancing in column.[16]

From his position on Marye's Heights, Brigadier General Pendleton reacted to Gibbon's maneuvering Federals. He ordered Lieutenant Norcom's gun section, positioned in gun pits along side the Orange Plank Road, sent to the far left of Marye's Heights. Taking position in a gun pit almost opposite the front of Gibbon's men, Norcom's section of twelve-pounder Napoleons opened an accurate fire on to the Federals. Norcom's two guns prevented Gibbon's force from replanking the disassembled bridge. These two Confederate guns were urgently needed at this point, but Pendleton erred by not ordering up other available guns from the rear as reinforcements. Pendleton had sent instructions to move Norcom's gun section assuming Captain Miller's two guns were still positioned alongside the Orange Plank Road. Unbeknownst to Pendleton, Barksdale had earlier sent this gun section to a position higher on the heights, just north of the Marye house, "Brompton." Norcom's change of position, ordered by Pendleton, greatly reduced Confederate firepower along William and Hanover streets, leading up the center of Marye's Heights.[17]

Gibbon's force was an inviting target for Norcom's Confederate gunners. Accurate artillery fire forced the Federals to disperse and seek cover. A company commander of the 20th Massachusetts, Captain Oliver Wendell Holmes, described the experience:

> Pleasant to see a d'd gun brought up to an earthwork deliberately brought to bear on you — to notice your company is exactly in range — 1st discharge puff ... and my knapsack supporter is knocked to pieces ... second discharge and man in front of me hit — 3rd whang the iron enters through garter & shoe into my heel — They have been firing hard ever since and as the stretcher is waiting for me — I stop.[18]

The future United States Supreme Court justice would receive his third wound of the war on this field. After recovering from his foot wound, Captain Holmes returned to duty and was offered a line officer's position with the 20th Massachusetts. Holmes turned the company commander slot down and sought a staff position. Holmes eventually secured a position as aide-de-camp on Sedgwick's headquarters staff of the Sixth Corps.[19]

As shot and shell explosions tore up the ground, Colonel Hall rapidly deployed Gibbon's Third Brigade behind a stone wall, which lined the sunken roadbed of the River Road. Henry L. Abbott of the 20th Massachusetts later praised Hall for his gallant performance. Abbott wrote, "But thanks to Colonel Hall, who showed wonderful coolness & self-possession, where many a man in an open space under heavy fire would have lost his head & destroyed us."[20]

Gibbon sent Colonel Laflin's brigade farther to his right in an attempt to cross the canal at another bridge, but he too was forced to seek protection from the intense Confederate shelling. The majority of Laflin's brigade took cover from the Confederate fire in abandoned entrenchments closer to the Rappahannock River. Two companies of the

15th Massachusetts were advanced a greater distance up the River Road, only to find that route blocked. By this time, skirmishers from Wilcox's brigade had taken position near the Oyster Shell Road, leading up the hillside on Dr. Taylor's property to "Fall Hill." The canal was an impassable obstacle, preventing Gibbon's infantry from closing with the enemy. Any attempt to repair the exposed bridges would have been suicidal. Gibbon later explained the reconstruction idea as not very feasible.[21]

Meanwhile, Gibbon sent forward into battery the six rifled cannon of Captain J.G. Hazard's Battery B, 1st Rhode Island. Hazard was on sick leave, and the battery was under the command of Lieutenant T. Fred Brown. Near the edge of the city, in the vicinity of the partially constructed Mary Washington Monument, Brown's battery of three-inch ordnance rifles rumbled into position. Artillery from both sides roared as Gibbon's infantry held fast for protection.

From gun pits on the Taylor property, Penick's Confederate gunners had difficulty depressing the muzzles of their guns enough to effectively engage Gibbon's exposed force. In an attempt to improve his field of fire, Penick pulled his guns out of the redoubts and fired from the open. This dangerously exposed the Confederate guns to incoming Federal artillery fire, emanating from Federal reserve batteries across the river. Penick was soon forced to limber up and reposition his guns near Moore's guns in battery on Stansbury Ridge.[22]

Galloping forward, Captain G.W. Adams' Battery G, 1st Rhode Island, struggled to get into a firing position on the open plain. A member of the 2nd Rhode Island recalled, "As they [Battery G, 1st Rhode Island] were crossing a small bridge over a stream, a shot hit one of the caissons and knocked it off the bridge." As enemy artillery fire increased, Adams advanced his guns and went into action throwing shells at Confederate gunners on the heights.[23]

Adams's six exposed guns instantly drew intense hostile fire. Adams's cannoneers worked feverishly to maintain a steady rate of fire as an accurate Confederate shelling took its toll. Battery G, 1st Rhode Island, suffered twenty-four killed or wounded, sixteen horses killed, and one gun carriage badly damaged. Because of the qualities shown on the morning of May 3, 1863, Major General Sedgwick requested that Battery G, 1st Rhode Island, be detached from the Second Corps, where it had been since the corps was formed, and placed in his own Sixth Corps, where it remained until the end of the war. Colonel Charles H. Tompkins, chief of artillery for the Sixth Corps, and Major John A. Tompkins, who commanded Sedgwick's First Division artillery, both originally hailed from the 1st Rhode Island Artillery and undoubtedly played a role in formulating this transfer.[24]

Forced to retire, Adams repositioned Battery G closer to the city adjacent to Lieutenant T. Fred Brown's battery. Batteries B and G, 1st Rhode Island, maintained a constant fire onto enemy positions to their front. To the rear of Fredericksburg, cannon muzzles also flashed as Sixth Corps rifled batteries continued to shell the heights to their front. Private Carlton Felch of Company C, 3rd Vermont, recorded in his diary, "Moved on the Bowling Green Road. Ball opened at 6 heavy cannonading some musketry..."[25]

In an attempt to assist Gibbon in his turning movement, the Sixth Corps commander sent over the 10th Massachusetts, 37th Massachusetts, and the 2nd Rhode Island. For protection from the shelling, these Sixth Corps regiments took position in and adjacent to the Fredericksburg Cemetery to the rear of Gibbon's busy cannoneers. With the main canal to their front, Gibbon's two Second Corps brigades were neutralized as they were pinned down by the cannonade that shook the ground they hugged. Importantly, Gibbon's maneuvers revealed for the first time the presence of Confederate troops to Sedgwick's far right front, atop Taylor Hill. The presence of Gibbon's Second Corps troops occupied the attention of Confederate infantry troops on Stansbury Ridge and Taylor Hill, preventing them from shifting to their right to support Barksdale's force entrenched along Marye's Heights. The destroyed bridges over the canal thwarted Sedgwick's attempt at a turning movement, while his efforts toward implementing this tactic consumed valuable time and delayed the Sixth Corps' advance toward Chancellorsville.[26]

Brigadier General Gibbon was irate over the lack of intelligence concerning the condition of bridges spanning the canal. This information should have been circulated among the commanders operating near Fredericksburg. Sedgwick had been convalescing from three wounds received at Antietam and was not a participant in Burnside's Fredericksburg Campaign. Once established within Fredericksburg, the canal must have been obvious to Sedgwick. The Sixth Corps commander apparently did not know the location or condition of bridges spanning the lengthy canal. Although Gibbon saw action during Burnside's campaign and somewhat knew the lay of the land, he had reason to complain, for the better part of his Second Corps division was dangerously exposed on a mission that was impossible to complete. Union intelligence reports made by signal stations and aeronauts simply failed to mention the canal or condition of bridges in their dispatches to Major General Butterfield, headquartered at Falmouth.[27]

From the Phillips house on Stafford Heights, acting Chief Signal Officer Captain Samuel Cushing attempted to open flag communication with Sedgwick, but failed. Cushing's earlier torch signals sent the night before had also failed to get a response from Sedgwick. Unable to "call" Sedgwick's signal officers, Cushing was certain his signals were being ignored. Unbeknownst to Cushing, Sedgwick was operating without signals per instructions issued by Major General Butterfield. Butterfield understood that the enemy could read Federal signals sent by flag or torch. Butterfield wrote Sedgwick, "I don't want any signal. It will betray our movement for miles. The enemy read our signals." Butterfield's order concerning the use of signals may very well have caused the poor flow of intelligence concerning the condition of the bridges spanning the canal.[28]

Butterfield failed to notify his own signal officer of these instructions issued to Sedgwick, and Cushing continued to signal across the river. Frustrated in his attempts, Cushing threatened to place Sedgwick's signal officers under arrest. Finally, Captain Cushing received a written explanation from the Sixth Corps' signal officer, Captain E. C. Pierce. Now enlightened, Cushing responded to Pierce, "Use your cipher (as heretofore) to send important messages. Tell General Sedgwick that messages may be sent to him giving him information regarding position of the enemy, which will not aid the enemy much, and may aid him."[29]

At his headquarters in the Chancellor house, Major General Hooker remained on the defensive as he waited to hear Sedgwick's advance. The Federal Third and Twelfth corps' troops held off attacks by Jackson's corps, led by Major General J.E.B. Stuart, as Lee attempted to reunite his force around Chancellorsville. During the fighting, the Union Army commander made the mistake of ordering back Sickles' corps from their position on the high ground of Hazel Grove. Major General Stuart immediately seized the vacated position. Thirty-one Confederate guns soon occupied Hazel Grove and opened on the Federals. The fire of several of these guns enfiladed a part of Hooker's line, while others commanded the area around the Chancellor house.[30]

Just after 9:00 A.M. on May 3, one of Lieutenant Colonel E.P. Alexander's Confederate cannoneers fired off a solid shot from Hazel Grove that struck the wooden pillar Hooker was leaning against. The concussion knocked Hooker to the ground and momentarily stunned the Union Army commander. Assisted by his staff, Hooker got up and was moved about a mile away from the house. Near the Bullock house, Hooker was laid on a blanket and received aid before he was again helped to his feet. As Hooker moved away, another Confederate shell landed in the exact spot where he had been lying. Accompanied by staff members and medical personnel, the stunned army commander mounted his horse and rode out of range of the Confederate shelling. Hooker's second in command, Major General Darious N. Couch, rode up to the mounted band of officers and fleetingly congratulated the army commander for not being badly injured.[31]

None of Hooker's subordinates, including Major General Couch, really knew the extent of Hooker's injury. Despite Hooker's contusions, he did not relinquish command of his army, which led many officers to believe he was not seriously hurt. Union corps commanders were left in a state of limbo as they awaited instructions from their commander. Couch recalled, "This was the last I saw of my commanding general in front.... He probably left the field soon after his hurt, but he neither notified me of his going nor did he give any orders to me whatever."[32]

Forty-five minutes later, Couch received orders to report to Hooker's new headquarters. Hooker instructed Couch to reestablish Union lines and strengthen this new defensive position. This was a significant error which further demoralized many Union foot soldiers. The Federal Third and Twelfth corps' troops had been desperately fighting to hold their position and should have been reinforced, not put on the defensive to await another assault by Lee. Hooker could not bring himself to advance his army to the offensive. Hooker imparted to Lee the advantage by abandoning an excellent fighting position when it was not necessary and not counterattacking with his larger army. Lee quickly seized the opportunity to realign his force as Confederate line officers closed several gaps in their lines.[33]

Fighting continued as Lee increased the pressure on the Federal position around Chancellorsville. Federal lines were battered, but Hooker was solidly established and far from being in jeopardy. Many of Hooker's infantry had not yet been engaged. Command decisions were immediately required, and more Federal troops needed to be committed to battle. Following orders, the angered Major General Couch made arrangements for Hooker's forces around Chancellorsville to fall back fighting to the new Federal position. Anchored on both ends by the Rappahannock, Hooker's new U-shaped defensive line had been earlier laid out by Captain Cyrus B. Comstock and prepared by members of the 50th New York engineers. Hooker's new position secured a line of retreat by way of the United States Mine Ford.[34]

Facing the heights behind Fredericksburg, Sedgwick attempted to develop the strength of his opponent dug in to his front. Any hopes of a turning movement to flank the Confederate position on Marye's Heights from the north had disappeared. The early morning fog had lifted, but the elaborate enemy entrenchments still shielded the defenders from view. Close to 9:00 A.M., Sedgwick directed Brigadier General Newton to advance a force toward the heights. Newton ordered his Third Brigade, under Brigadier General Frank Wheaton, to make the reconnaissance in force.[35]

The first line forward consisted of the 62nd New York and the 102nd Pennsylvania. Wheaton watched and noted, "Before the regiments were 200 yards from the brigade line they were fired on by heavy musket fire and apparently five pieces of artillery from the rebel works and rifle-pits not 250 yards distant." Wheaton's line was sent scattering by intense Confederate fire. Sedgwick harshly commanded, "Will some staff officer rally those men!" Nearby, the six ten-pounder Parrotts of Captain Jeremiah McCarthy's 1st Pennsylvania battery opened fire in response to the Confederate salvoes. Federal line officers, assisted by members of Sedgwick's staff, quickly stayed the retreat as men dropped to the ground for protection behind a slight rise. Wheaton sent forward the 93rd, 98th, and 139th Pennsylvania regiments to support the advanced position as Confederate riflemen continued to send bullets whizzing down at the bluecoats.[36]

Sedgwick witnessed the repulse and galloped out to the left of Wheaton's brigade line. He and his mounted staff immediately drew hostile rifle fire from the heights. After a few seconds of delay, Colonel Martin T. McMahon, Sedgwick's adjutant general, suggested the general retire from his exposed position. The Sixth Corps commander sharply exclaimed, "By heaven, sir, this must not delay us." Sedgwick turned his horse, named "Cornwall," and trotted back into the city.[37]

Having probed the north and center of the fortified Confederate position, Sedgwick next attempted to reconnoiter the southern flank of Marye's Heights. This section of Marye's Heights was locally known as Willis Hill. Howe's Second Division, positioned south of Hazel Run, advanced skirmishers to feel this sector of the Confederates' terraced fortress. Captain Orin Rugg of the 77th New York recalled, "Companies A, G, and F were ordered to deploy as skirmishers and advance and take a rifle pit and some buildings about halfway between us and the hills then held by the Rebs.... My Company (G) were just in front of the rifle pit and I ordered my men to fire then move forward which they did and with a yell we made the Rebs leave."[38]

Howe's skirmishers were checked. Confederate fire erupted from the base of Lee's Hill to their front as well as from the entrenchments below Willis Hill. Crossing portions of Howe's path was Hazel Run. This stream flowed three feet deep in some sections and in lower areas had overflowed its banks, producing a large boggy area which proved difficult to cross. The open nature of the ground, combined with the offset Confederate entrenchments, dangerously exposed Howe's flank to enemy fire, frustrating his attempt. Howe's skirmishers held fast for protection in the abandoned rifle pits, while the remainder of his force lay protected in ditches that lined each side of the Bowling Green Road.[39]

CHAPTER 7

Second Fredericksburg

Sedgwick's probes toward the Confederate position on the heights had used up time the Sixth Corps' commander did not have to spare. Shortly after 10:00 A.M. Sedgwick received orders from Hooker's headquarters: "You will hurry up your column. The enemy flank now rests near the Plank Road at Chancellorsville, all exposed. You will attack at once." Sedgwick anguished over the thought of sending forward his men on a frontal assault against a well-entrenched Confederate force, but he was out of options and "Nothing remained but to carry the works by direct assault."[1]

Every soldier of the Sixth Corps who peered out across the open plain, to the rear of Fredericksburg, shared Sedgwick's apprehension. Although soldiers of the Sixth Corps were not direct participants in the previous December's failed attempts to carry Marye's Heights, the great carnage suffered by the Army of the Potomac during Burnside's crushing defeat weighed heavy on their minds. Following the disastrous Fredericksburg Campaign, many soldiers of the Army of the Potomac commonly referred to the open plain to the front of Marye's Heights as the "slaughter pen." The landscape itself held ominous tidings as spring rains had washed out a number of shallow gravesites, exposing macabre views of Union dead, killed there the December last.[2]

Sixth Corps officers realized the best chance to succeed was to cross this no-man's-land as quickly as possible, thus reducing the exposure time to deadly enemy fire. Much to the regret of Sedgwick's foot soldiers, orders were issued forbidding the storming parties from capping their loaded muskets. Uncapped rifles would prevent attacking Federals from stopping to fire while in the open. Most line officers passed the order on, but many left it up to their troops to decide. Colonel Thomas S. Allen of the 5th Wisconsin refused to enforce the order, saying, "His men could be trusted."[3]

To the Federals' front, Confederate defenders were encouraged by Sedgwick's unsuccessful attempts to probe their fortified position. The gray soldiers were further motivated into raising a cheer upon the arrival of intelligence from Lee at Chancellorsville. The news regarding the previous night's successful assault by "Stonewall" Jackson enthusiastically spread across Early's defensive front.[4]

In light marching order, Federal storming parties formed in columns of four on William Street. Traveling west out of the city, William Street ran straight for half a mile

No Knapsacks,
haviksticks, etc.
-Just Rifle, Ammunida
+ bayonet

to the Confederate entrenchments at the base of Marye's Heights. Here, William Street became the Orange Plank Road. Almost half of this byway's twenty-foot-wide dirt roadbed was overlaid with eight-foot long pine planks, but many of the three-inch thick boards had suffered severe decay, as the road was in general disrepair. The wooden-planked road continued straight as it climbed west over Marye's Heights toward Chancellorsville Crossroads, and then some thirty miles farther to Orange Courthouse.

Williams St. turns into Orange plank Rd.

Along William Street stood the Light Division regiments of the 61st Pennsylvania and the 43rd New York, commanded by Colonel George C. Spear. Colonel Alexander Shaler, leading the 67th New York and 82nd Pennsylvania of the Third Division, formed directly behind Spear's lead column. Arranged in columns of four, members of the storming parties unslung their knapsacks and prepared for the assault. Many men exchanged personal items with their comrades to be forwarded home in case of their death. Others shook friends' hands, while most quietly sought divine providential safeguarding. After briefing the sergeants of the 61st Pennsylvania, Colonel Spear, comprehending the grave consequences, closed with, "You are dismissed and God bless you."[5]

Two hundred yards to Spear's left, Hanover Street ran parallel to William Street. Along this dirt roadway, Colonel Thomas D. Johns formed two columns of four consisting of the 7th Massachusetts followed by the 36th New York. Once Hanover Street left the city it also ran for half a mile directly to the base of the heights and continued west up the heights before winding south. Branching off Hanover Street and running along the base of the heights was the Telegraph Road. A four-foot-high stone wall edged parts of the sunken roadway, forming an ideal fighting position facing toward the city of Fredericksburg. This stone wall entrenchment commanded a gently sloping thousand-square-foot parcel of land known to locals as the Fredericksburg Fairgrounds. Adjacent trenches extended from either side of the stone wall, traversing the majority of the base of the heights. The Telegraph Road continued south across the small valley containing Hazel Run and up a slope over Lee's Hill in the direction of Richmond, some fifty miles distant.[6]

To the left and a short distance behind Newton's assaulting columns, the three remaining regiments of Colonel Burnham's Light Division rested along Princess Anne Street as they awaited developments. Arriving from Sedgwick's position, Burnham galloped up and broadcast, "Boys, I have got a government contract." The men shouted, "What is it, Colonel?" "One thousand Rebels, potted and salted, and got to have 'em in less than five minutes." Light Division line officers formed the 6th Maine, five companies of the 5th Wisconsin, and the 31st New York in line of battle along a drainage ditch running behind the city. The remaining five companies of Colonel Allen's 5th Wisconsin were given the position of honor as advanced skirmishers. Colonel John Ely's 23rd Pennsylvania, belonging to Shaler's brigade of Newton's division, volunteered to join Burnham's assault, extending the Light Division's battle line farther to the left.[7]

The gunners of Butler's 2nd United States, Battery B, were busy snapping lanyards as gun commanders trained their fire on the entrenched enemy to their front. All Federal batteries were instructed to redirect their fire toward the Confederate gun pits higher on the heights once the assaulting columns were ordered forward. Just prior to

A section of the stone wall below the heights. The photograph was taken from the sunken road toward what many soldiers of the Army of the Potomac referred to as "The Slaughter Pen" (Massachusetts MOLLUS Collection, U.S. Military History Institute).

the assault, Colonel Allen quickly advised the 5th Wisconsin. Gesturing toward the heights, he announced, "Perhaps you think you cannot take them; I know you can. When the signal forward is given, you will start at the double-quick, you will not fire a gun, and you will not stop until you get the order to halt! You will never get that order!"[8]

Observing from across the Rappahannock, Butterfield appeared to be caught up in the excitement of the impending attack and expressed this to Sedgwick by cipher:

> I wish to facilitate your operation in every way. Command me in any way, and I am at your disposal. Telegraph communication with the General via United States Mine Ford is broken. Will advise you when restored. I am of no service here while the line is down. If I can aid you on the field, command me. Butterfield. P.S. My orders were to remain here, from General Hooker, but I feel like disobedience now. Please consider this confidential.[9]

As Newton and Burnham's troops prepared, Sedgwick sent a staff officer to notify the commander of his Second Division, Brigadier General Howe, of the attack to be launched north of his position. Howe was instructed to assist. He responded quickly, ordering the eleven rifled cannon accompanying his division forward to shell the heights directly to his front. Under the command of Major J. Watts de Peyster, Captain Andrew Cowan's 1st New York Independent Light Battery and Lieutenant Leonard Martin's 5th United States, Battery F, unleashed salvoes toward the heights. Howe's infantry was commanded to drop their knapsacks and pile them alongside the Bowling Green Road as excited line officers rushed to deploy the two brigades.[10]

Howe's division formed in three lines of battle, just south of Hazel Run. The front line consisted of the 7th Maine, five companies of 21st New Jersey, and the 33rd New York, all from Brigadier General Thomas Neill's Third Brigade. Colonel

Colonel (later Brigadier General) Hiram Burnham, commander of the Light Division "Flying Division," Sixth Corps (Massachusetts MOLLUS Collection, U.S. Military History Institute).

Winsor B. French commanded the skirmishers as he deployed the 77th New York to the front of Neill's line. The 20th and 49th New York regiments, of Neill's brigade, were held in reserve on the Bowling Green Road. The commander of Howe's Second Brigade, Colonel Lewis A. Grant, formed the 6th Vermont, 26th New Jersey, and the 2nd Vermont directly behind Neill's line. Howe's trailing battle line, commanded by Colonel Thomas O. Seaver, consisted of the 3rd and 4th Vermont and the remaining five companies of the 21st New Jersey. The 5th Vermont of the First Vermont Brigade was assigned to support Cowan's six three-inch rifles in battery on the Bowling Green Road. Due to the boggy ground to Howe's front and the steep fortified embankments, officers of the Vermont regiments were instructed to leave their mounts and go forward on foot, as it was believed horses could not negotiate the terrain.[11]

Butterfield wired Hooker at 10:35 A.M., "Sedgwick at this moment commences his assault. He is on the old ground of December (1862). The force to his front is small, but active. Will post you speedily as to result." The booming Union guns pounding Marye's Heights temporarily went silent, as Sixth Corps gun crews worked feverishly to elevate the muzzles of their tubes in order to fire over the attacking blue columns. Along the roadways Federal line officers barked out the command, "Forward! Double-quick march," and the colors were advanced. With fixed bayonets Sedgwick's columns charged over wooden planks, placed to span the millrace flowing to the rear of the city.[12]

Immediately, Confederate batteries on the heights opened fire down the roadways at the advancing massed Federals. Before both columns had exited the city, a Confederate shell exploded directly on Hanover Street among the 36th New York, killing and wounding several men. Many Confederate cannoneers knew the exact ranges to numerous points across their defensive front. The distances of bridges, roads, even sheltered spots such as drainage ditches, and railroad cuts had been pinpointed long prior to the first battle of Fredericksburg, which greatly assisted the Confederate artillery crews. The scattered 36th New York re-formed and continued their advance up the roadway.[13]

Standing four paces apart behind the stone wall, the six hundred or so Mississippi infantrymen held their fire as they marked their blue targets. At just under two hundred yards from the entrenchments, Confederate musket fire erupted to the Federals' front. Along the roadways the lead elements of the condensed Union columns proved easy prey for Confederate riflemen. A member of Sedgwick's staff remembered, "The whole force moved on steadily, magnificently, without firing a shot, the men dropping like leaves in autumn."[14]

From his gun pit to the left of the stone wall, Lieutenant Norcom's section of Confederate twelve-pounder Howitzers punished the heads of Federal columns advancing up the roadways. From all over the heights Confederate artillery belched fiery death. Five-second shells sent shrapnel tearing into the quick-moving Federal formations. Losses were heavy. The column on William Street was almost swept away by canister and enfilade fire. Shortly after crossing the bridge spanning the millrace, Colonel Spear went down with a mortal wound at the head of his column. Deadly Confederate fire continued to flash to the Federals' front. Spear's splintered columns lost momentum and were forced to seek protection in gullies alongside the road.[15]

The Federals advancing along Hanover Street received artillery fire, but were spared

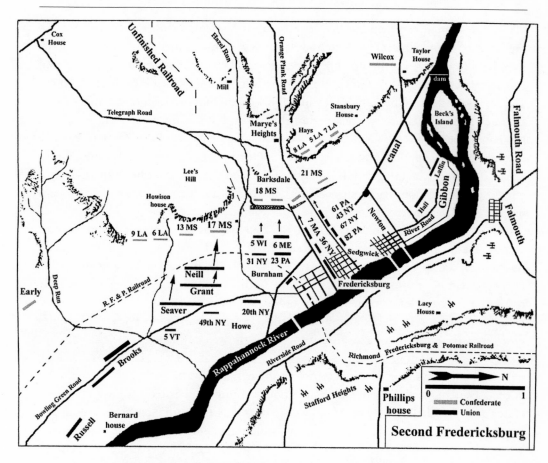

Second Fredericksburg: 10:45 A.M. May 3, 1863.

from rifle fire until they neared the stone wall. At roughly twenty-five yards from the defenders' muzzles, the cry of fire was heard and the stone wall appeared to explode with flame and smoke. Hundreds of whizzing rifle projectiles found their mark. The unerring Confederate rifle fire broke the head of Colonel Johns' column. Cries of retreat were heard, but others yelled, "Forward! Don't go back! We shan't get so close again." Regrouped and rallied by Johns, the column charged forward again, only to be staggered a second time. Advancing toward the entrenched enemy, the crazed Colonel Johns was hit by a rifle ball and severely wounded. His men fell back and dispersed into adjacent backyards on either side of the roadway.[16]

A short time after Newton's columns began advancing up the roadways, Burnham's regimental banners unfurled in the breeze, as his long blue battle line stepped off with a thundering "Hurrah!" Five companies of skirmishers from the 5th Wisconsin first appeared at a trot. Sergeant Benjamin Thaxter of the Sixth Maine remembered, "We all came to our feet with a TIGER and soon caught up with the skirmishers." Conspicuously leading the charge was Color Sergeant John A. Gray, who gallantly rushed ahead waving the regimental colors of the 6th Maine.[17]

Unlike the columns charging up William and Hanover streets, the advance of

Burnham's battle line was hindered by rugged, uneven terrain. Although open country, Burnham's path crossed muddy fields, many of which held standing water and were partially fenced. The distance Burnham's battle line had to travel on their cross-country route was also nearly one hundred yards longer than the course taken by regiments advancing along the roadways. The columns along the roads were able to significantly outdistance Burnham's battle line. Defenders on Marye's Heights were temporarily allowed to mass their firepower against the compact Federal formations charging four abreast directly up the roadways.

From among the surviving Federals pinned down on the sides of the roadways, a white flag appeared calling for a cease-fire. Colonel Thomas Griffin, commanding the 18th Mississippi, hastily acknowledged the Federals' white flag to his front and called to his men to cease firing. Brigadier General Barksdale reported, "Upon the pretext of taking care of their wounded, the enemy asked for a flag of truce after the second assault on Marye's Hill, which was granted by Colonel Griffin, and thus the weakness of our force at that point was discovered."[18]

Concurrently, Colonel Burnham's Federal battle line, oblivious to the white flag, continued to advance toward Marye's Heights. Moving through a small depression, the Federal battle line emerged onto the open plain and charged at a run across the fairgrounds toward the stone wall. Confederate artillery, positioned higher on the heights, recognized the attack and continued firing on Burnham's fast-moving battle line. After the appearance of the white flag, Colonel Humphreys of the 21st Mississippi recalled, "three columns of infantry seemed to rise out of the earth and rushed forward with demonic shouts — one from the valley in front of Marye's Hill, one on the Plank Road, and one from the valley of Hazel Run."[19]

Well to the front of Burnham's battle lines, Colonel Allen of the 5th Wisconsin urged his men forward as Confederate cannon fire thinned his ranks. Colonel Burnham received a minor head wound, which knocked him from his horse as his reduced Union battle line continued on. Screaming wildly, the blue lines surged forward. A young Confederate private recalled, "We all allowed that the whole Army of the Potomac were coming, you'uns kept up such a wicked yelling."[20]

To the far left of Burnham's battle line, the 23rd Pennsylvania and the 31st New York received intense fire from their left front, forcing them to seek cover. Members of the 5th Wisconsin and 6th Maine continued forward and reached the stone wall. The majority of Confederate cannon, positioned above on the heights, were now unable to depress their gun muzzles enough to damage the Federals. A deadly brawl ensued at the wall. Bayonets and rifle butts were used freely as from above Confederate rifle fire continued to drop Federals. Some surprised defenders dropped guns, swords, or anything that could slow their evacuation, while others desperately fought to the death. The adjutant of the 6th Maine, Charles A. Clark, claimed he "drove his sword into his adversary before he fell."[21]

Along Hanover Street, several companies of the 7th Massachusetts lay protected behind a board fence. With the Confederate defenders frantically responding to Burnham's sudden breach of the section of stone wall on their right, several Bay Staters were able to work themselves closer to the Confederate position. Unseen, the Federals gained a view behind a section of the stone wall. Federals observed some defenders reacting to Burnham's attack and others standing down due to the earlier flag of truce. A member of the 7th Massachusetts recalled, "In the sunken road were two Confederate lines of battle, the front line firing on our charging lines [Burnham's] on the left of the roads and the rear line sitting on their heels, with their backs against the terrace wall at the base of the hill and rear of the road."[22]

With the battle on, soldiers of the 7th Massachusetts quickly called, "Massachusetts colors to the front!" Within seconds, companies of Bay Staters charged up Hanover Street into the Confederate works. Squads of outnumbered defenders expeditiously evacuated the sunken road. Some remaining defenders were slain while resisting, as other confounded Mississippians were ordered to drop their guns and were taken captive.[23]

Shortly after Burnham's battle lines stepped off, Howe's three Federal battle lines went forward at the charge. Remaining to the right of Deep Run, Neill's and Grant's lines sounded off with a loud "Huzzah" as they advanced a short distance to the left of Burnham's battle line. Constant artillery fire roared from above as Confederate gun crews fired from gun pits on the Howison property, Lee's Hill, and Willis Hill. Confederate rifle fire flashed from the entrenchments stretching along the base of Lee's Hill. Private Wilbur Fisk of the 2nd Vermont wrote, "The rebels opened on us from every piece they had, from a 24-pounder to a pocket pistol."[24]

Neill's battle line quickly caught up with its skirmishers as they crested the railroad embankment. Fire from Louisiana and Mississippi troops forced the 21st New Jersey to drop to the ground for protection behind the railroad embankment. Exploding shells tore up the ground. The majority of the 33rd New York and 7th Maine continued charging toward the Confederate works between Lee's Hill and Willis Hill.

In the commotion, Howe's second battle line became mixed up as Grant's regiments crossed the R.F. & P. Railroad embankment. Several companies of the 26th New Jersey faltered, while others drifted left, entangling themselves with the advancing 2nd Vermont. Confusion reigned as deadly Confederate fire continued. The 26th New Jersey was made up of bounty men who were nearing the end of their nine-month enlistment. Originally promised garrison duty in Washington, they never expected to see combat. Instead, the tail end of their time in service would be spent attached to one of the hardest fighting brigades in the Union army, the First Vermont Brigade.[25]

This assault was the 26th New Jersey's baptism of fire. The majority of them broke, running for cover with their colonel, Andrew J. Morrison. The First Vermont Brigade commander, Colonel Lewis A. Grant, held little faith in the 26th New Jersey and had earlier instructed Lieutenant Frank Butterfield of the 6th Vermont to assist the untested 26th New Jersey during the assault. Butterfield and the 26th New Jersey's second in command, Lieutenant Colonel Edward Martindale, hurriedly separated the confused and scared troops at this critical time. To untangle his regiments, Grant shifted to his right and moved around several barns leading his men toward Confederate positions on Willis Hill.[26]

Lieutenant Colonel Martindale and Lieutenant Butterfield bellowed out commands to urge the terrified men forward. Several line officers of the 26th New Jersey acted as file closers and slapped the backsides of numerous Jerseymen with the broadsides of their swords in an attempt to move the panicked troops to the attack. Sergeant Major Amos J. Cummings recalled, "A shell exploded beneath the Lieutenant Colonel's horse, nearly lifting him from his saddle, but his only reply was 'Forward, men — act like Jerseymen!' [27]

Grant's Vermonters, followed by remnants of the 26th New Jersey, splashed through Hazel Run. Also unaware of any white flag, the right of Grant's line joined Maine and Wisconsin men of Burnham's Light Division, who were battling at the stone wall running along the base of Willis Hill. Burnham's force crashed into the front of the remaining Confederate defenders and overwhelmed them. Grant's blue lines swarmed into adjacent shelter-trenches on their right. Greatly outnumbered, the surviving defenders climbed out of the sunken roadbed and up the heights to escape capture. Pursuit of the outflanked Confederates was slowed as Federal troops continued to receive fire from Confederates entrenched higher on the heights.[28]

Along William Street, Spear's dispersed column, now led by Colonel Alexander Shaler, had reformed and rejoined the battle. Shaler grabbed a regimental standard in order to rally his men and galloped forward calling upon the 82nd Pennsylvania and the 67th New York to follow him. Confederate fire continued from above as Shaler "pushed forward with a supporting column pierced the enemy works and turned their flank." Shaler's New Yorkers poured through an entrance into the near vacant entrenchment and up the heights after the exiting defenders.[29]

The entire entrenchment along the base of Marye's Heights was now in Federal hands, but there was work yet to be done. Surviving 18th and 21st Mississippi troops joined several companies of the 21st Mississippi still firing from a line of entrenchments higher on the heights. Lieutenant Norcom's Confederate gun crews continued firing their guns until the Federals were nearly upon them. Unsupported by infantry, Norcom's cannoneers finally were forced to abandon their two pieces and ran to the rear to escape capture.[30]

On the slope of Willis Hill, Grant's Vermonters caught their breath in a vacated trench line. Colonel Grant called to his men, "Up now my brave boys and give it to them." Grant led his men forward only to receive a heavy volume of artillery fire that greatly thinned the Vermonters' ranks. While returning a brisk fire, the Vermonters were joined on their left flank by elements of the 7th Maine and 33rd New York These two regiments made up the right portion of Neill's advancing brigade. With one gallant rush these Union regiments, led by Grant, raced toward the second entrenched enemy position on the crest of Marye's Heights. To Grant's left, the bulk of Neill's regiments struggled to maintain battle formation as they fought their way through the rough terrain lining the ravine that held Hazel Run.[31]

Howe's remaining battle line under Colonel Seaver had also been sent forward at the charge. Initially slowed by boggy ground, Seaver avoided the pandemonium occurring to his right front and led his Vermonters left toward enemy entrenchments on Lee's Hill. At the double-quick, the 3rd and 4th Vermont regiments stormed over the R.F. & P. Railroad embankment toward the heights. From their gun pits on the Howison

A view across the Telegraph Road at Welford's Mill on Hazel Run. Marye's Heights is in background on the right (Massachusetts MOLLUS Collection, U.S. Military History Institute).

property, Captain Carlton's Confederate Battery fired a last salvo at Seaver's fast-moving Federals before hitching up and withdrawing to the rear. Fortunately for Seaver's men, from atop Lee's Hill Captain John Fraser's Georgia Battery was busy firing away from Seaver's direction at the exposed Yankees at the base of Willis Hill. Moving at the double-quick, Seaver's Vermonters maintained formation and crossed the exposed area to the front of Lee's Hill virtually unharmed.[32]

Colonel Monaghan, commanding the Louisiana infantry at the base of Lee's Hill, opened fire on Seaver's advancing Vermonters. Monaghan's defenders quickly realized they were in jeopardy of being captured by Neill's Federals, who were making inroads up Hazel Run to their left. Monaghan ordered back his outnumbered defenders from their forlorn position into entrenchments atop the heights to his rear.[33]

From Lee's Hill, guns of Captain Fraser's Georgia Battery switched to canister and pelted the Federals with iron as they advanced up Willis Hill and Marye's Heights. Expending his remaining supply of canister, Captain Fraser switched to short-range shell and even solid shot. The three guns of Captain G.M. Patterson's Sumter (Georgia) Battery were hurried from their position on the ridge behind the Howison house to a point on the Telegraph Road. Directed by Brigadier General Pendleton, Patterson fired at the Federals down near Hazel Run as well as at those clawing their way up the slopes of Marye's Heights. Four guns of the Washington Artillery, two each from Captain J.B. Richardson and Benjamin F. Eshleman's batteries, arrived in the vicinity of Lee's Hill and also were instructed by Pendleton to fire onto Marye's Heights.[34]

Neill led the 21st New Jersey, 7th Maine, 33rd New York, and 77th New York scrambling up the slopes of the ravine containing Hazel Run. Finding Willis Hill already taken care of by Grant's Vermonters and Burnham's troops, Neill swung left toward the roaring Confederate guns on Lee's Hill and the Telegraph Road. To the left of Neill's position, Seaver's Vermonters, having gained the protection of Lee's Hill, worked up and around the slope of the hillside. Receiving rifle fire from above, Seaver's men slowly gained position on the flank of the Confederate gun positions on Lee's Hill.[35]

Colonel (later Brevet Major General) Lewis A. Grant, commander of the Second Brigade, Second Division, Sixth Corps (Massachusetts MOLLUS Collection, U.S. Military History Institute).

Across the ravine, among the entrenchments atop Marye's Heights, chaos ruled. Barksdale's outnumbered defenders, though disordered, put up a determined resistance. Companies of Federals, led by Wisconsin, Vermont, and Maine men, overwhelmed pockets of stubborn enemy resistance as they gained the crest of Marye's Heights. En route, Captain Squire's two cannon of the Washington Artillery were captured. Just prior to his capture, Lieutenant Edward Owen of the Washington Artillery remembered, "Our last gun was fired when six or eight Yanks were in the entrance. It blew them to atoms." The battalion commander of the cannoneers from Louisiana, Colonel James B. Walton, surrendered personally to Colonel Allen of the 5th Wisconsin. Walton handed his sword over to Allen and exclaimed, "Boys you have just captured the best battery in the Confederate service." The Washington Artillery lost six guns in battery on Marye's Heights.[36]

Confederate cannoneers remained at their posts, gallantly firing as outnumbered gray infantry withdrew through their guns. Private William Stowe of Company F, 2nd Vermont, remembered, "I must say that their artillery men was gritty. They did not abandon their guns until our men had shot nearly all of them down and when they was loading it the last time our men shot the one from his gun before he could have time to fire. The rammer was left in the gun." Gun crews under Lieutenant J. Thompson Brown of Virginia remained servicing their cannons until overpowered. Brown's two smoking Parrott rifles were the last Confederate guns to be captured on Marye's Heights.[37]

Neill's regiments, advancing toward Lee's Hill, had pushed Confederate troops out of several lines of earthworks before gaining that summit. The flag of Colonel French's 77th New York was the first Second Division banner to be anchored atop this sector of the heights. Amongst the entrenchments, near a brick schoolhouse, Corporal Michael Lamey of Company F managed to seize the colors of the 18th Mississippi. The commander of the 18th Mississippi, Colonel William H. Luse, was also captured and taken prisoner. Second Division commander Brigadier General Howe rode to the 77th New York's position and shouted to his men, "Noble Seventy-Seventh, you have covered yourself with glory!"[38]

The 3rd and 4th Vermont regiments were instrumental in forcing the Confederate artillery to abandon their position on Lee's Hill. Leaving their support position on the Bowling Green Road, the 5th Vermont added their number to Seaver's assault of Lee's Hill. Seaver's troops joined with regiments of Neill's brigade. Two Confederate guns under Patterson were overwhelmed and captured by the Federals. One gun under Richardson was captured when its wheel driver and several of its horses were shot. Actively skirmishing, Seaver and Neill's men remained in contact with elements of Monaghan and Barksdale's infantry as the Confederates stubbornly relinquished ground to the rear of Lee's Hill.[39]

Atop Marye's Heights, celebration broke out amongst the victorious Federals in the captured earthworks. Federals randomly fired off rifles into the air as men rejoiced. The supposedly impregnable Confederate works to the rear of Fredericksburg were taken and the Confederates sent flying. Union officers worked to maintain order while attempting to gather their jubilant men. Regimental commanders on the heights quickly ordered out skirmishers as Confederate infantry and artillery were spied forming farther up the Orange Plank Road.[40]

In the Federal assault at Second Fredericksburg, Colonel Allen's 5th Wisconsin of the Light Division suffered the worst, with 193 men killed or wounded. The 5th Wisconsin's men were the first Federals over the stone wall at the base of Marye's Heights. After having gained the heights, Colonel Allen declared to his men, "It was like a journey to hell; but we have made the trip, boys."[41]

Without firing a shot, members of the 6th Maine were the second Sixth Corps regiment to have brawled their way into the Confederate works. Led by Lieutenant Colonel Benjamin F. Harris, the 6th Maine was first to plant its regimental standard on the crest of Marye's Heights. Color Sergeant John Gray, who conspicuously led the charge far to the front, remarkably reached the summit unscathed. Losses sustained by

Brigadier General (later Brevet Major General) Thomas H. Neill, commander of the Third Brigade, Second Division, Sixth Corps (Massachusetts MOLLUS Collection, U.S. Military History Institute).

the 6th Maine would total 169 men killed or wounded. This courageousness proved costly to the 6th Maine's officer corps as the regiment lost sixteen of twenty-one officers engaged, including Major Joel A. Haycock and four company commanders.[42]

Members of the 6th Vermont of Howe's Second Brigade were the second Federal regiment to gain the crest of Marye's Heights. The 2nd Vermont of Grant's First Vermont Brigade would follow closely up the heights and lose 108 of their number killed or wounded during the ascent. Color Sergeant Ephraim W. Harrington of the 2nd Vermont would later be awarded the Medal of Honor for advancing the national colors to the muzzles of the enemy's guns atop Marye's Heights. Following the assault, Lieutenant Colonel Martindale of the 26th New Jersey was highly commended by his brigade commander, Colonel Lewis A. Grant, and was given command of the 26th New Jersey. This was Colonel Grant's first engagement as commander of the First Vermont Brigade. Thirty years later Grant would be awarded the Medal of Honor for his leadership ability, displayed on Marye's Heights.[43]

From the assaulting columns along the roadways, Private James H. Luther of Company D, 7th Massachusetts, was amongst the first Bay Staters to jump over the stone wall and was responsible for capturing three defenders. Also from the 7th Massachusetts, Private James Holehouse and the wounded Corporal Lowell M. Maxham, both of Company B, had gallantly pushed on into the enemy works. These three enlisted men of the 7th Massachusetts would later all be awarded the Medal of Honor for their gallant efforts while capturing Marye's Heights. The 7th Massachusetts lost 150 men, killed or wounded, out of 400 engaged in the assault.[44]

Colonel Alexander Shaler, leading the 67th New York and 82nd Pennsylvania, had performed exceptionally well during the assault up William Street and the Orange Plank Road. For his gallantry he was brevetted to brigadier general of Volunteers on May 26, 1863. In 1893, Shaler would be awarded the Medal of Honor for his gallant service while rallying his troops at the base of Marye's Heights.[45]

After the assault, Sedgwick's Third Division commander Brigadier General Newton was quoted as saying, "If there had been one hundred more defenders on Marye's Hill we could not have taken it." Though the Confederates were greatly outnumbered, they violently resisted the assault. It was later reported that "Many of the defenders were slain in their place in the pits, where they stood till the last moment and resisted even as the Federals clambered over the wall." Without the added weight of Howe's assaulting brigades there was a good chance the Confederate force on Marye's Heights would have held.[46]

On Marye's Heights, Barksdale lost nearly six hundred men killed, wounded, or missing. Confederate reports on losses suffered near Lee's Hill are vague, while reports on the missing across Early's entire front only seem to have been partially reported. In the confusion, many regimental commanders were not sure if souls were captured or just straggling. Union accounts do claim large numbers of prisoners taken during Second Fredericksburg. After the fact, unofficial Federal accounts were likely inflated to enhance the Federal victory. Many Confederate casualty tallies were made at the end of the campaign, making it difficult to get accurate numbers for specific engagements. The provost marshal of the Sixth Corps, Major Thomas Hyde, recorded marching some 500 Confederate prisoners back into Fredericksburg after the assault on Marye's Heights.[47]

The violent hand-to-hand combat occurring during the assault led many Confederates to believe the attacking Federals were under the influence of alcohol. There undoubtedly were individuals who had fortified their courage with distilled spirits, but these were isolated instances. The majority of the attackers were likely affected by a surge of adrenaline brought on by the frenzied charge and ensuing combat. This assault proved to be one of the rare occasions during the war that the bayonet was actually used for its designed purpose. One account states that an attacker "...bayoneted two adversaries, and then brained a third with the butt of a musket." By actual count the adjutant of the 6th Maine, Charles A. Clark, stated that his regiment was responsible for bayoneting forty defenders on the way to the top of Marye's Heights.[48]

Many Confederate accounts of this assault claim the white flag was a Federal ruse used to turn the tide of battle. The numerous reports mentioning the white flag leave little doubt one did appear during the assault on Marye's Heights. However, the significance of the flag of truce in many cases has been overstated in Confederate reports. The majority of the attacking Federals, as well as many defenders on the heights, had no idea a local truce had been established. Not all defenders on the heights stood down after Colonel Griffin's brief exchange with the Federals asking for the cease-fire. Many defenders on Marye's Heights only learned of the white flag after the engagement.[49]

The pace of Sedgwick's assault was rapid and the duration brief. Numerous Federal accounts claim the assault lasted only ten to fifteen minutes, which demonstrates there was no time for a formal negotiated truce or any lengthy pause during the attack. No Federal accounts, official or unofficial found, make any mention of a flag of truce. A member of the Sixth Maine recorded that once his regiment charged, it took him only six minutes to reach the enemy fortifications. It is apparent Burnham's battle line double-quicked across the fairgrounds and

Colonel (later Brevet Major General) Alexander Shaler, commander of the First Brigade, Third Division, Sixth Corps (Massachusetts MOLLUS Collection, U.S. Military History Institute).

never stopped until among the defenders. The charge was much the same for Howe's attackers, as his lines only briefly paused in order to realign, all the while under fire. Burnham and Howe's attacking Federals never knew a white flag ever appeared during Sedgwick's assault on Marye's Heights.[50]

The flag-of-truce incident was an uncalculated happening, resulting from the bedlam of battle. The white flag was not a Yankee trick employed by Sedgwick's regimental commanders attacking Marye's Heights. The determining factors involved in Sedgwick's successful assault on Marye's Heights were the speed of attack, the high level of violence employed once among the defenders, and Sixth Corps' preponderance of numbers. Sedgwick's prudent use of Gibbon's force to widen his attack front had effectively lengthened and weakened the Confederate defensive line. This point was exemplified by one of the Mississippi defenders who wrote, "...they could have kept the enemy from gaining possession of Marye's Heights if they had of a shorter line to defend."[51]

Captain A.J. Russell's photograph shows slain Confederate defenders at base of Marye's Heights May 3, 1863. (Massachusetts MOLLUS Collection, U.S. Military History Institute).

The Sixth Corps' losses totaled 1,500 killed and wounded during the frontal assault on Marye's Heights. Within the city of Fredericksburg, surgeon Charles O. Leary, medical director of the Sixth Corps, and surgeon Charles F. Crehore, medical inspector of the corps, took possession of numerous dwellings and converted them into field hospitals. Major Thomas Hyde recalled, "The green slope was dotted all over with still forms in blue, and the prisoners were streaming down the hill in hundreds." Federal medical personnel were busy providing for the wounded within the city of Fredericksburg, while across the river at the Chatham manor preparations were made to receive the injured. The wounded eventually were moved to Potomac Creek Hospital, near Belle Plain, where they received aid until they embarked on their voyage north to general hospitals in Washington. Shortly after the storming of the heights, citizens of Fredericksburg claimed 3,000 wounded of both sides had been brought into their city.[52]

Later in his official battle report on the Sixth Corps at Second Fredericksburg, Sedgwick stated, "The gallant conduct of Colonel Burnham, in leading the Light Division on to the rifle pits in the rear of Fredericksburg, is worthy of the highest admiration. It is no disparagement to the other regiments of the corps to say that the steadiness and valor of the 6th Maine, 5th Wisconsin, 7th Massachusetts and the Vermont Brigade could not be excelled."[53]

CHAPTER 8

"A Force Yet to His Front"

During the assault on Marye's Heights, three regiments of Brigadier General Hays' Louisiana Tigers were positioned on Stansbury Ridge. They had helped thin the Federal storming party charging along the Orange Plank Road. From their elevated position, the Louisiana soldiers had a clear view to their right and quickly realized there would be no stopping the rapid moving blue infantry surging up the slopes of Marye's Heights. The only option for Hays was to pull back his force to prevent it from being flanked and captured. Hays wisely ordered his men to fall rapidly back toward the Orange Plank Road.

Farther up the ridgeline, Brigadier General Wilcox's brigade had been positioned near the Taylor house, "Fall Hill." Wilcox initially observed the combat on Marye's Heights and responded by sending Colonel William H. Forney and his 10th Alabama at the double-quick toward the fighting. Wilcox also galloped down Stansbury Ridge in the direction of Marye's Heights. Wilcox soon came upon Hays' troops moving toward the Orange Plank Road and was informed that the Yankees had taken Marye's Heights. Wilcox recalled the 10th Alabama and rode on to coordinate with Brigadier General Hays. Wilcox endeavored to convince Hays to remain with him to make a stand and contest any Union advance on Chancellorsville. The commander of the Louisiana Tigers declined, having been earlier instructed to rejoin his command. Hays led his men on a roundabout trek to rejoin their division maneuvering along the Telegraph Road.[1]

Brigadier General Brooks' First Division was not an active participant in Sedgwick's attack on Marye's Heights. Brooks' men viewed this "most brilliant" military exploit of the war from their protected position under the banks of Deep Run. Since first light, Early's Confederate troops could clearly see the bluecoated enemy massed near Deep Run and concentrated an accurate artillery fire on them. "But we were by no means fully protected, for, almost every moment, some poor fellow received the terrible assurance of the presence of shot and shell," remembered First Lieutenant George W. Bicknell of the 5th Maine.[2]

In response to the Confederate artillery fire booming down from the heights, Major John Tompkins returned cannonfire from the Bowling Green Road. The twelve three-inch ordnance rifles of Rigby and McCartney's First Division batteries exchanged shot and shell with Colonel Richard Snowden Andrews's Confederate gunners. Major Tompkins' smoking Union guns were unsuccessful in silencing the dug-in enemy batteries to his front.

Having dispersed the Confederates defending Marye's Heights, Newton's Third Division assembled atop the crest. Orders were sent down to Brooks, instructing him to advance his First Division. The Confederates opposite the First Division's front had not been driven off and still continued to be active as sporadic artillery fire continued. The bulk of Howe's Second Division also continued an angry skirmish with Confederates to the rear of Lee's Hill and along the Telegraph Road. Private Francis Brown of the 33rd New York recorded the action behind Lee's Hill "Two rebel regiments which we had not discovered before, pour a destructive volley into us. Many of our brave comrades are forced to bite the dust, still we do not yield our vantage ground, and the conflict has commenced. For forty minutes it was obstinately contested, neither party yielding its position."[3]

Several hundred yards south of Lee's Hill, near a pump house located on the Telegraph Road, Colonel William Monaghan reformed his 6th and 9th Louisiana on the Leach family's property. Brigadier General Barksdale gathered remnants of 18th and 21st Mississippi regiments and rapidly bolstered Monaghan's line. After retiring from Lee's Hill and the Howison property, gun sections from Carlton and Fraser's Confederate batteries took position on the right of Barksdale's line. Colonel Henry C. Cabell reported, "A line of battle was then formed at that place [Leach's], and Captain Carlton placed in position, supported by General Barksdale's brigade. His artillery continued to engage the enemy."[4]

Farther down the Telegraph Road, Major General Early was uncertain of developments on Marye's Heights. Riding in the direction of the combat he was soon informed of the Federals' capture of the heights. He immediately sent instructions for reinforcements to be sent toward the endangered area. Three regiments of Gordon's brigade threw back their left and formed to protect against a possible advance by Brooks's Federals up the ravine holding Deep Run. Early galloped farther up the Telegraph Road, and encountered Barksdale forming his line of battle on the Leach property. Barksdale described the situation, "Our center has been pierced, thats all, he said; we will be all right in a little while."[5]

Below the heights, behind the railroad embankment, Brooks was unsure if the Confederates near Deep Run were withdrawing or deploying for attack. To the rear of the Howison house, Howe's troops had their hands full with Barksdale's stubborn battle line as his men were dispersed several times by Confederate artillery fire. The ten-pounder Parrott rifles of Harn's 3rd New York Independent Light Battery and McCarthy's 1st Pennsylvania C, D Battery were advanced onto the Howison property and joined Howe's men battling Barksdale's troops.

From either side of the Telegraph Road thirteen Confederate artillery pieces, comprised of guns from Richardson, Eshleman, Patterson, Fraser, and Carlton's commands, exchanged canister blasts and case shot with the two Federal batteries. Several guns under

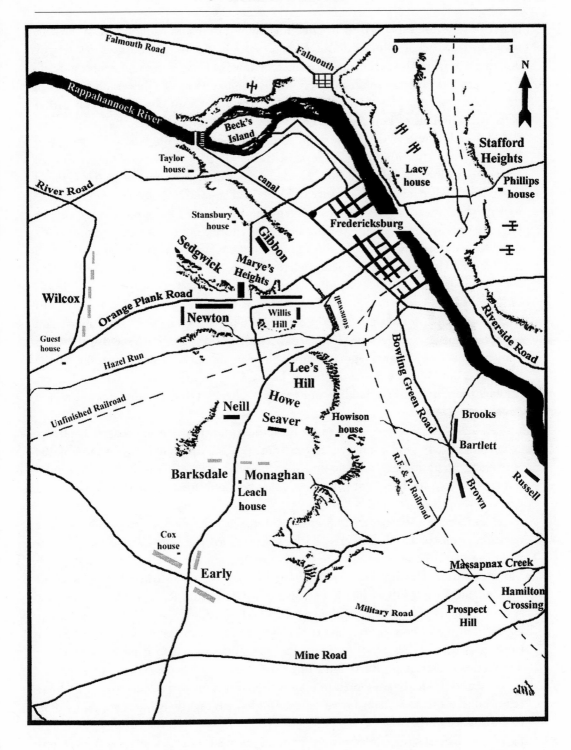

Skirmish at the Leach property along the Telegraph Road, 1:00 p.m. May 3, 1863.

Fraser and Carlton expended their remaining ammunition and had to retire to the rear. Fraser had a wheel of a limber destroyed and was only able to haul the gun to safety by utilizing a nearby caisson limber. Various companies of Hays' three regiments, en route from Stansbury Ridge, found their way to the combat along the Telegraph Road. On the Leach property, Hays joined Barksdale's line and reunited with the two earlier detached regiments of Louisiana Tigers, under Colonel Monaghan.[6]

Ten miles away at Chancellorsville Crossroads, the morning's fierce fighting had long subsided. After 10:00 A.M., Lee paused to align his force, while Hooker worked on strengthening his defensive line. Hooker's chief quartermaster, Brigadier General Rufus Ingalls, dispatched this message to Butterfield at noon. "General Hooker is doing well. We have plenty of fresh troops still left, but have gained no ground today, yet our lines are strong; but no doubt another desperate effort will be made to force our position. We feel confident that Sedgwick must press them fast. Answer me here. I will take it to General Hooker. He wants Sedgwick to press them." Butterfield responded, "Sedgwick is by this time 12:00 P.M. probably free from all obstacles of earthworks. He has carried the heights on the right of Telegraph Road (Marye's). Two lines of his troops have disappeared in the woods on the hills, and all seems going well. Will advise you further as soon as I can get word from Sedgwick." At 12:32 P.M., Butterfield again wired army headquarters, "Signal reports enemy still being driven on Sedgwick's right. To the left and rear of Howison house the enemy have taken a position on the Telegraph Road [Leach's property] and are holding our forces in check. They are hotly contesting the ground at this point."[7]

At 1:00 P.M., Warren reported to Butterfield the situation on Sedgwick's front, "General Howe reports a force yet to his front. Brooks' division was kept busy by the enemy's fire in position on our left, and after the heights were carried he had three miles to march to join us. He is not yet up." Hooker received this information around 2:30 P.M.[8]

Confederate artillerymen, bolstered by Monaghan and Barksdale's infantry, fought tenaciously on the Leach property. Early was provided the time to reposition Smith, Hoke, and Gordon's brigades at the Cox house near the intersection of the Telegraph and Mine roads. Having exhausted their ammunition, Early instructed Barksdale and the Confederate guns to withdraw one mile down Telegraph Road to his new position at the Cox house. Early had lost the key terrain of Marye's Heights and Lee's Hill, but his division was almost entirely intact. In short time, he was assembled and ready for battle near the Cox house. If pursued, Early was determined to make a stand at the intersection of Telegraph Road and Mine Road.[9]

Meanwhile, Early attempted to open communication with General Lee at Chancellorsville. Brother William Owen, chaplain of the 17th Mississippi, was sent riding to inform Lee of the Federal occupation of Fredericksburg and the current position of Early's Confederate division. Shortly after noon, the near frantic chaplain gave the Confederate commander the bad news about the Federals capturing Marye's Heights. Unbeknownst to Early's courier, Lee had already been informed of Sedgwick's victory by Lieutenant A.L. Pitzer of Early's staff. Pitzer, on his own enterprise, rode to Lee shortly after Marye's Heights had been carried. Lee immediately responded and put infantry in motion to reinforce Early.[10]

General Lee, in possession of key military terrain on the Chancellorsville line, again boldly divided his force in an attempt to drive the Federals back. After calming the excited chaplain, Lee confidently remarked to Brother William, "The Major [Sedgwick] is a nice gentleman; I don't think he would hurt us very badly, but we are going to see to him at once. I have just sent General McLaws to make a special call upon him." Lee had known Sedgwick ranked as a major while serving in the old army.[11]

Sedgwick's capture of Marye's Heights forced Lee to change his battle plan. Confederate staff officer Major J.E. Cooke noted his commander had to "...arrest the second advance upon the Federal main body [Hooker], and divert a considerable force to meet the attack on his flank." First Lieutenant Randolph H. Mckim observed, "When preparing an assault on Hooker's third line of entrenchments, which must have been fatal to the Federal Army, the arm of Lee was arrested by the news that Sedgwick has captured Marye's Heights at Fredericksburg, has swept Early out of his path, and is marching with 25,000 or 30,000 men on Lee's rear."[12]

Major General Lafayette McLaws' division of the Army of Northern Virginia's First Corps, accompanied by Brigadier General William "Little Billy" Mahone's brigade of Anderson's division, marched to Early's support. Lee sent the four guns of Captain Basil C. Manly's North Carolina Battery and four guns from Captain Edward S. McCarthy's Richmond Howitzers 1st Company for artillery support. In addition, the Southern commander also dispatched a fourteen piece artillery battalion from his Artillery Reserve, under command of the twenty-eight-year-old Colonel Edward P. Alexander. The total number of reinforcements sent to bolster Early's force amounted to nearly 9,000 men.[13]

The Confederates having pulled back from his front, Brooks assembled his First and Second brigades on the Bowling Green Road and marched toward Fredericksburg. Colonel William H. Penrose and his 15th New Jersey remained behind as rear guard and covered the withdrawal of Brooks' two brigades. Penrose was also assigned the task of gathering the First Division wounded left upon the field. Colonel Henry W. Brown, commanding the New Jersey Brigade, was counted amongst the First Division's wounded. Before being loaded into a wagon, Brown mistakenly assumed Penrose to be the senior officer on the field and gave command of his brigade to Penrose. In actuality, Colonel Samuel L. Buck of the 2nd New Jersey Volunteers was now the ranking colonel in the Jersey Brigade. Buck commanded a skirmish line and had earlier advanced with Brooks' First and Second brigades.[14]

A mile away near Franklin's Crossing, Brigadier General David Russell ordered in his Third Brigade perimeter pickets and began advancing up the Bowling Green Road. Mindful of Early's troops positioned a short distance away, Russell's First Division troops marched toward Fredericksburg. Accompanied by Williston and Parsons' twelve guns, Russell's force soon passed through the 15th New Jersey's picket line established by Colonel Penrose.

The sun had climbed, and the temperature was rising as Brooks' heavily laden troops advanced through Fredericksburg, en route to Chancellorsville. A member of the 96th Pennsylvania compared Fredericksburg's battle-scarred streets and buildings to the biblical description of "the destruction of Jerusalem." While marching through Fredericksburg, some First Division soldiers broke ranks and wandered about seeking treasures and souvenirs. Maneuvering and skirmishing through the previous night prevented Brooks' troops from eating or sleeping. After passing through the city, Brooks' First and Second brigades halted for fifteen minutes on the Orange Plank Road in order to renew themselves with water and hardtack, and to gather stragglers. On the Bowling Green Road, Russell's Third Brigade remained on the march, trudging along under an "uncomfortably warm" Virginia sun.[15]

Although an opportunity was apparent for Sedgwick to attack Early again, it was never an option for the Sixth Corps commander. The chance to destroy Early's division, along with the capture of the Confederate supply depot located at Hamilton's Crossing, would have to be ignored. Sedgwick's orders were clear and required him to press on in the direction of Chancellorsville Crossroads. Sedgwick's quandary was that his corps was still quite dispersed on and below the heights. He could not advance his corps piecemeal and was forced to wait for his divisions to consolidate.

The delay angered Sedgwick, but until his corps was safely reunited, the situation was out of his hands. The pressures of independent command were heightened for Sedgwick as rumors of suspected Confederate reinforcements arrived via Butterfield's headquarters at Falmouth. Sedgwick was informed that "There may be portions of Longstreet's troops with your opponents. If so, they are the first installments." News from Hooker's headquarters held no promise for assistance. Butterfield wrote, "Do not expect dispatches much from General Hooker at present. He wishes to hear constantly from you. He has been slightly hurt, but not at all severely. No firing for an hour...."[16]

As the Sixth Corps consolidated, the 77th New York's Surgeon George T. Stevens reported Sedgwick as being perturbed with Howe's pursuit of the Confederates skirmishing to the rear of Lee's Hill. Sedgwick believed the enemy on Lee's Hill would have been compelled to evacuate by Newton's troops, already occupying the adjacent Marye's Heights. Stevens recalled Sedgwick as being "highly displeased at the attempt, as the enemy was already virtually dislodged, and a short time would have brought General Newton upon the enemy's rear and flank." According to Stevens, Sedgwick "stigmatized the attack as useless, and an unnecessary effusion of blood."[17]

Howe's slant on the situation was quite different as earlier he was instructed on Sedgwick's order to assist in the assault. Once in the attack mode, Howe's Second Division was committed to battle as long as enemy fire continued to thin its ranks. It is also doubtful that the Confederates who were posted on one of the most prominent hills in the area, Lee's Hill, would have evacuated that high ground without having been forcefully driven away. At the time, the officers and men in Grant and Neill's brigades of Howe's division were unaware of Sedgwick's displeasure. The troops of the Second Division only knew that they had won a great victory. One New Jersey soldier recorded, "We were wild with delight."[18]

Atop the heights the assistant adjutant of Sedgwick's Second Division reported,

"Sir I have the honor to report that my division has taken five of the enemy's fortified works, one battery, and a large number of prisoners, the exact number I cannot now state, they are still coming in. My losses in officers and men has been considerable." Two Confederate guns were actually captured behind Lee's Hill, after their horses were shot down by the Federals. These two Confederate guns of Patterson's Sumter (Georgia) Battery B were later abandoned by the Federals and recovered by Early's troops.[19]

In his after action report, Brigadier General Howe recorded his two brigades captured two stands of colors, all of the armament of the works except one section of a field battery, some two hundred prisoners and all the enemy's camp equipage. General Lee's chief of artillery, Brigadier General William N. Pendleton, reported the total number of guns lost on Marye's Heights and Lee's Hill as being initially ten, and that two were afterward recaptured by Early's men. Many Confederate artillery horses were positioned to the rear, and Confederate gun crews were forced to haul off several cannon by hand in order to escape capture. The Confederate artillery on the heights also lost nine limbers, four caissons, and sixty-four horses.[20]

Immediately after Marye's Heights was carried by the Federals, Wilcox established his Alabama Brigade along the crest of hills that ran from the Orange Plank Road toward Stansbury Ridge. Wilcox's line formed 500 yards in front of a house located on the Orange Plank Road, owned by George Guest. To their front, four rifled guns from Moore and Penick's batteries began shelling the Federals forming on Marye's Heights. Wilcox reported, "This held the enemy in check for some time. At length they deployed skirmishers to the front and began to advance. This was slow and delayed by frequent halts, they seemed reluctant to advance."[21]

Federal skirmishers slowly worked forward on either side of the Orange Plank Road. The open terrain offered little protection from Wilcox's guns. Martin and Brown's Federal batteries were advanced atop Marye's Heights and shelled Wilcox's line. At 800 yards, contending artillery exchanged shells for some time as Federal officers under Newton scrambled to form a line of battle amongst the confusion.

Artillery roared as Wilcox's gunners switched to five-second shells, forcing Newton's skirmishers to slow to a halt. Rifle fire increased on Newton's front as Federal skirmishers pressed forward in the direction of the Guest house. Seeing that the Confederate line of battle to his front had no inclination of retiring, Newton extended his skirmish line to his left. The 2nd and 6th Vermont from Grant's brigade of Howe's Second Division skirmished on Newton's left, bolstering his line. Lieutenant Chester K. Leach of the 2nd Vermont recalled, "I never got into a place where the air was as full of lead as it was for the short time after we got on top of those heights." Private Wilbur Fisk of the 2nd Vermont wrote, "At the top of the hill we were met with a more terrific shower of bullets than before." The balance of Grant's brigade was battling along the Telegraph Road with Brigadier General Howe and the bulk of his Second Division.[22]

Gibbon's two Second Corps brigades followed the Sixth Corps up the heights, but due to the canal on their front had to detour through the streets of Fredericksburg. At the double-quick, Gibbon's columns moved to William Street and then advanced up the Orange Plank Road. Reaching the heights shortly after noon, Gibbon's men assisted

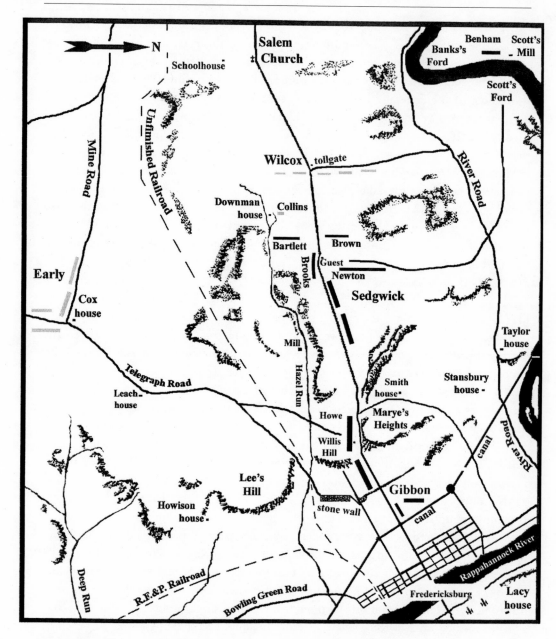

Delaying action by Wilcox at the tollgate on the Orange Plank Road, 3:30 P.M. May 3, 1863.

in securing the area and rounding up prisoners. Lieutenant T. Brown's Battery B, 1st Rhode Island, clattered along, following Gibbon's troops up the heights. Gibbon's First Brigade deployed along Stansbury Ridge, extending to the right of Newton's force positioned on Marye's Heights. Gibbon sent out skirmishers from the 7th Michigan and 82nd New York, under Captain George Ryerson. Immediately these Second Corps troops received rifle fire from Wilcox's Confederate skirmishers.[23]

Gibbon's advancing skirmishers pressured Wilcox's line. Newton's progress also began overlapping the right flank of Wilcox's line, endangering the Confederate position. Confederate gunners quickly limbered up and galloped up along the River Road. Wilcox left a strong skirmish line to screen the withdrawal of his five Alabama regiments. Before these skirmishers could extract themselves, one hundred and three sons of Alabama would be captured by Newton and Gibbon's advancing Federals. A Federal signal station near Banks's Ford observed Wilcox's expedient movement up the River Road and reported this information to Butterfield.[24]

From atop Marye's Heights, Sedgwick re-formed the bulk of Newton's division in column. With a line of skirmishers forward, he began advancing up the Orange Plank Road toward Chancellorsville. When reaching the Guest house, Sedgwick ordered a halt. He briefly spoke with homeowner George Guest and confidently told him, "We're after Cadmus [Wilcox] and we're going to pick him up." Sedgwick and Wilcox's paths had earlier crossed during the Mexican War, and they both were decorated for bravery. Brooks' First Division, having some distance to travel, was not up yet, and Sedgwick remained at the Guest house, not wanting to distance his divisions from one another.[25]

Sedgwick was eager to move on Chancellorsville. Sixth Corps staff members were unsuccessful in their search for guides familiar with the area ahead. The Sixth Corps commander was acutely aware of the importance of opening communication with Banks's Ford, somewhere along the Rappahannock off to his right flank. As the crow flies, Banks's Ford was two miles distant from Sedgwick's position at the Guest's house. A sharp bend in the Rappahannock River extended the distance to Scott's Ford almost a mile farther. Several riders were sent out to locate Banks's Ford and open communication with Benham's engineers.

Due to Confederate patrols or poor navigation on the riders' part, Sedgwick's first two attempts failed as his messengers never completed their mission. These riders may have attempted to reach Banks's Ford, while Benham's force was actually located a mile downriver at Scott's Ford. The provost marshal of the Sixth Corps, Major Thomas W. Hyde recalled, "Major [John A.] Tompkins was sent there with a message. He did not return. Captain [Henry W.] Farrar was sent. He came back to us some months after by way of Richmond exchange. Then General Sedgwick in impatience sent me. I did not take the road, but took a bee-line across country, most fortunately, for I was back in an hour, having seen no wandering Rebels."[26]

At the Guest house, Sedgwick remained anxious as he waited for his corps to assemble. Howe, having pursued some distance down the Telegraph Road, had placed quite a stretch between his division and Sedgwick's position. By advancing Newton's division up the Orange Plank Road, Sedgwick inadvertently extended that distance, along with the line of communication between himself and Howe. The men of Howe's two fatigued brigades had not had the opportunity to eat since the night before and were allowed to stumble back down to the Bowling Green Road to gather up their knapsacks.[27]

On the Bowling Green Road Howe's men celebrated their victory. The Second Division troops quickly refreshed themselves with water and hardtack as Brooks' First Division moved up the Orange Plank Road. There would be only a short rest for Howe's troops as drums soon rattled, calling the Second Division to fall-in. Howe marched his two brigades through the war-torn city of Fredericksburg after the "flying foe," and up the Orange Plank Road toward Chancellorsville. The day grew sultry, slowing the march and forcing trailing elements of the Second Division to collect stragglers. Heat victims dropped to the sides of the road as Howe's column proceeded up the roadway.[28]

The disbursement of his divisions, which earlier had aided Sedgwick by not allowing his opponent to quickly consolidate, now worked against the Sixth Corps commander. Sedgwick was forced to waste precious time assembling his weary corps along the Orange Plank Road. The developments causing the delay galled Sedgwick and appeared to have been the genesis of a turbulent relationship between him and Second Division commander Brigadier General Howe. Stormy seas between the two would continue until the autumn of 1863, when Howe was reassigned or demoted, depending on how one looks at it, to command the artillery depot at Washington.[29]

Sedgwick's success in capturing Marye's Heights necessitated the withdrawal of Confederate troops guarding Banks's Ford. To escape capture, Major Collins' 15th Virginia Cavalry and Lieutenant Cobb's two Confederate guns left their outpost and raced to rejoin Wilcox. Union officer Brigadier General Hunt, protecting the ford on the opposite side of the river, sent Major Alexander Doull across (swimming his horse) to ascertain the distance Sedgwick had advanced. Pontoons were positioned at Scott's Ford as engineers began the construction of a bridge. Telegraph wires were pulled across the rushing river by swimmers. This would be as far as these telegraph wires would be extended. No telegraph hook-up with the Sixth Corps would be attempted until the location and distance of Sedgwick's headquarters could be established.[30]

On the grounds of the Guest house, Sedgwick and Newton impatiently waited as the Sixth Corps consolidated along the Orange Plank Road. Shortly after 2:00 P.M., the head of the First Division column reached Sedgwick's position at the Guest house. It was decided that the First Division would lead the advance up the Orange Plank Road to Chancellorsville. Sedgwick was uncertain whether Gibbon's Second Corps troops were to join the Sixth Corps advance or not. With no authority to join Sedgwick, Gibbon's two brigades remained near Fredericksburg to secure the area and protect Sedgwick's three pontoon bridges.[31]

As the day progressed, Gibbon established outposts on Marye's Heights. Concerned with preventing the enemy from crossing the river at or below Fredericksburg, Gibbon deployed the bulk of his two Second Corps brigades below the heights, running from Hazel Run across the rear of the city. While Sedgwick advanced, Butterfield attempted to coordinate with Hooker in regards to instructions for Gibbon's 3,400 men. Awaiting orders, companies of Second Corps troops were engaged in collecting and transporting captured arms and equipment back across the river to Falmouth. Butterfield later that evening informed Gibbon, "General Hooker wishes you kept at Fredericksburg." Gibbon's infantry pulled back into the city. This now left the key terrain feature of the Fredericksburg area, Marye's Heights, unoccupied.[32]

Having withdrawn farther up the River Road, Confederate Brigadier General Cadmus Wilcox deployed Major Charles R. Collins and his squadron of fifty troopers of the 15th Virginia Cavalry. To provide early warning, Collins was sent riding cross coun-try to the Orange Plank Road. In a grove of pine trees, to the rear of the Downman house, "Idlewild," Collins' dismounted troopers positioned themselves on Sedgwick's line of march.[33]

Wilcox's brigade continued marching west up the River Road. Moving rapidly, Wilcox took a cross road back to a tollgate located on the Orange Plank Road. Wilcox deployed his brigade in the vicinity of the Morrison house, with regiments on either side of the Orange Plank Road. Two guns under Lieutenant James S. Cobbs were posi-tioned in the roadway. For want of ammunition, the two remaining guns of Penick's battery and Moore's Norfolk (Virginia) Battery withdrew 1,000 yards to the grounds of Salem Church. To Wilcox's front, Collins' dismounted squadron opened fire on the approaching Federals as they advanced up the Orange Plank Road.[34]

From column formation, Brooks deployed his First and Second brigades on either side of the Orange Plank Road in column of brigade fronts. The First New Jersey Brigade maneuvered over the uneven terrain on the right of the Plank Road. Regiments of Brigadier General Bartlett's brigade wheeled into position on the left. Four Federal batteries of Brooks's First Division remained in column along the roadway.

To the front of Brooks's brigade lines, six companies of the 2nd New Jersey, under Lieutenant Colonel Charles Wei-becke, crept forward as skirmishers. A steady fire was maintained by Collins' concealed Confederate troop-ers as well as Cobbs's two rifled Par-rotts at the tollgate. Brooks ordered Captain Rigby's six guns into battery to shell the grove of pines harboring Collins' dismounted horsemen. Under bombardment, Collins' courageous gray band of horsemen fired some final shots before yielding to the enemy skirmishers to their front. Falling back through Wilcox's posi-tion at the tollgate, Collins' men rode at the gallop to Moore and Penick's position at Salem Church. Skirmish-ers from Wilcox's battle line at the tollgate were thrown forward.[35]

Wilcox's brigade was aided by the good position they held. Sending shot and shell whizzing down upon the dueling Yankees, his intrepid force slowed Sedgwick's advance by com-pelling the Federals to deploy. Wilcox

Major Charles A. Collins (C.S.A.) (United States Military Academy).

knew these delaying tactics would only slow Sedgwick's much larger force and realized it would only be a matter of time before his line would be forced to retire. He did not know the situation at Chancellorsville Crossroads or the availability of reinforcing units if any, to his rear. After the campaign Wilcox reported, "I felt confident if forced to retire along the Plank Road, that I could do so without precipitancy, and that ample time could be given for reinforcements to reach us from Chancellorsville; and, moreover, I believed that, should the enemy pursue, he could be attacked in the rear by Early, reinforced by Generals Hays and Barksdale."[36]

Unbeknownst to Wilcox, Major General McLaws was steadily marching 9,000 Confederate reinforcements toward his position. McLaws' fatigued infantry marched down the partially macadamized Orange Turnpike. Potholes and settling had made the pike's crushed stone surface irregular and hindered the stride of McLaws's marchers. Alexander's artillery rumbled down the washboard surface of the Orange Plank Road, paralleling McLaws' route.

These Confederate troop movements did not go unobserved at Hooker's headquarters. A signal station reported, "The signal telescope discovers about several thousand troops due west from this point, about eight miles, counts seven colors — rebel battle flags. This would locate them at 5:00 P.M. Near Tabernacle Church by the photograph map. Is this not a column marching to meet Sedgwick and away from your front? Will get further information if I can." This valuable information never reached Sedgwick's position near the Guest house until events had rendered it useless.[37]

Brigadier General (later Major General) Cadmus M. Wilcox (C.S.A.) (Massachusetts MOLLUS Collection, U.S. Military History Institute).

Back at Chancellorsville, Lee observed Hooker's 86,000-man force as they strengthened their entrenchments. The thin gray line holding Hooker in check consisted of 21,000 men in the three divisions of Jackson's Corps, temporarily under the command of Major General J.E.B. Stuart. Augmenting Stuart's force were three brigades of Anderson's division, totaling 4,000 rifles. To mask the absence of troops Lee had earlier, at 1:00 P.M., instructed Brigadier General Raleigh E. Colston, commanding Brigadier General Isaac R. Trimble's division, to advance on the United States Mine Ford Road. Colston's maneuvering evoked lively artillery fire from Hooker's cannoneers. Colston's movements further discouraged Hooker from initiating any advance in the direction of Sedgwick's position. Hooker's infantry remained idle the rest of the day and continued to improve their breastworks.[38]

Brigadier General Benham had instructed Lieutenant Colonel William Pettes and his 50th New York Engineers to begin assembling a pontoon bridge at Scott's Ford shortly after 3:00 p.m. Under the charge of Colonel Clinton G. Colgate, sufficient quantities of bridging material to span the Rappahannock was forwarded eight miles up river to United States Mine Ford. This move fulfilled orders Benham had earlier received from Hooker's headquarters. Adequate amounts of bridging material to extend across the Rappahannock River twice, if required, remained with Benham at Scott's Ford.[39]

Once a pontoon bridge was completed at Scott's Ford, Brigadier General Hunt crossed to inspect the abandoned Confederate entrenchments. Hunt rode back across the river as Brigadier General Joshua T. "Paddy" Owen began crossing the four Pennsylvania regiments of his Philadelphia Brigade. Hunt instructed Owen to coordinate with Sedgwick for instructions before crossing his entire brigade. Riders were sent at the gallop toward the Sixth Corps' supposed position. In a short time, Owen's couriers found Sedgwick advancing along the Orange Plank Road. Sedgwick sent back the couriers with instructions for Owen to have his Second Corps troops remain at the ford to protect the approaches to that crossing.[40]

Shortly thereafter, Chief of Artillery Brigadier General Hunt received orders from Hooker to report to headquarters at Chancellorsville. Upon his arrival, Hunt explained the situation on Sedgwick's front. Many officers were present at headquarters as Hooker's artillery chief made his report. After hearing of Sedgwick's progress, Colonel Charles S. Wainwright recorded the popular consensus among the attending officers, "Lee will draw off heavily to attack Sedgwick and of course we shall pitch in this afternoon."[41]

CHAPTER 9

Salem Church

En route to link up with Early's force, McLaws paused to rest his weary troops in a line of entrenchments near the junction of the Orange Turnpike and Mine Road. Earlier that spring, General Lee had ordered these rifle pits dug as a contingency position to the rear of Fredericksburg. Two miles east of these entrenchments, Salem Church stood on the south side of the Orange Plank Road. The red brick church was situated on the edge of a large irregular-shaped clearing. Beyond the church and on either side of the clearing was a wooded ridgeline, Salem Ridge, covered with young second growth timber.

From the Orange Plank Road, this asymmetrical two-hundred-fifty-yard-wide band of wilderness extended far to the south. It stretched to the north for a mile before it dropped off toward Banks's Ford on the Rappahannock River. Bisecting this tract of woods, the Orange Plank Road continued across a large open clearing east toward Fredericksburg. Intersected by several small ravines, this clearing sloped gradually downward for 1,000 yards before reaching a slight rise near the tollgate and Wilcox's position.

Major James M. Goggin of McLaws' staff rode to Wilcox and reported that three brigades of reinforcements were en route to join him. Wilcox coordinated with Goggin, recommending to McLaws that he position his brigades out of view from the Federals in the strip of woods along the ridge near Salem Church. Wilcox's brigade fired at the Federals and maintained a brisk skirmish until almost 4:00 P.M. Sedgwick's preponderance in numbers forced Wilcox to leave his wounded and withdraw his brigade at the double-quick, up the Orange Plank Road.[1]

Wilcox raced across the open field into the wood line. A short distance into the wood, the trees parted where Salem Church stood to the left of the road. Sixty yards southeast of the two-and-a-half-story Baptist church stood a small log schoolhouse. Wilcox posted one company of the 9th Alabama in and around the wooden structure. The men cut holes in the chinking between the logs to use as firing ports. Wilcox placed another company in and around Salem Church. Members of these companies unable to fit in the buildings deployed behind a row of bushes hedging the border of the property surrounding the churchyard.

Wilcox positioned the bulk of his brigade directly behind the church on either side of the Orange Plank Road. To the south side of the Orange Plank Road, behind a wattled fence lining a small dirt lane, Wilcox deployed the 8th and 10th Alabama regiments. North of the road, behind a rail fence bordering the edge of a field extending to their rear, the 11th and 14th Alabama formed. Exhausted from maneuvering and fighting, the men from Alabama faced into the wood line and dropped to the ground to rest. Wilcox withdrew a short distance to the rear with the remaining companies of the 9th Alabama, forming a small reserve line directly behind the 10th Alabama.[2]

On Brooks' arrival at the tollgate, Parsons' six ten-pounder Parrotts went into battery on the right of the road and shelled the woods on Salem Ridge. Wilcox reported, "The enemy then threw shells to the right and left of the church, through the woods, endeavoring to reach our infantry." In order to expedite their advance on Chancellorsville, Brooks' infantry brigade commanders did not have their men unsling their knapsacks. Regimental commanders quickly dressed their two lines and maneuvered their men to form an extended battle line across the Orange Plank Road.[3]

On the left of the Plank Road, from left to right, Brigadier General Bartlett

An 1884 photograph of veterans visiting Salem Church. The Orange Plank Road runs east-west behind the cameraman's location. Wilcox's battle line faced east and ran perpendicular to the right end, or entrance end, of the church. Brooks attacked from the west approaching the left end, or backside, of the church (Massachusetts MOLLUS Collection, U.S. Military History Institute).

deployed the 5th Maine, 96th Pennsylvania, and the 121st New York. To the right of Bartlett's line, Colonel Brown placed the 23rd New Jersey with their right resting on the wooden plank road. The 1st and 3rd New Jersey regiments were aligned by Brown to the right of the road. Brooks extended Brown's line farther to the right by having Colonel Gustavus W. Town deploy the Third Brigade regiments of the 95th Pennsylvania (Gosline's Zouaves) and 119th Pennsylvania. Brooks had detached these two regiments from Russell's Third Brigade earlier that morning, while positioned below the city of Fredericksburg. Two companies of the 3rd New Jersey were ordered out with the 2nd New Jersey's advanced skirmishers to cover sufficiently the Federal's front. Bartlett would advance the 16th New York as a reserve, a short distance to the rear of the 121st New York.[4]

On the grounds of Salem Church the Confederate cannoneers of Moore and Penick's batteries had remained silent while Wilcox positioned his regiments. Shortly after Wilcox's line was established, McLaws' reinforcements began arriving from Chancellorsville. Moore's battery fired off one volley, and then both batteries were ordered to the rear as McLaws' Confederate infantry came up in column. From the tollgate Union artillery peppered the woods in the vicinity of the church as Mahone's and Kershaw's brigades, unobserved by the distant Federals, filed into line. McLaws reported, "The batteries of the enemy were admirably served and played over the whole ground."[5]

Kershaw's regiments were sent to the right, as Mahone was directed to position his men toward Wilcox's left. Mahone was instructed to march a considerable distance and leave an interval between his troops and Wilcox's battle line. Brigadier General Paul J. Semmes' brigade, following close behind, would fill this gap. With his left resting near Smith's Run, Mahone immediately sent out into the thickets the 61st Virginia as skirmishers.

The Confederate batteries following McLaws' infantry had departed the Chancellorsville front, low on ammunition. Alexander's artillery battalion arrived well after the fighting started and would remain to the rear of McLaws' line in the vicinity of the Perry house. Ordnance wagons from Lee's front would be the last to arrive at Salem Church.[6]

Believing that he only had one Confederate brigade retreating to his front, Brooks pursued quickly. Brown and Bartlett's Federals advanced up either side of the Orange Plank Road. Parsons' six gun battery in action at the tollgate continued firing as Brooks' Union battle lines gallantly advanced at common time (a fast walk) shoulder to shoulder. To their rear, teams pulling Williston's and Rigby's twelve Federal guns rumbled up the Orange Plank Road. Both batteries found positions on a slight rise of ground to the left of Parsons' booming guns near the tollgate.

Before all of McLaws' troops were positioned, Wilcox's Alabama troops were actively engaged with Brooks' skirmishers to their front. Wilcox's skirmishers drifted back into the woods as Federal skirmishers continued forward and reached a rail fence. McLaws, accompanying Semmes' brigade, rushed to deploy the Georgians into the interval on Wilcox's battle line. Semmes reported, "Marching by the right flank, the most rapid mode of forming — being on the right by file into line — was executed under the fire of the enemy ... A position was never more gallantly taken or more persistently and heroically held...."[7]

McLaws ordered up Brigadier General William T. Wofford's brigade, who had temporarily been left to the rear to protect against a suspected Union cavalry advance from the south. Semmes' brigade took position along an embankment that afforded them an excellent firing position. From left to right, McLaws' battle line consisted of Mahone, Semmes, Wilcox, Kershaw, and Wofford's brigades.

Federal skirmishers bounded over a fence and cautiously entered the tangled thicket. Federal artillery ceased as the blue-clad lines neared the tangled band of woods. Following their skirmishers, the main Union battle line reached the wood line and halted. A small rail fence that crossed some of the Federals' path was laid flat. Isaac O. Best of the 121st New York remembered receiving the order, "fix bayonets and forward, double quick, charge" imme-

Major General Lafayette McLaws (C.S.A.) (Massachusetts MOLLUS Collection, U.S. Military History Institute).

diately upon entering the underbrush. Major General Wilcox reported, "...they [Federals] made a slight halt; then, giving three cheers, they came with a rush, driving our skirmishers rapidly before them." Once in the wood, the Federal battle line was instantly slowed by dense brush, and most alignment quickly became distorted. Federals were now greeted by increased fire coming from the rifles of recently arrived skirmishers thrown forward by McLaws' regimental commanders.[8]

From their position in the buildings, the riflemen of the 9th Alabama could hardly miss the slowed Federals as they struggled to advance through the tangled wood. Fighting their way through the brush, the main Union line joined their battling skirmishers as a sharp fire poured from the schoolhouse. Companies of the 121st New York rushed the schoolhouse and captured all inside as Confederate skirmishers outside the building fell back, disappearing into the thicket.[9]

From in and around Salem Church, stubborn Confederate skirmishers thinned the blue line as they gained the clearing or fought their way through the unyielding underbrush. Companies of the 23rd New Jersey dashed forward to Salem Church and surrounded it, capturing the Confederate riflemen inside. Confederate skirmishers were driven across the clearing, while other adjacent skirmishers wove a path through the growth of small trees back to their main battle line.

The Federals pressed on. The center of the Union line advanced across the clearing forming an apex as adjacent regiments were slowed by heavy brush. Some Federals

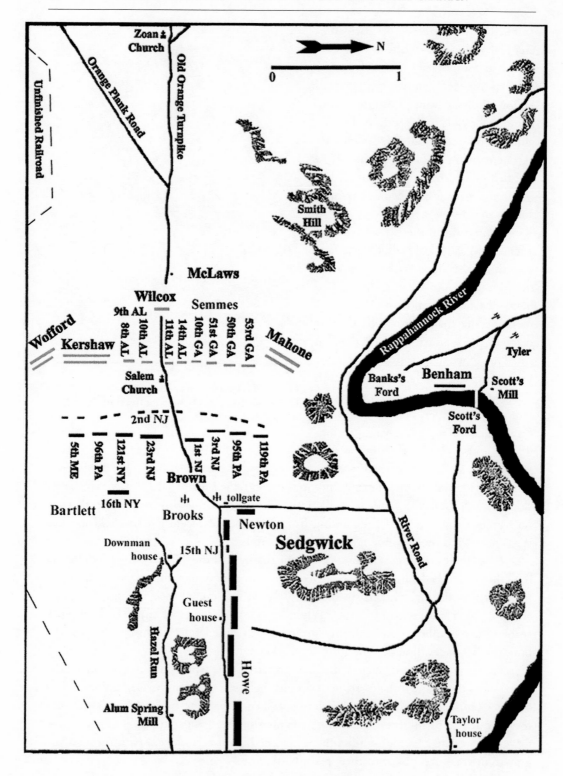

Battle of Salem Church, 4:30 P.M. May 3, 1863.

units found themselves in such thick and tangled brush they were barely able to make headway. Retiring Confederate skirmishers gained Wilcox's concealed battle line, which now rose to its feet. To the Federals' astonishment, a tremendous volley exploded to their front. With telling effect, the smoky blast tore through the thickets, killing and wounding many surprised Federals. Bartlett reported, "The woods were thick with harsh, unyielding undergrowth, with little large timber. It afforded no protection to our troops from the showers of bullets which were rapidly thinning our ranks, but retarded their advance so much that nothing but the most unflinching bravery could make them withstand their fearful loss while overcoming so many natural obstacles."[10]

To Wilcox's left, Semmes' brigade fired as fast as they could on their arrival. The Georgians' fire cut great gaps in the lines of the struggling Federal attackers. John L.G. Wood of the 53rd Georgia recalled, "We just did have time to form our line behind a brush fence before the Yanks drove our skirmishers in. Company D, E, F, G, H, I, K, commenced firing as soon as they formed their lines as the Yanks were 75 yards of them in full view. The 50th Ga. regiment doubled quick into the fight without having time to form a line."[11]

The action became general as the disjointed lines of Federals fought their way through the thickets, attempting to engage their foe. Near Salem Church, Brown's Jerseymen fought hard as Colonel E. Burd Grubb rushed forward companies of the 23rd New Jersey and almost reached the blazing battle line of the 10th and 11th Alabama. Grubb's nine-month regiment fought bravely as thick smoke obscured the gray enemy to their front. Federal walking wounded made for the rear as well as men stricken with panic.[12]

To the right of Brown's Jerseymen, Colonel Gustavus W. Town struggled to advance the 95th Pennsylvania through the wood. On Town's right, Colonel Peter C. Ellmaker advanced the 119th Pennsylvania. Town's men received heavy fire from Semmes' Georgians to their front and right. The Confederate battle line overlapped Ellmaker's right and elements of Semmes' brigade were able to pour a destructive enfilade fire into the 119th Pennsylvania, checking their advance. To the front of the 95th Pennsylvania, more than a hundred men quickly became casualties. Among

Colonel Henry W. Brown, commander of the First Brigade, First Division, Sixth Corps (John Kuhl Collection).

the victims were Colonel Town and Lieutenant Colonel Elisha Hall, who both received mortal wounds while encouraging the 95th forward.[13]

From his position on the Orange Plank Road, Brigadier General Bartlett saw his advanced regiments were in need of support. Bartlett sent in the 16th New York on the right of Salem Church. Helping to anchor the battling Federals near the church, the 16th New York sent volley fire toward the obscured Confederates battling to their front. Voluntarily advancing with the 16th New York was their gallant chaplain, Francis B. Hall. Unarmed, this man of the church assisted many wounded New Yorkers while urging his troops to stand fast near the church. Hall's efforts while performing his duties as a noncombatant would win him the only Medal of Honor issued to a chaplain for performing his duty unarmed.[14]

In the thick smoke, various Federal regiments recoiled and again surged on. Led by Colonel Emory Upton, the 121st New York managed to reach and pierce Wilcox's blazing battle line. Several companies of the 10th Alabama were sent flying out of the lane into the field to their rear. Companies of Grubb's 23rd New Jersey pushed forward and joined Upton's men, who had charged past the left flank of the 8th Alabama and lodged themselves in the dirt lane. Positioned with his reserve to the Confederates' rear, Wilcox twice hollered to his men, "...look at that damned Tenth, steady Ninth Alabama."[15]

Colonel (later Brevet Major General) Emory Upton, commander of the 121st New York of the Second Brigade, First Division, Sixth Corps (Library of Congress).

From Upton's left flank two companies of Colonel Young L. Royston's 8th Alabama wheeled to their left and poured a destructive fire into Upton's battling bluecoats. Colonel Royston, a giant of a man at six-foot-seven, went down with a severe wound as his men determinedly loaded and fired. Lieutenant Colonel Hilary A. Herbert assumed command of the 8th Alabama. Squads of Upton's New Yorkers and Grubb's Jerseymen were mowed down as they attempted to hold their advanced position in the lane.

The battle raged on either side of the Orange Plank Road as smoke from musket fire filled the air along with deadly projectiles that clipped through the thickets before hitting their targets. Private L.G. Wood recalled, "The struggle became furious immediately after the pickets were drove in.... It sounded like a large cane break on fire and a thunder storm with repeated thunder claps, one clap following the other."[16]

Colonel William Penrose and his 15th New Jersey steadily advanced up the Orange Plank Road. Orders reached Penrose: "hasten forward and form on the right of the brigade, who is driving the enemy." Reaching the tollgate, well after the deadly ball had opened, Major General Sedgwick immediately sent Penrose into the fray on the right of the Orange Plank Road. Among the confusion, advancing in good order, Penrose briefly halted and ordered his men to unsling knapsacks before hollering the command, "Forward, Guide Center." The 15th New Jersey charged into the smoky woods and came upon the 3rd New Jersey, who were by this time nearly all played out. Private Edmund Halsey, a member of the 15th New Jersey, remembered, "I don't think we had advanced twenty yards before we caught a terrific volley. The command was given, 'Fire by file–commence firing.'"[17]

Brigadier General (later Brevet Major General) Joseph Bartlett, commander of the Second Brigade, First Division, Sixth Corps (Massachusetts MOLLUS Collection, U.S. Military History Institute).

Across the Orange Plank Road, in front of Upton and Grubb's advanced positions, a yelping Rebel yell arose from Wilcox's Confederate reserve line. Among the din of battle, Major Jeremiah H.J. Williams hollered the command, "Forward, 9th Alabama!" Strengthened by re-formed companies of the 10th Alabama, Williams charged with the bayonet and drove the survivors of the 121st New York and 23rd New Jersey out of the lane, back toward Salem Church. Upton reported, "The firing became very heavy on both sides, and was maintained about five minutes. It was impossible to remain longer.[18]

Adjacent Confederate units furiously exchanged smoky blasts of musket fire with the Federal units on their front. Upton and Grubb's bloodied regiments fell back past the struggling 96th Pennsylvania, who had received heavy fire from parts of the 8th Alabama as well as the 3rd South Carolina and the 3rd South Carolina Battalion of Kershaw's brigade. Companies of Pennsylvanians stood to their work and fired while others began to fall back. The rattle of massed rifle fire was earsplitting. Captain Jacob Haas of the 96th Pennsylvania wrote, "I ordered my men to put in a volley which they did with fine effect I think. At any rate it saved us in some measure for had they got their 1st volley on us I think somebody would have been hurt. And then the circus commenced.... We fired as fast as we could and Johnny Reb done the same."[19]

The 5th Maine on the extreme left of Bartlett's line had been ordered to lie down as a lively fire erupted from the obscured Confederate battle line to their right front. Laboring to see the enemy, the Maine men managed to sustain their position while steadily firing to their front. Through the tangled brush, the Mainers could catch glimpses of butternut clad troops maneuvering towards their left. These Confederate troops were parts of Wofford's brigade marching to extend Kershaw's line farther south. In the smoky confusion, elements of Wofford's maneuvering brigade mistakenly fired into Kershaw's troops deployed on McLaws' line. Kershaw sent back a color bearer who waved a Confederate banner, to notify Wofford's men that friendly troops were to their front.[20]

To the front of Kershaw's line, Federal Lieutenant R.P. Wilson of Bartlett's staff

rode forward to the 5th Maine's position and yelled to Colonel Clark S. Edwards, "For God's Sake, Colonel, get your men out of this as quickly as possible, for you are nearly surrounded." Edwards quickly ordered a volley to be fired and withdrew his Federals out of the thicket down the slope towards the tollgate. During this excitement several participants remembered more than one Maine soldier who neglected to withdraw his ramrod from his gun, firing it with the bullet. Skirmishing as they retired, the 5th Maine reached the vicinity of the tollgate minus 75 of their number in killed or wounded.[21]

While the battle raged, Newton's regimental commanders had been busy marching by the flank, extending Federal lines to the right of the Orange Plank Road. Newton instructed the 2nd Rhode Island to advance and link up with the 10th Massachusetts, who were established on a slight rise to their right. Riding forward, Newton observed groups of Federal troops falling back and called out, "We are being badly

Colonel William H. Browne, commander of the Second Brigade, Third Division, Sixth Corps (Massachusetts MOLLUS Collection, U.S. Military History Institute).

driven; hurry up and help them!" Regiments of Newton's Second and Third brigades were sent forward.[22]

Among the fugitives fleeing to the rear came an adjutant of a New Jersey regiment seeking help. He excitably explained that his hard-pressed regiment, who were almost out of ammunition, needed support. Colonel Horatio Rogers immediately advanced his 2nd Rhode Island regiment to assist. On their right, the 10th Massachusetts also advanced across the field in line of battle. The 10th Massachusetts was able to establish a line at the edge of the wood and commenced firing to their front. With company officers to the front, the majority of the Rhode Island men continued forward and charged into the woods.[23]

Rogers' Rhode Island men advanced and reached the right flank of several companies of the battling 15th New Jersey. Farther to the front, parts of Colonel James P. Simms' 53rd Geor-

Brigadier General (later Brevet Major General) John Newton, commander of the Third Division, Sixth Corps (Massachusetts MOLLUS Collection, U.S. Military History Institute).

gia had gained the flank and rear of the 3rd New Jersey. Elisha Hunt Rhodes of the 2nd Rhode Island recalled, "Men were falling here and there, but 'Close up and forward' was the command and we kept on.... The Rebels had as prisoners a regiment of New Jersey troops with their colors. We succeeded in releasing the troops and recapturing the colors." Although Confederate reports indicate the flag of the 2nd Rhode Island as being captured, it appears it was the flag of the 3rd New Jersey that was temporarily seized and recaptured during this chaos.[24]

Along his battle line, Colonel Rogers grabbed his 2nd Rhode Island regimental standard three times and gallantly waved it over his head to rally his hard-fighting Rhode Islanders. Engulfed in smoke, the Rhode Islanders' position became untenable as they received heavy fire. Rogers hastily withdrew his men out of the woods. Rogers reported, "Maintaining this position for some time, losing heavily, til I thought support must have arrived, I ordered the regiment back to the edge of the woods there, the men cheering as they cleared the woods. Here we met our three left companies and the 10th Massachusetts." When well out of the woods, Colonel Henry L. Eustis, commanding the Second Brigade as Colonel William H. Browne had been wounded, ordered both regiments back across the littered field to join Sedgwick's reserve line.[25]

On the other side of the Orange Plank Road, Brigadier General Wilcox seized the moment and sent his Confederate brigade forward at the charge. Union line officers near the church strained to hold their men to their work, but the Federals could not stand the shock of Wilcox's counterattack. Groups of Federals gave way and made tracks to the rear.

Led by Wilcox's Alabama troops, the Confederates chased the Federals through the thickets to beyond Salem Church. Among heavy firing, Major Williams' men were able to liberate the Confederate captives at Salem Church, while in turn capturing a detachment of the 23rd New Jersey. Falling back through the confusion, squads of Federals sought cover behind the buildings, but to their surprise they quickly found themselves prisoners. A captain of the 9th Alabama remembered, "So hotly was the ground contested that at one time during the fight your men were at one end of the church and ours were at the other. We had literally converted the House of God into a charnel house and had pushed aside the Book of Life and were using the instruments of death."[26]

Advancing with a Rebel yell the 10th and 51st Georgia regiments, led by Brigadier General Semmes, joined Wilcox's counterattack. Private Fred West of the 51st Georgia wrote, "Then one of those wild shouts so terrible to the Yankees was heard along our lines and the rebel lines were in charge upon them. They could not stand this and fled before us in wildest confusion." All sense of order was lost as companies of various Union regiments broke, while others held their ground. Segments of Major Oliver P. Anthony's 51st Georgia fought their way forward through the smoke and heavy brush. Unknowingly, several charging Confederate regiments gained the rear of battling Federal troops, forcing many hard-pressed Yankees to retreat through Rebel lines.[27]

To Semmes' left, his remaining two regiments, the 53rd and 50th Georgia, did not get the word to charge as they were heavily engaged with the 15th New Jersey and 2nd Rhode Island, who were supported by the 10th Massachusetts. Firing furiously, Semmes' Georgia troops on this section of the Confederate battle line had expended much of their supply of ammunition. Semmes reported, "The enemy's main attack being directed against my left, the Fifty-third and Fiftieth Georgia; reinforcement after reinforcement being pressed forward by him during the continuance of the fight." By the

Brigadier General Paul J. Semmes (C.S.A.) (U.S. Military History Institute).

end of the battle, members of the 50th Georgia claimed to have expended almost sixty rounds of ammunition per man. Their ammunition exhausted and rifles fouled, the 50th Georgia reluctantly retired to the rear of Mahone's troops deployed to their left.[28]

Mahone's brigade was also unable to follow up on Wilcox's countercharge due to Federal activity on their right front. A member of Mahone's brigade noted, "In our front the brunt of the action fell upon the 61st Virginia regiment, under Colonel Virginius Despeaux Groner, which command was deployed as skirmishers to cover our formation, and which held the enemy back with great firmness maintaining its line after the last cartridge had been expended for some time under heavy fire."[29]

In response to the Federals maneuvering toward his left, McLaws directed the trailing two regiments of Wofford's brigade to the left in support of Mahone's sector. McLaws reported, "I now strengthened the left of Mahone's, which was strongly threatened, with two regiments from Wofford's brigade, on the right ..."[30]

Federal regiments from Wheaton's Third Brigade of Newton's division were advancing, marching by the flank, from the Federal reserve line. In an attempt to stop the retreat, Newton sent the 102nd and 93rd Pennsylvania regiments marching by the oblique to the right of the Orange Plank Road. At the double-quick, Wheaton's line moved down into a hollow, across a small stream and up the opposite slope. Cresting the slope, the 93rd Pennsylvania and the 102nd Pennsylvania bravely advanced on, only to receive blasts of buck and ball, fired from the smoothbore muskets of Semmes' charging Georgians.[31]

Wheaton's exposed Federal ranks were quickly thinned as the Pennsylvanians angled to their left and returned fire. Wheaton wrote, "To sustain this line many minutes was evidently impossible, and I immediately dispatched a staff officer to the rear to bring up troops with which to form a second line." A second blue line was formed as Newton advanced the 139th Pennsylvania and the 7th Massachusetts, anchoring the Federals' far right. Heavy volley fire erupted from the 139th Pennsylvania and the 7th Massachusetts allowing Wheaton's battered regiments to perform a quick, but orderly, withdrawal to the rear.[32]

Along the Orange Plank Road Wilcox and Semmes' fierce countercharge swept Brooks' Federals down the slope toward the tollgate. As most of Bartlett and Brown's retreating Federals cleared Sedgwick's reserve line, artillery opened a devastating fire on Wilcox and Semmes' attackers. Sedgwick personally assisted in directing the busy Union gunners. Before the Confederates retired, the cannon blasts forced them to seek cover from the hail of iron hurled at them by the Federal gun crews. Lieutenant Williston reported, "During this action, the enemy carried a large red battle-flag, crossed with white, which was knocked down twice by shots from my section."[33]

The well-manned Federal batteries of Rigby and Parsons poured shells into the attackers. When in range, Williston's six twelve-pounder smoothbores showered the charging "Johnnies" with double-shot canister, halting their pursuit. Private Fred West, with the 51st Georgia, experienced the Federal artillery fire. "They opened fire on us a battery of artillery nearly enfilading our lines from right to left — opened upon us with grapeshot. Our friends were fighting behind us and shooting into our ranks and it was

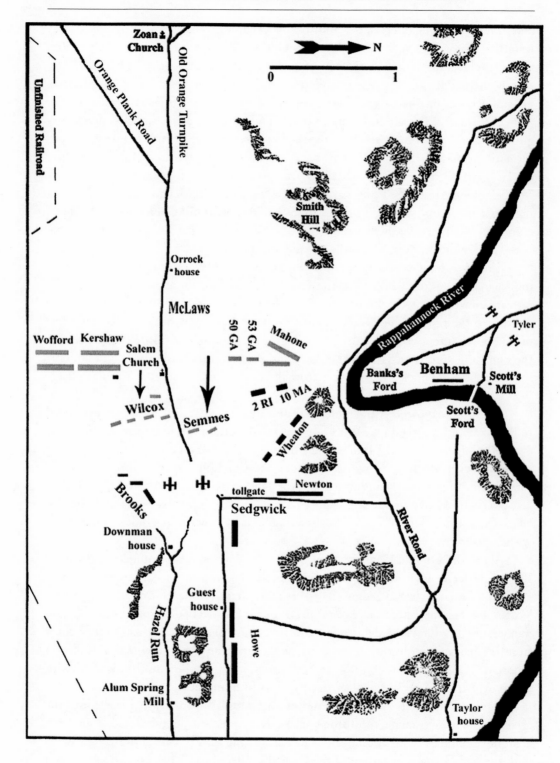

Wilcox's counterattack at Salem Church.

evident we could not remain in this position of unsupported advance, and fell back to our place in line, but we brought out 117 prisoners with us." The 51st and 10th Georgia came within 100 yards of the booming Federal guns on Sedgwick's reserve line. Lieutenant Colonel Willis C. Holt of the 10th Georgia reported, "After pursuing them for half a mile, and finding that General Wilcox's brigade had stopped, and we were far in advance, without any support, General Semmes ordered us to fall back, which was done in good order."[34]

Posted close to the Orange Plank Road in support of a Union battery was the 62nd New York of Newton's Third Division. While Brooks' two brigades raced to the rear, Corporal Edward Browne Jr. stood defiantly to the front of the Union reserve line waving the stars and stripes. Browne took a wound to the side. He held his ground, providing the retreating Federals something to rally on and demonstrated to the enemy that the Federals were not in complete panic. Remaining anchored with the colors as panic led others to the rear would earn Browne the Medal of Honor.[35]

To the rear of the Union guns, the scene was pandemonium. Elements of Bartlett and Brown's brigades continued to the rear, spreading confusion among Federal reserve units. Regimental officers, assisted by Brooks' staff, struggled to maintain order and prevent a general panic. Newly promoted First Lieutenant Daniel Wheeler of the 4th Vermont desperately tried to restore order. Transferred from the Second Division, Wheeler was aid-de-camp assigned to the First Division staff of Brigadier General Brooks. As an aide-de-camp, Wheeler was not required to be at the forefront of battle, but while attempting to stem the retreating tide, his horse was shot from under him and he received a flesh wound. Another conspicuous figure in this bedlam was Major John C. Gilmore of the 16th New York. Major Gilmore struggled to re-form elements of his retreating brigade. Both Wheeler and Gilmore would later be awarded the Medal of Honor for their efforts at Salem Church.[36]

In the waning daylight, Wilcox and Semmes pulled back their victorious Confederates to their original position behind Salem Church. Sedgwick advanced Newton's reserve line forward to the protection of the littered crest in preparation for an attack, but daylight was gone and it was deemed unwise to attempt the woods again. Brigadier General David Russell of Brooks' division took charge of this front line, establishing the 18th New York, 32nd New York, and the 49th Pennsylvania. To Russell's right, Colonel Eustis aligned the 2nd Rhode Island and 7th Massachusetts, while Brigadier General Wheaton maintained his front with the 139th Pennsylvania. Butler, Cowan, and Harn's batteries, who had been held in reserve, were brought forward as Williston, Rigby, and Parsons' batteries were sent to the rear to fill their limbers.

Sedgwick, unaware of the exact whereabouts of Early's division, ordered Major General Howe to guard against a possible Confederate flank attack. Howe's Second Division, in column along the Orange Plank Road, faced left and threw out skirmishers. After investigation, Howe found nothing developing on his front and placed his division at rest alongside the roadway. The Third Division commander, Brigadier General Newton, called Howe's actions into question. Newton was annoyed at Howe for not being readily available to support another attempt to carry Salem Ridge. However,

Newton's anger was misdirected as Howe was acting on Sedgwick's instructions. It appears Sedgwick was uneasy about the location of Early's Confederate division, last seen on the Telegraph Road. If an opportunity to launch another attack was let to pass, Newton's displeasure with Howe should have been leveled at his good friend "Johnny Sedgwick."[37]

Howe's Second Division troops spent a restless night as Union ambulance wagons rumbled down the Orange Plank Road loaded with groaning wounded crying out for water and help. Many of Sedgwick's wounded were promptly evacuated from Salem Ridge and hauled over the Rappahannock via the pontoon bridge positioned below Fredericksburg. This difficult task was completed under the direction of Captain W. H. Robinson, chief of the Ambulance Corps for the Sixth Corps.

The atmosphere was thick with clouds of gunpowder smoke, making the air bitter and sulfurous. Night had come on, and Sedgwick ordered all his ammunition trains forward from Fredericksburg. The road to Chancellorsville was blocked. Federal infantry turned their attention to cleaning rifle barrels as ammunition was distributed among the regiments. Regimental commissary wagons loaded with rations accompanied Sedgwick's munitions train. Knapsacks belonging to Newton's division, which earlier in day had been dropped in the streets of Fredericksburg, were also forwarded by wagon up the Orange Plank Road. Sedgwick's Light Division and Newton's Third Division had been without their knapsacks since before the storming of the heights behind Fredericksburg.[38]

McLaws' troops across the battlefield were not in much better shape, although Federal knapsacks unslung and left on Salem Ridge were found to be a much needed boost to Confederate morale. "Each Federal soldier bore on his back in this fight a well-packed knapsack with several days' rations in his haversack," wrote Colonel John C.C. Sanders of the 11th Alabama. These encumbrances were, as usual, immediately thrown away.... A Yankee knapsack is a Rebel's prize of war...." The night would prove relatively quiet as contending warriors slept under arms.[39]

Members of the 95th Pennsylvania witnessed a gruesome sight:

> In getting over a post and rail fence, in our front, during the heat of battle, one of our party (a brave young fellow) was shot dead just as he had reached the top most rail; there he fell, and remained equipoised in death, to the surprise and horror of all around; after we had fallen back, and during the night a gentle breeze rocked the corpse to and fro in its aerial position, the moon shed a halo about the head and face of this 'somebody's darling,' and a rebel picket made the scene more hideous by the flash of his rifle, which seemed to come from beneath the dead soldier.[40]

To the front of Newton's line, Corporal Peter McAdams of the 98th Pennsylvania braved enemy picket fire and ran out between lines to rescue a wounded friend. Carrying the man back on his shoulders, McAdams drew cheers from his comrades as well as nearby Confederate pickets. This unselfish act would later earn McAdams the Medal of Honor.[41]

In the fierce engagement at Salem Church the Sixth Corps lost 1,523 in killed, wounded, and missing. Bartlett's Second Brigade, First Division, lost 580 men out of a total of 1,500 officers and men engaged. The rifled muskets of Wilcox's Alabama troops proved extremely effective against Colonel Emory Upton's 121st New York. In the New Yorkers' first engagement, the 121st lost 48 killed, 173 wounded, and reported 55 missing, totaling 276 casualties out of 453 men engaged. This was the heaviest loss sustained by any Union regiment in this battle.[42]

Although Colonel Upton's casualty count differed slightly, his recollection of the 121st New York's loss at Salem Church is insightful:

> Of four hundred and fifty-three taken into action, two hundred and twenty-seven were killed and wounded, and this in their first fight. The killed amounted to eighty. Of these, sixty-two were left dead on the field; seventeen were from one company.... Nearly the whole loss was inflicted at a range varying between four and eight rods [approximately 65 to 80 feet], and in the space of about five minutes.[43]

Sedgwick's First Division commander, Brigadier General Brooks, was concerned about the repulse his troops had suffered in the battle at Salem Church. Recognizing the roughhandling his troops had received, Brooks commented to Lieutenant Daniel Wheeler of his staff, "Twenty-five years in the army, Mr. Wheeler, and ruined at last." The engagement at Salem Church ultimately had no adverse effect on Brooks' military career as complaints and critiques remained within the Sixth Corps. Brooks' Third Brigade commander, Brigadier General David Russell, was very outspoken about the hurried advance used by his division commander. Observers noted Russell as being "very much put out," because Brooks attacked without his entire division present. Russell claimed if Brooks had waited for the arrival of his Third Brigade, "it would have made all the difference in the world."[44]

Brooks' rapid advance has been critically viewed on the grounds he went forward minus one of his three brigades, and that the two brigades

Brigadier General William T.H. Brooks, commander of the First Division, Sixth Corps (Massachusetts MOLLUS Collection, U.S. Military History Institute).

sent in were minus one regiment each. Sedgwick's advance up to this time had been hindered by the dispersal of his corps and Wilcox's delaying tactics. The Sixth Corps commander was more than anxious for Brooks to advance in order to make up time on his move to Chancellorsville. Although Brooks was not at full division strength, the addition of the 95th and 119th Pennsylvania detached from the Third Brigade placed his strength at two full brigade-size elements. To Sedgwick's knowledge there was only one Confederate brigade retiring to his front. These odds appear to justify Brooks' advance, especially since Newton's entire Third Division was directly following in column. The First Division's rapid advance reveals Sedgwick's desire to comply with the army commander's instructions. Regardless of Brooks' hasty advance, the Southern triumph at Salem Church resulted from the fighting tenacity displayed by Southern soldiers on the field, Wilcox's selection of a good fighting position, and the element of surprise.

A few weeks after Salem Church, Brooks would leave the Sixth Army Corps due to poor health. He accepted a garrison position in Pittsburgh, Pennsylvania, as commander of the newly formed Department of Monongahela. Brigadier General Horatio G. Wright took command of the Sixth Corps' First Division. Brooks was promoted to major general on June 10, 1863. In April 1864, the War Department revoked his promotion to major general. Bully Brooks' connections with the December 1862 attempted cabal to oust Major General Ambrose Burnside as commander of the Army of the Potomac cost him the promotion, not the repulse suffered at Salem Church. In April 1864, Brigadier General W.T.H. Brooks returned to combat duty in Virginia. Brooks performed well at Cold Harbor and during the Petersburg Campaign, but reoccurring health problems persuaded the forty-three-year-old brigadier general to resign from the army on July 19, 1864.[45]

The Confederates sustained less than half the number of casualties that the Federals did at Salem Church, approximately 650 men. Wilcox's brigade lost 75 killed, 372 wounded, and came up with 48 missing, for an aggregate of 495 casualties during the campaign. Brigadier General Wilcox stated that his brigade was "furiously attacked by superior forces, and not only stood their ground, but repulsed the enemy with great loss." Colonel Lucius Pinckard's 14th Alabama paid a high price for their valor, losing 13 dead, 104 wounded, and 34 missing, for a total loss of 151 men. Colonel Pinckard was counted among the wounded.[46]

In his after action report, Brigadier General Semmes described this two-hour engagement at Salem Church as "one of the most severely contested of the war ..." adding, "the brunt of the battle fell upon his brigade.... The loss of the brigade in this battle was severe." The 10th Georgia suffered the worst in Semmes' brigade, sustaining 128 casualties out of 230 soldiers engaged. An aide to Brigadier General Semmes, W. R. Stilwell of the 53rd Georgia, wrote home to his brother, "I was at the battle of Wilderness Church at Chancellorsville and Salem Church, the latter place is where our brigade suffered so much. Out of 1,461 men we lost 581, killed and wounded [throughout the entire campaign].... Men never fought better than our Reg. did at Salem Church."[47]

CHAPTER 10

"I Find Everything Snug Here"

As the tumult of battle died away at Salem Church, First Lieutenant Charles Atkins, from Cowan's 1st New York Battery, departed the city of Fredericksburg. Atkins' gun carriage had been damaged that morning by Confederate artillery fire and had undergone repairs. Atkins moved out, anxious to rejoin the Sixth Corps advancing on Chancellorsville. Accompanying the three-inch ordnance rifle were several battery wagons and two wagons of rolling forage. The small column rumbled toward the heights and the Orange Plank Road, which would lead them to Sedgwick's position near the tollgate.

In the dwindling daylight, the unsuspecting column neared Marye's Heights. Confederate Major General Early observed the scene and wrote, "The approaching darkness rendered objects very indistinct, and we therefore watched the approaching piece until it got within a few hundred yards of us, when the drivers suddenly discovered who we were, wheeled rapidly and dashed to the rear." Early's artillery opened on the surprised Federals from their position on the ridge at the head of Deep Run. The frantic Federal column skedaddled back to the safety of Fredericksburg. The gun and battery wagons arrived unscathed, but accurate Confederate artillery fire forced the Federals to abandon the two forage wagons. This incident was the first indication for the Federals occupying Fredericksburg that Early's Confederates remained along the Telegraph Road in force.[1]

While positioned at the head of Deep Run, Early received this cipher from General Lee:

I very much regret the possession of Fredericksburg by the enemy. I heard today of their taking of the hills in the rear of the city, and sent down General McLaws with two brigades of Anderson's division and three of his own, to unite with the forces under you, and endeavor to drive them back. I heard this afternoon that he halted at Tabernacle Church.... If they are attacking him there, you could come upon their left flank. and communicate with General McLaws, I think you would demolish them. See if you cannot unite with him, and together destroy him. P.S. I understand that Wilcox is with him also.[2]

Lee also wrote to McLaws at Salem Church:

I presume from the firing, which I hear in your direction that you are engaged with the enemy.... I have just written Early, who informs me that he is on the Telegraph Road, near

Mrs. Smith's house, to unite with you to attack the enemy on their left flank. Communicate with him, and arrange the junction, if necessary and practicable. It is necessary that you beat the enemy, and I hope you will do it."[3]

In the vicinity of Chancellorsville, Hooker's entrenched force clearly heard the din of battle originating from the direction of Salem Church. Surprisingly, as battle sounds rolled over the countryside, Hooker remained idle. Eighty-six thousand Union troops awaited developments behind their U-shaped defensive position along Mineral Spring Road and Hunting Run. Approximately 35,000 of Hooker's Federals had yet to test their mettle in this Union offensive. Awaiting orders, his infantry was kept busy fortifying its new position with earth and logs. To Hooker's front, Stuart and Anderson's 25,000 Confederate troops awaited action as they maintained their sparsely held front. More entrenching conducted by the Federals reassured Lee that no advance would be made against him from that sector. Lee had seen the best of "Fighting" Joe Hooker.

On top of Salem Ridge, field hospitals had been established to the rear of McLaws' lines. Confederates collected the mangled wounded of both armies in wagons of all description, including many vehicles marked with the "U.S." insignia. Prior to the battle, the Baptist Church had been temporarily used to store furniture and belongings of some of Fredericksburg's displaced citizens. These items were quickly deposited outside the bullet-pocked brick church as the chapel was converted into a field hospital. Surgeons, assisted by attendants, busily dressed wounds and gave relief to the injured. On the grounds surrounding Salem Church the Confederates gathered weapons and accouterments from Federal casualties as ordnance wagons distributed ammunition. The commander of the 24th Georgia infantry, Colonel Robert McMillan, described the scene at Salem Church:

> Here hundreds and hundreds of wounded of both armies were brought for surgical attention.... After the house (of worship) was filled, the spacious churchyard was literally covered with wounded and dying. The sight inside the building, for horror, was, perhaps, never equaled within so limited a space, every available foot was crowded with wounded and bleeding soldiers. The floor, the benches, even the chancel and pulpit were all packed almost to suffocation with them. The amputated limbs were piled up in every corner almost as high as a man could reach; blood flowed in streams along the aisles and out the doors; screams and groans were heard on all sides, while the surgeons, with their assistants, worked with knives, saws, sutures, and bandages.[4]

Sedgwick's adjutant, Lieutenant Colonel Martin McMahon, recalled the uneasiness of the night:

> We slept in line that night with the dead of the day's battle lying near us. The stretcher bearers with their lamps wandered here and there over the field, picking up the wounded and loaded ambulances rattled dismally over the broken Plank Road. Sedgwick scarcely slept that night. From time to time he dictated a dispatch to General Hooker. He would walk a few paces apart and listen; then returning would lie down again in the damp grass, with his saddle for a pillow and try to sleep. The night was inexpressibly gloomy. Fires were not allowed to be lighted, and there was not even the excitement of a picket alarm to relieve the singular stillness.[5]

During the night Major General Warren, who had been assisting Sedgwick, used the bridge at Scott's Ford and returned to Hooker's headquarters. Arriving at 11:00 P.M., Warren found Hooker asleep. When the commander was awakened, it was noticeable that he was not fully recovered from his injury. Warren asked if there were any instructions for Sedgwick. Hooker replied, "None." Warren learned, after full conference with Hooker, "that the army [near Chancellorsville] was now in position to court an attack from the enemy, and no longer needed the assistance of Sedgwick."[6]

The much-fatigued Warren took it upon himself to write Sedgwick, informing him of the situation. Warren's message was sent just after midnight, but did not reach Sedgwick until six and a half hours later. The delay in transit of this dispatch illustrates how Sedgwick, in effect, was left to his own devices. The situation on Sedgwick's front could and did change quicker than the amount of time it took for most dispatches to reach him. Warren wrote:

> I find everything snug here. We contracted the line a little, and repulsed the last assault with ease. General Hooker wishes them to attack him tomorrow, if they will. He does not desire you to attack again in force unless he attacks him at the same time. He says you are too far away for him to direct. Look well to the safety of your corps, and keep up communication with General Benham, at Banks' Ford and Fredericksburg. You can go either place, if you think best. To cross at Banks' Ford would bring you in supporting distance of the main body, and would be better than falling back to Fredericksburg.[7]

Warren's assessment of the situation at Chancellorsville was not completely accurate. The chief engineer had been without sleep for more than a day, and he was truly exhausted when he penned this dispatch to Sedgwick. Warren was somewhat correct in stating that Hooker wished the enemy to attack him. It was also true that Hooker's position was solid, even after being dealt a hard blow by Jackson's flank attack. Warren was under the impression that the army commander did not want Sedgwick to attack unless Hooker attacked first. This was not what Hooker had in mind. Hooker had shied away from the offense for the last three days. Recognizing that Sedgwick's advance had been checked, Hooker

Chief Topographical Engineer of the Army of the Potomac, Brigadier General (Major General from May 3, 1863) Gouverneur K. Warren (Massachusetts MOLLUS Collection, U.S. Military History Institute).

wanted and expected Lee to attack his entrenched army near Chancellorsville. Warren, like the majority of Hooker's subordinates, was not quite comfortable with the army commander's idea of remaining on the defensive.

Warren wrote to Sedgwick, explaining what appeared to be the logical steps needed to engage and defeat the Army of Northern Virginia. The recommendations contained in Warren's dispatch were little more than suggestions for Sedgwick. Hooker's intentions were not clear as the army commander had retired for the night without issuing specific orders for Sedgwick. Warren's dispatch to Sedgwick was an attempt to help, but actually was misleading. After the fact, Warren realized his letter had taken on greater importance and possibly could be viewed as misguiding, especially to Hooker's point of view. Warren later attempted to retrieve his battle reports from headquarters and modify them. A paper shuffle involving an unknown number of officers seems to have occurred, and various reports were not available until nearly three months after the campaign, while others could not be found.[8]

Warren's attempt to assist Sedgwick held little promise without Hooker's endorsement. The Confederates were strongly positioned to Sedgwick's front and prevented him from advancing on Chancellorsville. Without updated orders from Hooker, Sedgwick was not authorized to vary from his objective of advancing on Chancellorsville. Left to his own by Hooker, Sedgwick was forced to let the situation on the Sixth Corps' front dictate to him the course of action to be taken. The only development that could improve the Sixth Corps situation, besides positive orders from Hooker, was an offensive move initiated by Hooker at Chancellorsville. Lieutenant Elisha Hunt Rhodes of the 2nd Rhode Island, Third Division Sixth Corps, lamented, "Our wounded have been captured in Fredericksburg and nothing but good generalship can save the dear old Sixth Corps." [9]

In the dark night, Sedgwick's lines were realigned as line officers attempted to account for their men. As the Federals established a perimeter, Daniel M. Holt, assistant surgeon of the 121st New York Volunteers, became disoriented. The much-fatigued Holt marched his squad of medical attendants back to what he thought was the rear of Sedgwick's line. Holt recounts the event:

> I rode along, where I saw just ahead of me, not more than three rods distant, a moving line of battle, up to which I rode and asked an officer — a captain who was leading his company, "What brigade is this?" to which the answer came, "Kershaw's!" ... After imparting to me this cheering piece of news, the officer to whom I addressed the inquiry, asked me: "To what regiment do you belong?" "The 121st" says I, at the same time halting my men who were close upon my heels. "Halt! Halt! Halt!" ran all along the line in answer to mine for my men...."The 121st what?" says the interrogator. "The 121st N. York" says I. "What rank do you hold?" says Johnny Reb, for so was he. "Surgeon!" says I. "Well, doctor, I think you will have to dismount. I am very sorry to say you have fallen into the hands of the Rebels this time, and there is no help for you!" ... While still upon my horse, an officer rode up in a great rage, inquiring as he advanced, "Who had the audacity and authority to call a halt at this time?" ..."By what authority did you do so?" ..."Who are you sir?" "Surgeon Holt of the 121st Reg. N.Y. Vols. of the federal Army!"—"Federal army be damned! and you too!! Captain place a guard over him and his men and keep them safe until morning!"[10]

Placed under guard, Holt and his men were led through the littered battlefield to Salem Church. Upon entering the church, Holt found Confederate medical personnel were working feverishly to save lives. Outside against the building, piles of rifles were stacked next to a bloody heap of amputated arms and legs. Inside, Holt found dozens of wounded men suffering and dying, many from his own regiment. He and his attendants quickly went to work assisting the wounded of both sides. The surgeon was treated as a guest and had the opportunity to meet several Confederate general officers. In accordance to an 1862 agreement concerning noncombatants, Holt and his men were free to return to Union lines shortly after the Chancellorsville Campaign.[11]

As the first streaks of dawn appeared, Wheaton sent out four companies from the 62nd New York Volunteers (Anderson Zouaves) to reconnoiter to the right of the Sixth Corps' line. A short distance above Banks's Ford, the New Yorkers were quick to encounter Mahone's Confederate pickets strongly posted near Smith's Run. Captain Tyler C. Jordan's Bedford (Virginia) Battery was also positioned on the Smith property, preventing Sedgwick from forcing his way up the River Road.

At 6:20 A.M. Sedgwick, from his position near the tollgate, wrote Butterfield:

I am anxious to hear from General Hooker. There is a strong force in front of me, strongly posted. I cannot attack with any hope of dislodging them until I know something definite as to the position of their main body and ours. I have sent two or three messengers to Banks' Ford, but none have returned, nor have I heard from the General since yesterday."[12]

Along Sedgwick's front, musket and artillery fire erupted periodically as the Federals shifted troops. The tension between contending armies was somewhat reduced as a small herd of cattle suddenly appeared between skirmish lines. Panic stricken, the bawling bovines bolted back and forth until they made their escape in the direction they had come. A Sixth Corps soldier of Third Brigade, First Division, recorded the scene, "...a herd of cattle is between our skirmish line and the rebels, and it is very amusing to see them run and bellow, first to the right, then to the left, with tails straight out"[13]

On the Chancellorsville front, Major General Richard H. Anderson's three brigades had been positioned on Lee's right to prevent Hooker and Sedgwick from uniting. Anderson's men were deployed on the River Road until approximately 7:00 A.M. of Monday May 4, when three brigades under the command of Brigadier General Henry Heth relieved them. The previous night, Heth had taken command of Major General Ambrose Powell Hill's division after "Lil Powell" Hill received a painful wound to the calves of both legs. Lee instructed Anderson to gather his troops and march his men up the Mine Road to reinforce McLaws at Salem Church.[14]

At dawn this same day, from the vicinity of the Cox house, Early advanced in two lines of battle north up the Telegraph Road toward Lee's Hill. Early's goal was to connect with McLaws' right flank, somewhere near Salem Church. Through a misunderstanding, Colonel John B. Gordon sent forward his brigade prior to Early's planned jump off time. Angered by Gordon's premature advance, Early quickly reacted by advancing his remaining brigades to Gordon's support. Fortunately for Gordon's brigade, Lee's Hill by this time had been abandoned by Sedgwick's force. The only people in the area were a handful of women who had come out from Fredericksburg to comb the area for wounded. Gordon was unaware at the time of the fact that if the reoccupation of Marye's Heights proved unsuccessful he would have been court-martialed by Major General Early for disobeying orders. This incident was the start of a rocky relationship between Early and Gordon. Many quarrels would flare up between these two Confederate officers throughout the rest of the war.[15]

From Lee's Hill, Gordon moved toward the Orange Plank Road and discovered a large body of Federals at rest along the Orange Plank Road. The twenty-pounder Parrott rifles of Captain Archibald Graham's First Rockbridge (Virginia) Artillery were immediately put into action on the high ground overlooking Hazel run. The Virginians' shells fell among Howe's surprised Federals as Gordon sent forward his gray infantry skirmishers. Colonel Richard S. Andrews, commanding the artillery battalion accompanying Early, recounted the scene:

> A Federal battery placed on the right and left of the Downman's house opened upon Graham, their shell, with few exceptions, failing to reach us, whilst his twenty pds. Parrotts reached them very easily and soon silenced their guns, and they limbered up and ran off to the rear. As they had their guns within a few feet of Mr. Downman's house (in fact, as near as the porch would allow them to be placed) it was impossible to avoid damaging the house very seriously.[16]

Colonel (Brigadier General from May 7, 1863, and Major General from May 14, 1864) John B. Gordon (C.S.A.) (Massachusetts MOLLUS Collection, U.S. Military History Institute).

Caught off guard by the shelling, Howe's men scrambled for protection. Gordon advanced a battle line, which quickly caught up with his skirmishers near Hazel Run. Howe hastily sent forward the 33rd New York as skirmishers. Several regiments of Howe's Third Brigade formed on the slope to receive the Confederate attack. Gordon's force dashed ahead and engaged the 33rd New York as spirited skirmishing ensued. Captain James M. McNair of Company F, 33rd New York wrote, "The Regiment was thrown forward as a forlorn hope, trusting that by desperate fighting we might hold the enemy in check.... The enemy were rapidly flanking us, when we were ordered to fall back on the run."[17]

The uneven terrain hindered the alignment of Gordon's charge and dangerously exposed the Confederate left flank. Fortunately, the fire from Graham's Parrott rifles was accurate and the bombardment sent Howe's lines running for cover on the far side of the Orange Plank Road. The terrain favored the Federals as Gordon's infantry encountered thick brush-covered slopes bordering the valley containing Hazel Run. The bulk of Gordon's force plunged across the watercourse and continued, wet to the shoulders, up toward the enemy.[18]

During the action a riderless horse bolted into Gordon's lines. Confederate rifle fire had unhorsed the Union officer riding the beautiful coal-black mare. A member of Gordon's staff managed to seize the horse's rein and calm the frantic beast. The timing of this horse's arrival could not have been better as Gordon's own horse was quite exhausted and partially disabled. Gordon quickly changed mounts and to his surprise found this new charger a "superb battle horse." Gordon named the horse Marye after the heights on which she was captured. He rode this clever filly for the duration of the war.[19]

Howe was able to re-form a portion of his command along the roadbed of the Orange Plank Road, while others fell back to the cover of abandoned Confederate earthworks. Graham's two twenty-pounder Parrott rifles continued lobbing shells in the direction of the protected Federals. As Howe's Second Division fell back, the 31st Georgia captured several squads of the 33rd New York, a commissary wagon, and several Federal signal personnel. This thirty-minute skirmish gave Early possession of Marye's Heights and cut Sedgwick's line of communication with Fredericksburg.[20]

By 8:00 A.M., Early had advanced the remainder of his division up the Telegraph Road and reoccupied Marye's Heights. The remaining guns of Lieutenant Colonel Andrews' Confederate artillery battalion accompanied his advance and occupied gun emplacements on the heights behind Fredericksburg. Across the river on Stafford Heights, Federal reserve artillerymen observed the Confederate banners of Early's division appear on Marye's Heights. Federal heavy artillery shelled Early's division as they maneuvered to support Gordon's brigade facing Sedgwick.

Barksdale attempted to advance into the city of Fredericksburg, but Gibbon's two Federal brigades stood in his way. Gibbon placed his twelve guns and Lafflin's brigade across the river to protect the approaches to the three pontoon bridges spanning the Rappahannock. Gibbon's Third Brigade, under Colonel Hall, entrenched to the rear of the city facing Early's troops on the heights. Barksdale observed the numerous guns of the Federal artillery on Stafford Heights as well as Gibbon's entrenched infantry and wisely called a halt. Barksdale's men would have been easy targets for the Federal artillery located across the river had he sent his brigade across the open fields to recapture Fredericksburg. Barksdale informed Early of the situation. The much irritated Early instructed Barksdale to "desist from the attack on the town and to dispose of his brigade so as to resist any advance from that direction." Barksdale moved his brigade into their former position behind the stone wall at the base of Marye's Heights.[21]

With Barksdale's Mississippi brigade and four batteries of Pendleton's artillery positioned on Marye's Heights, Gibbon's Second Corps brigades were contained. To the rear of Fredericksburg, Colonel Hall sent forward Captain William Plumer's 1st Company Massachusetts Sharpshooters, "Andrew Sharpshooters," to return an annoying fire produced by Confederate marksmen entrenched on the heights. According to Hall, "Several Rebel officers were dismounted, and many men were struck by the bullets of this company." Gibbon's role in this campaign became negated by battlefield developments, but the mere presence of his two brigades yielded benefits. Gibbon's troops prevented Early's force from reoccupying the city of Fredericksburg. More importantly for Sedgwick their presence held the attention of Confederate troops on their front, which could have been used in an attack on the Sixth Corps.[22]

Major General Early, atop Lee's Hill, now set his sights on Sedgwick's corps. Among the maneuvering Confederates on Marye's Heights, captured Federal signal officers Captain P. Babcock and Captain Joseph Gloskoski managed to escape from Early's reoccupying force and found their way to the protection of Sedgwick's line.

Disregarding Butterfield's instructions forbidding the use of signals, the escaped signal officers immediately established a Federal call station at the Guest house. With no telegraph wires extending beyond Scott's Ford, this flag station would prove vital for the Sixth Corps. Within the range of enemy rifle fire, this signal station provided the only communication link between the Sixth Corps and headquarters on the opposite side of the river. For several hours on the morning of the May 4, information to and from Sedgwick was wigwagged over the heads of Early's Confederate troops. The Union signal station positioned in the charred remains of the Phillips house, located on Stafford Heights, used a powerful telescope to view the Sixth Corps' messages.[23]

Butterfield's headquarters on Stafford Heights had a good sense of what was developing on Sedgwick's front, but obviously Hooker had little idea. Concerned only with his immediate front, Hooker requested Sedgwick to send him any troops being held in reserve. At 8:00 A.M., Butterfield sent Sedgwick a message that read, "He desires that if any portion of your force is available, and can be spared, they be moved in a central position, near where they can support Howard or be thrown right or left, as required. He [Hooker] is under the impression that you have three brigades in reserve...."[24]

Butterfield was busy observing Early's force on Marye's Heights. To Hooker he wired, "Forces engaging Gibbon in front of Fredericksburg seem to imperil our communication with Sedgwick. I fear the staff officer who left here with a copy of Warren's dispatch will not reach him. From the tenor of that officer's statement, I judge Sedgwick was waiting to here from you. It is important that he should get Warren's dispatch. Gibbon just advised me that deserter reports Longstreet's force in direction of Bowling Green." It could only have been obvious to Hooker that Sedgwick's situation was rapidly worsening.[25]

Shortly after 8:00 A.M., Sedgwick received a message that originated from Hooker's headquarters at 6:00 A.M. The dispatch read, "The General commanding desires that you telegraph to him your exact position. What information have you respecting the force of the enemy in your front and rear? What is your own strength? Is there any danger of a force coming up in your rear and cutting your communications? Can you sustain yourself acting separately or in cooperation with us?" This dispatch to Sedgwick was closely followed by one from Butterfield, "The enemy are advancing on Fredericksburg, reported to have possession of Orange Plank Road. One brigade just reported advancing, now, 8:00 A.M., a column reported coming on the Telegraph Road."[26]

The 8th Pennsylvania Cavalry crossed the pontoon bridge at Scott's Ford that morning and reported to Sedgwick. Sedgwick's situation had rapidly changed and offensive maneuvers were no longer a consideration. This meant cavalry was of no use to the Sixth Corps' commander. Sedgwick sent the cavalry toward Howe's position, closer to the river. Howe, recognizing the terrain as not being favorable for cavalry, instructed Major Pennock Huey and his Union horsemen to cover the approaches to Scott's Ford.[27]

Sedgwick was unable to advance due to McLaws' entrenched force on his front and now was cut off from Fredericksburg by Early's division to his rear. The Sixth Corps was forced to draw back into a defensive position that took the shape of three sides of a parallelogram. The Federal line officers made good use of the terrain, positioning their troops along crests of hills that rolled through the wooded area. This drawing-in of the Sixth Corps' perimeter safeguarded Sedgwick's interior line, which would allow for the unmolested transfer of troops to any sector of his line. More importantly, the Sixth Corps' only workable escape route, Scott's Ford, remained secure within the new perimeter.

The Sixth Corps signal station located at the Guest house was compelled to stop communicating when Sedgwick contracted his line. Fortunately for Sedgwick, at Scott's Ford, Benham had sent over Second Lieutenant Conard F.M. Denicke by boat to establish a signal station within the lines of the Sixth Corps. Driven off several times by Confederate sharpshooters, Denicke finally established himself on the River Road and opened signal communication with the Federal flagmen at Scott's Ford. Sedgwick again had a reliable communication link with Butterfield, who had telegraph communications with Hooker near Chancellorsville.[28]

Sedgwick's battle line contraction placed Howe's Second Division facing east, toward Fredericksburg. Bolstered by Martin and Rigby's batteries, Howe's left rested close to the Rappahannock River and his line extended nearly one mile south to the Orange Plank Road. Facing south, basically parallel to the Orange Plank Road, was Brooks' First Division. Parsons and McCartney's batteries were placed in position on Brooks' line, which extended almost to the tollgate. Newton's Third Division, still confronting the Confederates along Salem Ridge, held the tollgate area and brought the Union line back toward the Rappahannock River. Positioned on the left of Newton's line were Harn and Cowan's batteries. A short distance to the rear of the center of Newton's line, Williston and McCarthy's guns were positioned along a slight rise of ground. Sedgwick's five-mile-long defensive line was anchored just above Banks's Ford by Butler's battery, supported by Burnham's Light Division.

At 8:30 A.M., Sedgwick responded to Hooker's earlier inquiry, "I am occupying the same position as last night. The enemy made an attack on Howe; did not amount to much [Early's reoccupation of Marye's Heights]; I think I have made secure my communications with Banks's Ford [Scott's Ford]. I think they will attempt to drive me back. I await instructions."[29]

Again at 9:00 A.M., Sedgwick informed Hooker:

I have secured my communications with Banks's Ford [Scott's Ford]. The enemy is in possession of the heights of Fredericksburg in force. They appear strongly in our front, and are making efforts to drive us back. My strength yesterday morning was 22,000 men. I do not know my losses, but they were large, probably 5,000 men. I cannot use cavalry. It depends upon the condition and position of your force whether I can sustain myself here. Howe reports the enemy advancing upon Fredericksburg (from the Heights).[30]

Sedgwick felt his force was quickly becoming outnumbered and that his corps was in grave danger. From his balloon across the river, Professor Lowe fueled Sedgwick's anxiety by overestimating the size of Early's force reoccupying Marye's Heights. Lowe informed Sedgwick that 15,000 enemy troops, nearly double the actual size of Early's force, had taken position between the Sixth Corps and Fredericksburg. Additional discouraging news reached Sedgwick telling him that a ten-car Confederate train had pulled into the depot at Hamilton's Crossing.[31]

From Hooker's staff, headquartered at Chancellorsville, came the following: "The commanding general directs that in the event you fall back, you reserve, if practicable, a position on the Fredericksburg side of the Rappahannock, which you can hold until tomorrow." Shortly after, another message reached Sedgwick, "I enclose substance of a communication sent last night [Warren's]. Its suggestions are highly important, and meet my full approval. There are positions on your side, commanded by our batteries on the other side, I think you could take and hold. The general would recommend as one such position the ground on which Dr. Taylor's is situated."[32]

These dispatches originating from Hooker's headquarters contained the commander's endorsement. In actuality, these recommendations were created and sent by headquarters' staff officers, who had little knowledge of the brewing situation on the Sixth Corps front. Hooker still had not sent positive orders to the Sixth Corps commander. These latest dispatches from army headquarters did make it clear to Sedgwick that Warren's advice met with Hooker's approval. Sedgwick was again sanctioned to act as he saw fit.

From his headquarters at Falmouth, Butterfield forwarded a message to Hooker that originated from Gibbon positioned at Fredericksburg. Gibbon wrote, "One brigade of division in town, the other and batteries this side at bridges, if forced out of town; and he [Sedgwick] has gone away I had better withdraw at once and take up the bridges." Butterfield replied to Gibbon, "Hold on to the last extremity, until further orders. Sedgwick holds same position as he did." At 10:27 A.M., Butterfield wired Gibbon, "You perhaps had better take up your lower bridge and get boats out of water, and hold engineer force ready to work on others. Use your discretion." At 10:35 A.M., James H. Van Alen of Hooker's staff notified Butterfield, "The General says, that Gibbon's command is to remain where it is. The bridges, of course, are to remain. It would seem from your dispatch that Gibbon and the enemy are retreating from each other." Several hours later, Gibbon used his own discretion and reduced the size of his perimeter by removing his lower pontoon bridge near the destroyed railroad trestle.[33]

On Marye's Heights, Early was frustrated in his attempts to coordinate with McLaws at Salem Church. He was uncertain about the strength of the Federal force to his immediate front and needed to ascertain the size and exact position of the enemy's line. The two Union brigades of Brigadier General Howe's Second Division defended the sector of Sedgwick's line, opposite Early's division. Howe had positioned the 49th New York, 7th Maine, 77th, 20th, and 33rd New York regiments of Brigadier General Thomas H. Neill's Third Brigade on his left. The right of Howe's mile-long line was held by Colonel L.A. Grant's First Vermont Brigade, which extended right toward the Orange Plank Road.

Early's force had not encountered much Union artillery fire from Sedgwick's line while reoccupying the heights. Around 11:00 A.M., to develop the enemy's strength, Early sent forward Brigadier General William Smith's brigade. Smith's skirmishers exchanged a lively fire with the advanced Federal picket line of Neill's brigade, positioned on the left of Howe's line. In a short time, Neill's pickets were forced to retire upon their main battle line as Smith's Virginians rapidly advanced. Upon nearing the Union battle line, Smith's attackers received heavy artillery and rifle fire from Neill's Federals. Smith's brigade charged but encountered a galling fire. After some spirited fighting, Smith was forced to retire through canister blasts provided by a section of twelve-pounder Napoleons belonging to Battery A, 1st United States, under Captain J.H. Rigby. Early wrote, "The 13th and the 58th Regiments became heavily engaged, and the 49th and 52nd slightly."[34]

Early's testing of the Union line was done with some force. While the 58th Virginia fell back, their regimental standard was seized by Neill's Federals. Corporal John P. McVeane of the 49th New York shot the gallant color bearer of the 58th Virginia and secured his flag. Several companies of the 58th Virginia sought protection from the intense Union artillery fire in an abandoned house. Soon the Federals surrounded the wooded dwelling, and the Virginians were taken captive. Corporal McVeane would later be awarded the Medal of Honor for capturing this battle flag. Two hundred prisoners of war were the result of the efforts put forth by Colonel Daniel D. Bidwell's 49th New York and members of the 7th Maine. Lieutenant Colonel Seldon Connor, commanding the 7th Maine, wrote home, "This little victory was the work of a single company of the 7th Maine and two companies of the 49th New York."[35]

Sedgwick immediately reported to Butterfield and Hooker, "General Howe has had a sharp fight and has taken a flag and 200 prisoners." Early wrote of the captured members of the 58th Virginia, "They were thus captured by their own misconduct, the enemy sending to take possession of them, which I could not prevent without bringing on a heavy engagement."[36]

From Marye's Heights, Early sent Lieutenant A.L. Pitzer to report his division's situation to McLaws at Salem Church. Early suggested that McLaws move to the attack with two of his brigades. Early would join in with three of his own brigades once McLaws had made contact with the Yankees. McLaws felt the enemy was too strongly posted on his front for him to initiate the attack with his force. McLaws, the ranking officer on the field, wrote back stating that he wanted Early to initiate the attack. McLaws believed his battle plan would force the Federals to expose their flank to an attack by his Confederate brigades.

In the meantime, McLaws informed General Lee of the situation and requested reinforcements. Lee explained that Anderson was on his way to Salem Church to assist him. McLaws gave orders postponing any attack until Anderson's infantry was up. Early was informed of the reinforcements that were en route to Salem Church. From a Federal officer captured near Banks's Ford, General Lee had learned that Sedgwick commanded his own corps as well as Reynolds' First Corps. The source of this false information might very well have been the Sixth Corps' missing courier, Captain Henry W. Farrar, earlier sent by Sedgwick to open communication with Banks's Ford. This captured information made Lee hold back from attacking Sedgwick until he had consolidated his force and equaled the odds.[37]

Anderson arrived at Salem Church around noon and began maneuvering his 4,000 Confederate troops into position. Lee arrived at Salem Church shortly after Anderson and took charge. Much to Lee's displeasure, Sedgwick's troop dispositions between McLaws' line and Early's had not been fully reconnoitered. Lieutenant Colonel Porter Alexander recalled Lee's anger over the situation and concluded, "Nobody knew exactly how or where the enemy's line of battle was and it was somebody's duty to know." Alexander's artillery battalion was resting in park along the Orange Turnpike, awaiting orders, when Lee reached the vicinity of Salem Church. Time was of the essence, but McLaws had failed to fully develop the enemy's position while waiting for Anderson's arrival.[38]

Brigadier General (later Major General) William Smith (C.S.A.) (Massachusetts MOLLUS Collection, U.S. Military History Institute).

Instructions were quickly given as Anderson's fatigued troops deployed. Colonel Alexander sent thirteen rifled pieces of Major Robert A. Hardaway's battalion to Smith's Hill, located just above Banks's Ford. One of these guns was a twelve-pound Whitworth breech-loading rifle, commanded by Lieutenant W.B. Hurt. Hardaway expected to find prepared firing pits on Smith's Hill, but instead his tuckered cannoneers found only four prepared positions and were forced to fell trees to clear fields of fire. Eight additional guns from Alexander's battalion soon joined Hardaway on Smith's Hill. Hardaway, one of the best artillery marksmen in the Confederate army, instructed his rifled cannon crews to direct their fire toward the Federal guns positioned on the north bank of the Rappahannock.[39]

Anderson continued to deploy his brigades as skirmishers quickly advanced in order to define the Sixth Corps' defensive line. Once in position, Lee's combined force would total 23,000 soldiers. Confronting him were 19,000 troops under the Sixth Corps banners of the Greek Cross. Lee wanted to hit Sedgwick's troops from two sides with a coordinated general attack. The brigades of Hays, Hoke, and Gordon, from Early's division, were to attack in cooperation with the brigades of Carnot Posey, Edward A. Perry, and Ambrose R. Wright, from Anderson's division, positioned to their left opposite the Orange Plank Road. Once Early's and Anderson's assault struck the Union line, McLaws' entrenched troops were to advance to the attack and connect with Anderson's left in order to sweep the Sixth Corps from the field.

Awaiting word from Hooker, Sedgwick anxiously remained ready as the enemy made preparations for an attack. A young officer of Sedgwick's staff, fully aware of his corps' predicament and a bit apprehensive, commented to Sedgwick that the situation appeared gloomy:

"General, it looks as if the Sixth Corps is going to close its career today." "It has somewhat that appearance," said the General. "Then," said the young officer, with much honest intensity, "if the Sixth Corps goes out of existence today, I hope it will be with a blaze of glory that will light the history of this war for all time." The General smiled and said, "I will tell you a secret; there will be no surrendering."[40]

Shortly after noon on May 4, Sedgwick received permission from Hooker to lay a second bridge at Scott's Ford. Hooker's message read, "I expect to advance to-morrow morning; will be likely to relieve you; you must not count on much assistance unless I hear heavy firing. Tell General Benham to put down the other bridge, if you desire it." Sedgwick immediately signaled Brigadier General Benham to lay the bridge close to the first one. Benham ordered Lieutenant Colonel Magruder of the 15th New York Engineers to begin constructing a second bridge at Scott's Ford. Sedgwick acknowledged Hooker's message, "I shall do my utmost to hold a position on the right bank of the Rappahannock until tomorrow."[41]

The day progressed slowly as Anderson's fatigued troops trudged into attack position. Sedgwick's defensive line crossed the Orange Plank Road, which denied Anderson the use of that road for deployment. Anderson's men were forced to maneuver over uneven terrain as advance skirmishers felt their way through the thickets to locate Sedgwick's line. Two remaining batteries of bronze Napoleons from Alexander's battalion, under the charge of the twenty-five-year-old West Point alumnus Major Frank Huger, were sent to coordinate with Anderson's brigades.

Near Marye's Heights, Early had deployed his division. In order to personally orchestrate the attack, Lee and his staff rode down to Early's position. From Early's left to right, the order of battle was Brigadier General R.F. Hoke's Brigade of North Carolina "Tar Heels," Brigadier General Harry T. Hays' "Louisiana Tigers," and Colonel

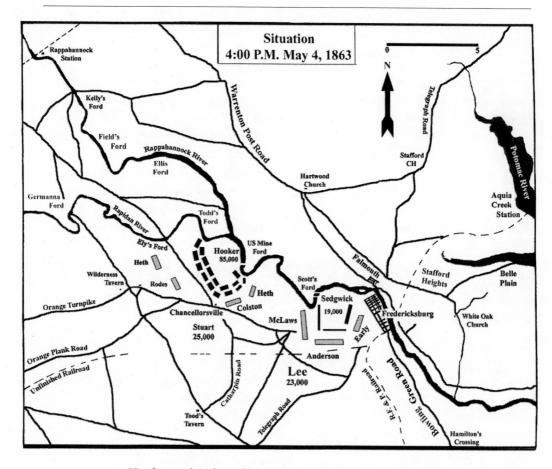

Hooker and Sedgwick's positions: 3:00 P.M. May 4, 1864.

John B. Gordon's brigade from Georgia. Smith's brigade was placed in a reserve position connecting with Barksdale's men deployed to the front of Marye's Heights. Early's troops slaked their thirst with water hauled from Hazel Run as they anxiously waited for the attack to commence. Three cannon shots fired in close succession from Colonel E.P. Alexander's gunners would signal the step-off time for Lee's assault.[42]

Due to the rolling terrain, Pendleton had difficulty effectively deploying most of his artillery. On Early's front, Confederate infantry laid positioned along hillsides above and forward of the majority Pendleton's guns. The mission of many Confederate gun crews became the suppression of Federal artillery positioned across the river. Captain H.M. Ross's Battery A, of Lieutenant Colonel A.S. Cutts' Sumter (Georgia) Battalion, and Captain H.H. Carlton's Troup (Georgia) Battery were the only two batteries able to locate firing positions capable of assisting Early's infantry assault. Ross and Carlton's guns found elevated positions on a knoll between the Telegraph Road and the Downman house. These eight Confederate guns would only be useful at the opening of the upcoming attack. Once gray battle lines stepped off, the artillery would be forced to cease fire to prevent injuring their own men.[43]

Nothing had changed throughout the day on Sedgwick's front except for an increase in Confederate troop strength. Remarkably, the Union forces at Chancellorsville remained idle for the entire day. As Sedgwick awaited orders from Hooker, the time appeared to creep by slowly. Tense Union soldiers nervously waited for developments as blue Virginian skies became gray from a hazy overcast. Major Mason Tyler of Sedgwick's First Division observed, "All that afternoon we watched Rebels moving through the woods on our front, and every now and then uttering the Rebel yell, at times apparently forming into lines of battle and preparing for attack. It was one of the most anxious six or seven hours that I ever spent."[44]

CHAPTER 11

Battle for Scott's Ford

A courier from E.S. Allen's Federal balloon detachment, operating in the vicinity of Banks's Ford, rode to Brigadier General Howe with a dispatch. The message, directed

Brigadier General (later Brevet Major General) Albion P. Howe, commander of the Second Division, Sixth Corps (Massachusetts MOLLUS Collection, U.S. Military History Institute).

to Sedgwick, explained that a large Confederate force was assembling on the heights behind Fredericksburg. Howe forwarded this dispatch two miles up the Orange Plank Road to Sedgwick and anxiously awaited instructions from the Sixth Corps commander. Howe, an artillery graduate of West Point, believed the enemy would force his left in an attempt to sever his communications with Scott's Ford. The Second Division commander carefully studied the rolling terrain and decided to occupy two positions, one in front of the other, in order to cover all likely Confederate avenues of approach.

Consisting of Brigadier General Neill's Third Brigade, Howe's front line was placed in a commanding position along the military crest of a ridgeline. Neill's battle line was anchored near the River Road by the 20th New York. Extending right, the 77th New York, 33rd New York, 7th Maine, 49th New York, and 21st New Jersey positioned themselves along the high ground. Each regiment sent out detachments of skirmishers to their front. Also on line with

Neill's brigade was the 5th Vermont from Howe's Second Brigade. Just south of the Orange Plank Road, the 5th Vermont formed in a small gully near the Guest house, in support of four guns belonging to Parsons' New Jersey Light, Battery A. Lieutenant Colonel John R. Lewis of the 5th Vermont sent out two companies to the front of the Guest house to provide early warning. Lewis' skirmishers connected with the left of the 27th New York, who formed the far left of Brooks' First Division skirmish line extending up the Orange Plank Road.[1]

In a covering of wood, higher and to the rear of Neill's line, Howe positioned regiments of Colonel L.A. Grant's Vermont Brigade. This reserve line, running left to right, consisted of the 4th Vermont, 26th New Jersey, 2nd Vermont, 6th Vermont and the 3rd Vermont. Grant's men erected hasty entrenchments by felling small trees and stacking knapsacks to their front for protection. Slightly ahead of this line, between the 3rd and 6th Vermont, Captain James Rigby rolled the six ten-pounders of his 1st Maryland, Battery A, into position. The Second Division's chief of artillery, Major J. Watts De Peyster, also positioned here a two-gun section of ten-pounder Parrott rifles belonging to Lieutenant Martin's 5th U.S., Battery F. Martin placed his remaining four ten-pounder Parrott rifles on some high ground to the left of Howe's reserve line.[2]

Around 5:30 P.M., McLaws' signal guns sounded and Early's gray lines advanced with a Rebel yell. Neill's Union skirmishers emptied their rifles before making tracks back toward their main battle line. Howe's Federal artillery opened on the attackers, sending shells crashing in the direction of the rapidly moving Confederates. The left of Early's attacking line grazed the left of Brooks' First Division skirmish line and then fell heavily on Howe's right center.

As soon as Early's troops had crossed the Orange Plank Road, Brigadier General Hoke, advancing the left of Early's battle line, received a severe bullet wound to the shoulder. Colonel Isaac E. Avery took command of Hoke's brigade. Continuing forward over the rolling terrain, the North Carolinians became entangled with the left regiment of Hays' brigade. Captain Hamilton Jones of the 57th North Carolina remembered the advance as "exceedingly difficult, and anything like true alignment was out of the question...." In the smoke and confusion Hoke's men accidentally fired into Hays' men, and the attack became disjointed. Several regiments of Hays' Louisiana Tigers continued forward on the run, outdistancing the Confederate battle lines to their left and right. Lieutenant Henry Handerson of the 9th Louisiana recalled, "Owing to the rapidity of our charge, the brigade became inextricably confused."[3]

On command, Neill's line let go a tremendous volley that slowed the Southern attackers. From atop his horse, Brigadier General Neill hollered the command, "Forward Third Brigade!" The charge sounded as Neill's command echoed down the line, and the boys in blue surged forward toward the Confederates. Major Thomas W. Hyde remembered, "I took my place with my regiment and we charged upon them with a defiant hurrah. The shock was terrible." Colliding with the distorted Confederate battle line, Neill's men fought bravely until the remainder of Hays' and Hoke's brigades rejoined the combat.[4]

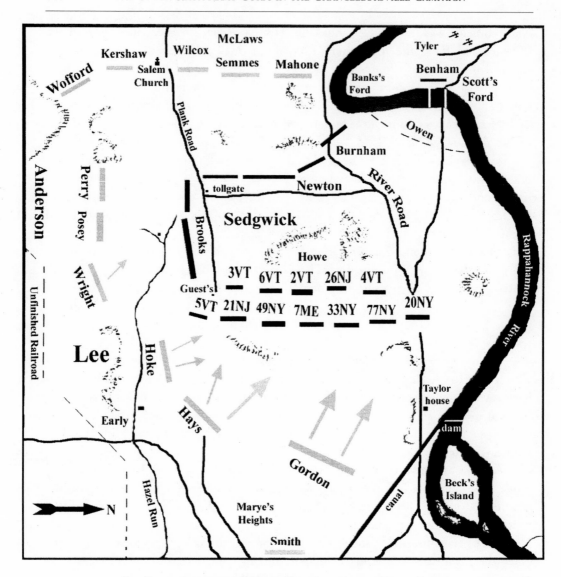

Battle for Scott's Ford (Banks's Ford) 5:30 P.M. May 4, 1863.

Assailed with great fury by large numbers of Confederates, Neill's brigade was cut up badly. Colonel Ernst Von Vegesack was unable to contain his 20th New York, which broke to the rear running. This caused great confusion among Rigby's six guns in battery to their rear. Brigadier General Neill was injured when his horse landed on him after it had been shot from under him. The smoke hung heavy in the air as Confederate lead found its mark. A large part of the 21st New Jersey ran for the rear as their colonel, Gilliam Van Houten, was taken down by a serious wound that would later claim his life while in the hands of the Confederates. Major Hyde of the 7th Maine described Neill's brigade as "smashed like a pitcher thrown against a rock."[5]

Toward the right of Neill's broken line, the 5th Vermont had thrown forward its right and poured a devastating fire into the flank of Hoke's charging Confederates. The fire from the Vermonters' Springfields was accurate. Colonel Grant observed the effect of their fire and claimed the 5th Vermont were able to "disable a much greater number of the enemy than there were in the regiment." Overwhelming numbers of Confederate attackers nearly cut the 5th Vermont off, but Colonel Lewis was able to withdraw his regiment through a depression to Howe's reserve line.[6]

Major De Peyster's two Parrott rifles ripped gaps in the ranks of the charging Confederates. The cries of battery commanders for two-second fuse and one-second fuse were heard just before De Peyster's smoking guns were drawn off to the rear of Howe's reserve line. From the Federals' reserve line, Howe instructed Lieutenant Colonel Martindale's 26th New Jersey to advance across a ravine slightly to his right in an attempt to prevent the enemy from gaining a section of woods. Sergeant Major Amos J. Cummings wrote, "Hardly had this been done before the woods on our left and the ridges to our front were covered with 'Butternuts,' who were gallantly surging upon us like an immense wave, exciting each other with wild shouts and firing very rapidly." Maintaining a brisk fire, the Jerseymen quickly found themselves being outflanked as Hays' Louisiana Tigers rushed past their left. Martindale attempted to change front, but Hoke's Confederate regiments to his immediate front sent most of the 26th New Jersey running to the rear.[7]

To escape, many of the Jerseymen fled through Captain Rigby's Union battery, who were also frantically attempting to withdraw to the rear. A team of horses from Rigby's battery became unmanageable and bolted, stranding one gun. Rigby stated, "As soon as I perceived this, I drew my saber, and by hard blows, forced the infantry to assist in drawing the piece from the field, which was done by attaching a prolonge [drag rope]." Rigby cursed the retreating blue infantry. Sergeant Major Cummings of the 26th New Jersey stopped and rallied a squad of his men to help drag off the gun. The Confederate attackers were soon upon them and a wild melee ensued; clubbed rifles were used freely. Elements of the 3rd Vermont rushed into the brawl, which allowed the Jerseymen to haul the three-inch ordnance rifle to safety. Sergeant Major Cummings would later be awarded the Medal of Honor for his actions, while saving the gun.[8]

On a knoll to the rear of the attacking Confederates, General Lee and Major General Early watched Hays' Tigers charge. Both officers were elated with the progress made to their front. Grabbing his hat and throwing it on the ground, Early exclaimed, "Those damned Louisiana fellows may steal as much as they please now!" This remark referred to theft charges earlier leveled against some of Hays' unruly Louisiana Tigers.[9]

Once the left of Neill's line had fled from their advanced position, Colonel C.B. Stoughton's 4th Vermont became hotly engaged on Howe's far left. Just as Howe had earlier predicted, Early was attempting to smash the Federals' left in order to sever their line of communication with Scott's Ford. Federal reserve batteries across the river had opened an accurate fire on Gordon's Georgia brigade and temporarily slowed their initial advance. A company commander in the 13th Georgia, Captain William R. Redding, remembered the bombardment, "We were subject to a tremendous shelling from the opposite side of the river...." Private Urbanus Dart Jr. of the 13th Georgia wrote,

"On we went climbing hills 40 to 50 feet high and so steep we had to climb on hands and knees. One battery in our rear just across the river, another on our left flank, and two in front all throwing shells ... and canister."[10]

In support of a section of Martin's battery, Colonel Stoughton's 4th Vermont held a commanding position and delivered heavy rifle fire into the Confederate attackers to their front. Gordon's determined attackers forced Martin's section to hitch up and race to the rear. Colonel L.A. Grant was quick to send the 5th Vermont to his far-left in support of the 4th Vermont. Sounding off with a Rebel yell, Gordon's regiments pressed forward in the direction of Scott's Ford.

To shore up Howe's left, Sedgwick's Chief of Artillery Colonel Charles H. Tompkins directed Lieutenant John H. Butler's battery toward Howe's position. Bouncing down the dirt way leading from Newton's battle line, Butler reported to Brigadier General Howe. Butler's six twelve-pounder Napoleons quickly went into action on a slight rise of ground that dominated a large area to the left front of Howe's battling line. Butler's Battery G, 2nd U.S., commenced raking the approaching attackers with canister, forcing many exposed Confederates into ravines and depressions for cover.

While Butler punished the attackers, Martin reestablished his section 200 yards to the left of Butler and began firing. Rigby had also re-formed on Howe's reserve line and sent percussion and combination shrapnel shells into the charging enemy masses. Returning fire, Gordon's troops were met with a hail of minie bullets and canister as they pressed Howe's line. As the attack raged, the 5th Wisconsin and the 31st New York were sent from Burnham's front to bolster Howe's left. Guided into position by Sedgwick's adjutant, Colonel McMahon, these Light Division troops joined the battling Vermonters and poured rifle fire through the heavy smoke into the determined gray attackers.

Brigadier General Howe sent Major Thomas Hyde racing

Brigadier General (later Major General) Harry T. Hays (C.S.A.) (Massachusetts MOLLUS Collection, U.S. Military History Institute).

Lee's May 4, 1863, attack on Sedgwick's Sixth Corps as seen from a sandbag-entrenched battery constructed just north of Falmouth, Virginia. A view of the battle for Scott's Ford (Leslie's Illustrated Newspaper).

to Sedgwick for more reinforcements. The corps commander sat bestride his mount next to Brigadier General Newton as Hyde's horse galloped up and skidded to a halt. The messenger excitedly reported the developments on Howe's front. Sedgwick immediately instructed Newton to send reinforcements toward the fighting.

Newton dispatched the 98th Pennsylvania of Wheaton's brigade at the double-quick down the Orange Plank Road to assist Howe. Lieutenant Colonel George Wynkoop's 98th Pennsylvania arrived and fired toward the advancing enemy who were nearing a lightly defended area on Howe's disarranged right. Brigadier General Wheaton remembered, "The most advanced Rebel battalions of the attacking column were within fifty yards of a low furze fence.... Lieut. Col. Wynkoop reached the fence first and checked the rebels who found the unexpected line to meet them." Following close behind Wynkoop was Brigadier General Wheaton's entire brigade, guided to the endangered sector on Howe's right by Major Hyde. Wheaton's remaining four regiments arrived at the double-quick, solidly anchoring Howe's embattled right, and assisted in rounding up numerous prisoners.[11]

Neill's imprudent Federal counterattack would cost his Third Brigade almost 1,000 men before they could extract themselves from their deadly dilemma. The Third Brigade's forced withdrawal dangerously exposed Howe's right flank, but owing to the sloping contours of the ground, the impetus of Early's attack veered right, down a ravine toward the front of the Vermonters in Howe's reserve line. After seeing the Union line falter, the Confederates sensed another push might send the Federals running for the river. The winded Rebels rushed onward through the ravine. From behind their barricade, the unseen 2nd, 3rd, and 6th Vermont regiments rose to their feet and fired. The deadly volley hammered the attackers, carpeting the ground with Confederate corpses. One of Hays' men wrote, "A wall of fire on three sides. The air was fairly hissing with round shot, grape, canister, and minie balls." With rattling ramrods, the Vermonters rapidly fired at will. Erastus H. Scott of the 3rd Vermont remembered, "...all jumped to their feet and poured it into them as fast as we could load and fire."[12]

Many of the Vermonters had recently been issued new waxed waterproof cartridges. This might have helped increase their volume of fire, which made their fire appear as one long continuous volley. Each Vermont regiment fired accurately into the startled Confederates as they neared their front. According to Private William Stowe of the 2nd Vermont, "...their dead covered the ground as gray as a badger in front of us." "Our loss was very heavy," one Confederate attacker wrote, "some regiments losing half their number in killed, wounded, and missing."[13]

Grant's fighting Vermonters presented an unbroken front, holding their ground as the Confederates obstinately remained active on the center and left of their battle line. In the smoky dusk, the Confederates recoiled and maintained their fire, refusing to retire. Among the roar of battle, Colonel Elisha L. Barney yelled, "Charge, boys, charge," and the 6th Vermont advanced, breaking the remains of the Confederate attack. A Vermonter wrote, "They raised the cry when within ten rods of us: Rally on the Plank Road. It was half a mile back and thither their broken columns ran in perfect confusion."[14]

Brigadier General (later Brevet Major General) Frank Wheaton, commander of the Third Brigade, Third Division, Sixth Corps (Massachusetts MOLLUS Collection, U.S. Military History Institute).

Barney's 6th Vermont swept forward several hundred yards to the opposite side of the ravine to their front. Lieutenant Colonel Martindale's re-formed 26th New Jersey gallantly charged forward on the right of Barney's men, causing great disorder among the enemy and sending survivors running to the rear. A member of the 26th New Jersey remembered the final enemy thrust:

> The 6th Vermont lay behind a little rise of ground, awaiting the onset of the Rebel host. Although the enemy was at least three times their number, for there was a whole brigade of them, the gallant Vermonters let them come on until they were actually within a few feet of them, and then, rising, poured in a volley which literally decimated the foe. They fled hastily, and the Sixth Corps was saved. It was now our turn and the Vermonters, followed by the 26th New Jersey, pressed forward on the flying foe, until we reached the brow of the hill from which they had come. As we went we took a great number of prisoners.[15]

Accompanied by his staff, Early rode forward and encountered retreating elements of his shattered division. Confederate officers worked to stop the retreat and re-form their units as Early ordered up the 49th and 52nd Virginia regiments from Smith's brigade. Having re-formed some of his troops, Early recalled, "...it had become too dark to make any further advance, and I did not hear either of the other two divisions engaged.... Hays and Hoke's brigades were put in line of battle across the Plank Road, at the point where they had been rallied." Smith's two Virginia regiments were advanced to the front as Early reestablished his battle line.[16]

The Vermont brigade commander, Colonel L.A. Grant, positioned in the center of Howe's line, lost contact with the 6th Vermont. In the growing darkness, Grant feared they may have been captured. Grant sent his acting aide-de-camp, Lieutenant Franklin G. Butterfield, to locate his wayward regiment. Forward of the main Union battle line, Butterfield found Barney's 6th Vermont in contact with Confederate skirmishers to their front. If the 6th Vermont did not retire from their exposed position, their flanks would surely be turned. Butterfield finally persuaded Barney's stubborn Vermonters to fall back to the main Union line as he commanded a skirmish line, screening the regiment's withdrawal. For his composure under fire Butterfield would later be awarded the Medal of Honor.[17]

To the left of Early's battling brigades, Major General Richard H. Anderson's brigades also advanced to the attack. Moving through the thickets across the uneven terrain, Brigadier General Ambrose "Rans" Wright's Georgians drifted to their left, making only slight contact with the Union skirmishers of Brooks' division. In straying to his left, Wright cut off Brigadier General Carnot Posey's brigade and interfered with Brigadier General Edward A. Perry's brigade of Floridians. Wright's direction of advance greatly diminished the effectiveness of Anderson's advance and reduced the area of maneuver for Brigadier General William T. Wofford's brigade positioned to Wright's left. Confusion ensued as the remaining daylight disappeared.[18]

Behind the Union line at the start of this attack, Sedgwick, Bartlett, and Russell sat atop their horses discussing the situation. Suddenly, close to a large brick house opposite the Orange Plank Road, a Confederate battle line appeared through the thickets. Sedgwick turned to Captain McCartney, who commanded Battery A, 1st Massachusetts, and said, "Captain, can you start those fellows up a little? The captain replied, "I will try," and jumped from his horse, sighted a gun and then pulled the lanyard." The shell slammed into the house, causing great damage. Immediately the remaining five brass twelve-pounders of McCartney's battery opened with a roar and effectively sprayed the wood to their front with large shotgun-like blasts of canister.[19]

McCartney's fire was accompanied by the discharges of a two-piece rifled section of Parsons' battery, which pounded the area to their front. Posey's Mississippians and Wright's troops were unable to advance through this hail of iron. Only making light contact on this front, Anderson's Confederates halted. The attack was launched so late in the day that darkness prevented Confederate line officers from coordinating further attacks. A British observer on Sedgwick's staff, Captain Harry G. Hore, was positioned on Brooks' line and described the carnage that occurred on the First Division's front.

Writing home to his cousin in England, the captain wrote, "Good God, dear girl, it was awful, the dead seemed piled heaps upon heaps, the shot went right through them, completely smashed the front of the columns." Hore's disquieting description seems a bit of an exaggeration, unless he viewed Confederate casualties on Howe's, not Brooks First Division front. To the front of Brooks, Anderson's losses during this disjointed assault only amounted to eighty-nine men across a mile-long avenue of approach. Anderson's brigades were quite fatigued, which exacerbated coordination problems, preventing his gray lines from working in concert. Brooks reported the Confederate attempt as "very feeble as the skirmish line, aided by a few rounds of fire by the battery of McCartney, not only repulsed but dispelled the whole line."[20]

Newton and Burnham's Union battle lines only saw limited skirmishing as McLaws never really advanced his Southerners to the attack. McLaws' right portion of his line did slowly advance, but because of delay and the lack of daylight, no serious attack developed in this sector. McLaws' Confederate troops, entrenched along Salem Ridge, were instructed to hold their front and join the attack as soon as Anderson's troops engaged the enemy. McLaws reported, "The darkness of the night, ignorance of the country, and the events transpiring on the other end of the line, prevented that co-operation which would have led to a more complete success; but I believe that all was gained that could have been expected under the circumstances. The enemy had several batteries (sixteen guns) in front of the left of my line, sweeping every approach from my left."[21]

McLaws' excuses for not joining the attack were rather weak, especially when closely reviewed. He stated the darkness of the night prevented him from attacking. Lee's attack was launched late in the day, but well before sunset. Once the attack commenced, Early managed to fight on his front for nearly an hour before darkness had set in. Ignorance of the country should not have been a factor as McLaws' division had spent the previous winter encamped in that general vicinity. Prior to the war, Brigadier General Mahone had been instrumental in the construction of the Orange Plank Road and had extensive knowledge

Major General Richard H. Anderson (C.S.A.) (Massachusetts MOLLUS Collection, U.S. Military History Institute).

of the area. Mahone's brigade was positioned on the left of McLaws' inactive line for the entire day. While his men rested, McLaws should have thoroughly reconnoitered and developed a strategy for the pending assault. During the attack, Wright's misdirected trek held some consequences for McLaws' far right, but his center and left were simply never advanced to the attack.

Apparently, McLaws' failure to attack was influenced by the strength of the Union defensive position to his front. Sedgwick's chief of artillery, Colonel Charles H. Tompkins, had done a masterful job of positioning the Sixth Corps artillery. His Federal battery placements commanded the open ground on McLaws' avenues of approach, which troubled McLaws. McLaws hesitated to assault, and daylight disappeared along with the opportunity to attack. Colonel Tompkins had skillfully orchestrated Sedgwick's artillery throughout the entire campaign, maximizing the effectiveness of his fifty-four guns. After the campaign, Sedgwick, an old artilleryman himself, commented on Colonel Tompkins' performance: "...his management and dispositions of the artillery, was worthy of the highest praise."[22]

Major General McLaws' performance during the Chancellorsville Campaign did impact Lee's later decision not to promote him to corps command. Some feel McLaws had been slighted by Lee and not promoted to corps command for the reason that he hailed from the state of Georgia, and not Virginia. This fact may have had some influence, but McLaws' sluggish execution on May 4 certainly did not advance his chance for the promotion to corps command in Lee's army. Lee was so disappointed in McLaws' performance that he wanted to reassign him out west, but Lieutenant General Longstreet stuck up for his former West Point classmate and spoke to Lee about retaining McLaws. Lee reluctantly agreed and said that Longstreet was now responsible for McLaws.[23]

At the outset of Lee's May 4 attack, Hardaway's Confederate guns on Smith's Hill commenced a fierce bombardment directed at eight Federal guns entrenched on the opposite side of the river. The eight guns of Tyler's Federal reserve were soon bolstered by the fire of four more Federal guns located farther downstream. From across the river, Federal gunners returned an accurate fire onto Smith's Hill and silenced five Confederate guns. The remaining gun crews under Hardaway were greatly hampered by the Federal fire, but continued to yank lanyards launching shells at the enemy guns on the far bank. Due to problems with the McAvoy fuse-igniters on the ammunition, many of the Confederate shells fired by Hardaway's eighteen guns extinguished in flight. Approximately only one in fifteen shells exploded, which in effect meant that the Confederate gunners were essentially shooting solid shot. Under such a disadvantage, Hardaway still claimed to have silenced six Federal cannon on the far bank.[24]

More importantly than destroying Federal batteries, Hardaway's duel drew annoying Federal artillery fire away from McLaws' entrenched infantry on Lee's left flank. Even with this advantage, the usually dependable McLaws hesitated as daylight faded along with the opportunity to destroy Sedgwick's Sixth Corps.

On Howe's Second Division front, Colonel L.A. Grant's Vermonters sent nearly 1,500 Confederate prisoners to the rear. Due to darkness and the contraction of the

Federal line, a majority of prisoners were able to slip away into the night. When the fighting ceased, Grant's men actually brought off 400 prisoners, many from the 8th Louisiana. Twenty-one Confederate officers were among the captives. Colonel Trevanion D. Lewis of the 8th Louisiana personally handed his sword over to the First Vermont Brigade commander, Colonel Grant. Sergeant Robert J. Coffey of Company K, 4th Vermont, would later be awarded the Medal of Honor for single-handedly capturing two officers and five privates of the 8th Louisiana. Colonel Leroy A. Stafford of the 9th Louisiana surrendered his sword to Colonel Barney of the 6th Vermont. Colonel Davidson B. Penn of the 7th Louisiana was another regimental commander counted among the Vermonters' captives. Penn tendered his sword to General Seaver of the 3rd Vermont, who reportedly "declined to take it from an officer who had shown such daring courage on that bloody field."[25]

Federal rifle fire from the left of the Louisiana Tigers' position took down Early's youngest and most promising brigade commander, Brigadier General Robert F. Hoke. Hoke's severe shoulder wound took this twenty-five-year-old combat commander out of the war until the end of 1863, when he returned to duty in his home state of North Carolina. The command of Hoke's brigade devolved upon Colonel Isaac Avery of the 6th North Carolina. Upon Hoke's recovery, he continued to perform well and his natural leadership abilities earned him a promotion to major general on April 20, 1864.[26]

Colonel L.A. Grant's regimental commanders fluidly shifted their Vermonters to meet emergencies, while raking the enemy with accurate fire. Butler, Rigby, and Martin's Union cannoneers greatly assisted in the repulse of Early's attack on May 4, 1863. Private Wilbur Fisk of the 2nd Vermont observed, "At every discharge the grape could be heard rattling against the trees like throwing a handful of pebbles against the side of a building. No enemy could stand such a fire, and they were soon driven back."[27]

Three brigades of Early's division were roughly handled in this assault, but the exact numbers of casualties are difficult to tabulate. Throughout the entire campaign, Major General Early

Brigadier General (later Major General) Robert F. Hoke (C.S.A.) (Southern Historical Collection, Wilson Library, The University of North Carolina at Chapel Hill).

only reported 136 killed, 838 wounded, and some 500 missing, which he believed were stragglers. Hays and Hoke's brigades lost nearly 850 casualties in their May 4 assault on the Sixth Corps. Gordon and Smith lost just over a total of 400 men on that day. Due to the number of Confederate prisoners able to slip away in the dark, many Union reports were inaccurate and placed the number of enemy prisoners at almost twice the number of missing Early had reported.[28]

Confederate soldiers captured in these engagements were marched under guard to Belle Plain. A sizable natural depression nicknamed "The Punch Bowl" was encircled by sentries and used as a makeshift holding area before prisoners of war were shipped north to Washington, and imprisoned. Once in Washington, commissioned officers were separated and taken to the Old Capital Prison, at all times being very well cared for. Lieutenant Edward Owen, captured on May 3, noted the prison accommodations in his diary: "Very well fixed. 6 of us in a room with beds 329 of us in our crowd." Enlisted prisoners were temporarily detained at the Soldier's Rest and then sent to Fort Delaware, located on Pea Patch Island in the Delaware River before being exchanged.[29]

Abraham Lincoln's general-in-chief of the army, Major General Henry W. Halleck, officially stopped the prisoner exchange program on May 25, 1863. The majority of the Confederate soldiers captured during the Chancellorsville Campaign managed to be exchanged by special agreement, enabling them to fight with Lee in July of that year, at Gettysburg, Pennsylvania. Prisoner of war exchanges somehow continued at City Point, Virginia, until Lieutenant General Ulysses S. Grant assumed overall command of the Union armies in March 1864. Grant's discontinuance of prisoner exchanges swelled the populations of prison camps, both North and South. Living conditions deteriorated rapidly, while death rates rose due to disease brought on by poor sanitation and inadequate rations. In the North, Fort Delaware became an infamous prisoner of war camp. Though a much smaller internment center, the fort's unhealthful living conditions were not much better than the deplorable situation found in the stockade at Georgia's notorious Andersonville prison.[30]

The battle for Scott's Ford (Banks's Ford) cost Brigadier General Neill's Federal brigade 732 casualties. Colonel L.A. Grant's First Vermont Brigade suffered considerably less, losing 22 killed, 163 wounded, and 93 missing for a total of 278. Many of Grant's missing were wounded or killed on the field, and when the Federals' lines were contracted, had to be left were they fell. The number of casualties inflicted on the Confederates by the Vermont Brigade was large; their firepower stunted Early's assault. After the attack, Brigadier General Howe told Colonel Grant, "You have reason to be proud of your men. They did well yesterday and have done well now. They have saved the day."[31]

In a letter to his father, Lieutenant Colonel Samuel E. Pingree of the 3rd Vermont wrote of this engagement, "Probably but little will be said of the part taken by the troops from my state — We have no hired correspondents here like New York, Pennsylvania, and Massachusetts — but I express the fact well known and acknowledged by the troops of this army that the Vermont brigade saved the entire Sixth Corps from destruction or capitulation."[32]

CHAPTER 12

"An Immediate Reply Is Indispensable..."

Smoke from weapon discharges settled on the ground as darkness gripped the land. The moon rose, brightening the night as ground fog appeared in the many hollows that crossed the rolling terrain. The Vermont Brigade formed a new line across the River Road. Their left rested on the Rappahannock, and the men prepared to repel any attack. Neill's brigade extended Howe's line toward the Guest house, where it connected with Brooks First Division. Brooks' men still paralleled the Orange Plank Road up to the tollgate, where Newton's division continued the Sixth Corps' defensive line back toward the Rappahannock River.

Not hearing from Hooker, Sedgwick issued orders around 6:45 P.M. for his corps to prepare to withdraw. Sedgwick called upon the engineering skills of Third Division commander Brigadier General Newton, to lay out a defensive position near the ford. Newton rode to meet with Brigadier General Benham at Scott's Ford, and preparations for the movement immediately began. Under the protection of thirty-six cannon of the Union's Artillery Reserve, a new defensive position was chosen along the hills close to Scott's Ford. All noncombatants, including surgeons and wounded, were sent in the direction of Scott's Ford. Pickets from Owens Philadelphia Brigade re-crossed the river and took a covering position on the north bank.[1]

The majority of Sedgwick's wounded eventually were assisted across the Rappahannock River. Not all wounded were fortunate enough to be collected and lay with the dead of the Sixth Corps on the field. Delayed by sporadic Confederate artillery fire, the construction of Sedgwick's second bridge continued and would not be completed until 10:20 P.M. Both bridges were covered with dirt and sod in an attempt to muffle any noise created by rolling wheels or tramping feet.[2]

In preparation for the Sixth Corps's withdrawal, Colonel Thomas O. Seaver's 3rd Vermont, under command of Lieutenant Colonel Samuel Pingree, was positioned to the rear of the First Vermont Brigade at a point overlooking Scott's Ford. Quite a distance to the front of Howe's main line, Colonel Seaver, the Second Division general officer of the day, deployed the 5th Vermont and two companies of the 6th Vermont as

138

a strong skirmish line. Adjacent regiments also established picket outposts to their immediate front. The First Vermont Brigade and Neill's brigade remained deployed with their left resting on the river as the balance of the Sixth Corps began retiring to the established defensive positions around the ford.[3]

Lee was fully aware that his effort to destroy Sedgwick's Sixth Corps had failed. He knew that Sedgwick was in a precarious situation and was attempting to contract his lines in an attempt to escape. Lee wanted to deny Sedgwick the opportunity to firmly establish himself on the south side of the river but more importantly wished to wreck as much of the Army of the Potomac as possible. To drive Sedgwick over the river was not enough. Lee knew if the Federals safely recrossed the Rappahannock, pursuit would be all but impossible. The elimination of Sedgwick would allow Lee to reunite his army and turn his attention to those people concentrated near Chancellorsville under "Fighting Joe Hooker."

For the first time in his military career, Lee gave orders for a night attack. Early's division was still recovering from their abrupt repulse, and Anderson's men were much exhausted from maneuvering. From Lee's headquarters at the Downman house, orders to advance were sent out to McLaws. From McLaws' division, Kershaw and Wofford's brigades slowly advanced a skirmish line in the direction of the Sixth Corps. The 8th and 9th Alabama regiments of Wilcox's brigade also began advancing from McLaws' battle line. Coordination problems soon arose as darkness and ground fog hindered the advance of the probing Confederates.[4]

Alexander and Hardaway's Confederate batteries increased their volume of fire as the sounds of movement indicated a Union withdrawal. In the dark, Federals could hear the loud reports of artillery and track the arcing enemy shells by their glowing fuses. A Sixth Corps soldier recalled, "When we got down near the pontoon bridges, we found the enemy thought he had their range and was dropping shells toward from several directions. The firing was like so many graceful curves of rockets...." Sedgwick's artillery responded to the Confederate shelling with battery fire until orders to retire were received. To hasten the artillery's withdrawal, Sixth Corps battery commanders directed their men to fire individually by piece. At intervals, each gun was discharged, then quickly limbered up and hauled toward Scott's Ford.[5]

After the bulk of the First Division began retiring, Brigadier General David A. Russell personally withdrew the remaining Union picket line in front of Salem Ridge. Russell dismounted and worked along the line saying, "Quietly, men, quietly; don't make any noise." But the jingle of infantrymen's accouterments revealed their movements and provoked enemy fire.[6]

In the dark, sporadic skirmishing broke out as the First Division regimental commanders withdrew their troops. Unable to see clearly to their front, lines of Federal troops would fire toward suspected probing Confederates and fall back through a second line that would fire and do the same. A member of the 27th New York wrote, "...troops were so anxious that one man loaded three or four charges into his rifle thinking he had fired each time, and another rammed home a minie ball without pouring the powder charge in first."[7]

As muzzle flashes stabbed the darkness, First Lieutenant Forrester L. Taylor, commanding Company H, 23rd New Jersey, responded to the cries of wounded soldiers and returned outside the protection of Union lines to rescue several wounded members of his company. The life saving errands would win Taylor the Medal of Honor.[8]

Newton's picket line remained in place, while individual regiments of the Third Division retired to the defensive positions around Scott's Ford. Separated from his division, Brigadier General Wheaton dispatched forty-five men, under Lieutenant Edward H. Morris of the 62nd New York (Anderson Zouaves), to investigate the area to his right front. Finding no Union troops in the darkness on his right and front, Wheaton began moving down the Orange Plank Road in an attempt to secure communications with his division commander. In the dark confusion, Wheaton came upon First Division soldiers moving hastily towards Scott's Ford. Finally locating Newton, Wheaton was instructed to move his brigade on to the ridge running along Dr. Taylor's property. Newton continued facilitating the withdrawal of his Third Division with Lieutenant Colonel McMahon, who was in charge of the crossing.

Brigadier General David A. Russell, commander of the Third Brigade, First Division, Sixth Corps (Massachusetts MOLLUS Collection, U.S. Military History Institute).

Wheaton's detachment of Union skirmishers, sent out earlier under Lieutenant Edward Morris, provided vital early warning while the remainder of their brigade withdrew. In contact with the enemy and delaying their pursuit, the members of the 62nd New York were unable to break off contact until all were captured or killed. Wheaton reported, "...it was impossible for the gallant little band (45 in number) to escape capture."[9]

Wofford's Confederate troops slowly advanced as far as the River Road, where they regrouped. In the dark night, brisk skirmishing erupted far to Wofford's left as Wilcox's 8th and 9th Alabama, accompanied by regiments from Kershaw's brigade, continued to advance through the hazy fog.

Poor visibility hampered the Confederate pursuit as units stumbled into each other, causing much confusion. Slowly advancing in the direction of Banks's Ford, the troops pressed the far right of Sedgwick's contracting line.

Burnham's Light Division held Sedgwick's extreme right. Around 10:30 P.M., pickets posted to the front of the Light Division were shocked to find that the adjacent Federal pickets to their left had withdrawn without informing anyone. Isolated in the dark, officers of the 6th Maine rode out to investigate. Groping in the wooded darkness, the officers came upon Wilcox's Confederate battle line readying to attack. Racing back to their lines, the Maine officers sounded the alarm as rifle fire broke out with a flash. The Confederates were in such close proximity that one hundred fifty enlisted men and thirteen officers from the 31st New York, 43rd New York, and 61st Pennsylvania surrendered without a fight. The balance of Burnham's Light Division took off down slope, running for the Rappahannock River. Many of the fleeing Federals dropped any equipment that could hinder their escape.[10]

The 6th Maine managed to fire a volley before making a dash over a cliff to the dark river bank. Working their way through the blackness, disorganized groups of soldiers from the Light Division made their way downstream to Sedgwick's new position near Scott's Ford. Years later, in 1894, Lieutenant Charles A. Clark of the 6th Maine received the Medal of Honor for extracting his regiment from this exposed area.[11]

Slowly, Kershaw's and Wilcox's pursuing troops advanced and took position in the abandoned earthworks overlooking Banks's Ford. During this commotion, on Sedgwick's right, several Confederates penetrated fairly close to Sedgwick's position at Scott's Ford and threw up rockets to mark the position. Captain Basil C. Manly's Company A, 1st North Carolina Artillery, accompanying Wilcox's brigade, opened fire on the ford from their position on the River Road. Union reserve batteries across the river responded to the muzzle flashes of Manly's guns and slowed this battery's fire.[12]

On the far left of the Union line, an officer of Sedgwick's staff rode up and reported to Brigadier General Howe. The rider informed Howe of Sedgwick's intentions to have the Second Division fall back to Scott's Ford. Howe did not see the necessity of withdrawing from his hard won position. He responded, "I will not leave this position until I get a positive order to do so." More to the point, Howe was still angry over Sedgwick's previously made remarks concerning his handling of the Second Division's assault, to the rear of Lee's Hill. Howe believed Sedgwick's instructions given the day before were vague, and that he had endeavored to follow them out the best he could. To ensure Sedgwick got his gist, Howe requested a positive order from his commander to emphasize his point. The messenger quickly returned to Sedgwick, and in a short time Howe received a positive order from his commander to fall back. Before Howe could execute this order, the Second Division commander received an addendum to that order. He was required to hold his position for one hour, which Howe did.[13]

At 10:30 P.M., after the completion of the second bridge, Howe withdrew his Second Division toward assigned defensive positions around Scott's Ford. He quietly filed Neill's brigade and part of Grant's Vermonters into position on the right of Newton's division, positioned snugly behind abandoned Confederate entrenchments. To illustrate the growing friction between Howe and Sedgwick, Howe later claimed in his rather poignant testimony to Joint Committee on the Conduct of War that he did not know that the other divisions had withdrawn. Howe went as far to say, "I have considered that by the movement made at the time by the other two divisions of the corps, my division was virtually turned over to the enemy." Although darkness had set in, Howe must have been fully aware of the withdrawal being conducted directly to his rear. He also had to have recognized his division's proximity to the river and Scott's Ford, which naturally made his force the best positioned to remain as rear guard.[14]

As Howe's and Sedgwick's personality conflict simmered, the sterling soldiers of Colonel Lewis A. Grant's First Vermont Brigade remained in position and became the rear guard for the Sixth Corps. To the Vermonters' front, spirited skirmishing commenced. The 2nd and 3rd Vermont and the remaining companies of the 6th Vermont advanced to support Colonel Seaver's battling skirmish line.[15]

From his vantage point across the river, Brigadier General Tyler, commanding the Union guns overlooking Scott's Ford, notified Butterfield, "Communication with General Sedgwick is at present full and open by two bridges and by messenger or telegraph. His main body is, however, below the crest of the hill, opposite the ford, under full fire of artillery. I consider his command in great danger."[16]

At 11:50 P.M. on May 4th, Sedgwick wrote Hooker, "My army is hemmed in upon the slope, covered by the guns from the north side of Banks's Ford. If I had only this army to care for, I would withdraw tonight. Do your operations require that I should jeopord it by retaining it here? An immediate reply is indispensable, or I feel obliged to withdraw."[17]

Brigadier General Benham rode to Sedgwick's location to discuss the situation with his former West Point classmate. Benham strongly advised Sedgwick not to recross the Rappahannock without Hooker's express consent. Benham urged Sedgwick to let Hooker be responsible for the decision to withdraw. Sedgwick, recognizing the wisdom behind his friend's words of advice, immediately dispatched a rider with a second message for Hooker. Sedgwick's intentions were for the second rider to overtake the first, and for his first message not to be sent. This was not to be as telegraph operators immediately sent the dispatches in the order received. Sedgwick's first message arrived at Butterfield's headquarters at 12:50 A.M. and was promptly forwarded to Hooker. Following close behind the first, Sedgwick's second dispatch reached Butterfield's Headquarters and was also quickly forwarded to Hooker. Reaching Hooker at 1:00 A.M. Sedgwick's second message read, "I shall hold my position, as ordered, on the south side of the Rappahannock."[18]

After reading Sedgwick's first message, Hooker immediately replied through Butterfield, "Withdraw. Cover the river, and prevent any force from crossing. Acknowledge." This was the order Sedgwick was waiting for. He promptly answered, "General Hooker's orders received. Will withdraw my force immediately." Ten minutes after responding to the Sixth Corps commander's first message Hooker responded to Sedgwick's second message. Hooker stated, "Yours received, saying you should hold position. Order to withdraw countermanded. Acknowledge both." Hooker's second reply to Sedgwick was delayed in transit and in the interim the Sixth Corps commander had begun the crossing of his corps.[19]

In the fog and darkness, the main elements of the Sixth Corps had begun the crossing just before 2:00 A.M., Tuesday May 5. The previous day's marching and fighting had left Sedgwick's troops extremely fatigued. The hilly terrain made the night withdrawal slow and difficult. Several instances witnessed various Sixth Corps units massed near the bridgeheads as they waited to cross. The commander of Brooks' First Brigade, Colonel Samuel Buck, was badly injured as he dislocated his shoulder when his horse slipped and stumbled into a rifle pit. The command of the New Jersey Brigade devolved back upon Colonel William Penrose.[20]

A short time into the withdrawal, as the tail end of the 2nd Rhode Island was crossing, the ropes anchoring one pontoon boat in the upper bridge were hit by Confederate artillery. A few soldiers ended up in the water, but there were no deaths or injuries due to the explosion. Repairs were quickly completed, and the flow of Sixth Corps troops continued.[21]

The men of the First Vermont Brigade "received the orders to retire with some astonishment." In the confusion, Colonel Grant's Vermonters knew nothing more than they had repulsed all attacks from the enemy and did not want to leave this hard fought field. The Vermonters obeyed orders and through a light rain fell back slowly. Halting frequently, they formed a new line of battle to guard the bridgehead as Howe's Third Brigade began crossing into the darkness of the far side. Private Henry Houghton of the 3rd Vermont recollected falling back to the bridges, "...one little circumstance shows the caution we took not to attract the attention of the enemy by anything that would catch their eye: it was quite a light night and we were ordered to take our cups from the outside of our haversacks and place them inside, and trail our arms barrels down, that they would not glisten in the light."[22]

Throughout the night, Lee's artillery regulated their fire in an attempt to conserve ammunition. The Union troops who had crossed the river earlier moved a short distance from the ford and fell to the ground from exhaustion and slept. Throughout the restless night, the Federals were annoyed by accurate Confederate artillery fire. Earlier, during the daylight hours, Lieutenant Colonel E.P. Alexander had taken the time to establish points of direction for night firing on the area around the fords. This was perhaps the first instance of the employment of indirect fire by the Confederate artillery. Alexander remembered, "I did a little shelling of their lines just for fun, & not only that, but I got the range and direction of Banks' Ford,.... I sat up there all night long firing shell at the ford." Alexander's periodic artillery barrages, provided mostly by the Virginia batteries of Jordan and Parker, threatened Sedgwick's crossing. Two additional sections under Hardaway bolstered Alexander's nighttime barrage and caused considerable commotion among Federal Sixth Corps troops after their crossing.[23]

At 3:20 A.M., Hooker's reply to Sedgwick's second dispatch reached the Sixth Corps commander, canceling his orders to withdraw. These latest instructions arrived too late; the majority of the Sixth Corps troops had already made the river crossing. Sedgwick responded, "Yours just received, countermanding order to withdraw. Almost my entire command has crossed over." Headquarters near Chancellorsville failed to follow up after not receiving Sedgwick's acknowledgment of Hooker's second set of orders.[24]

Colonel Grant was able to cross the majority of the First Vermont Brigade prior to the bridges being disconnected. A short time later Major Charles. P. Dudley of the 5th Vermont withdrew the final skirmishers of the Sixth Corps' rear guard to the banks of the Rappahannock. Just before daylight, Dudley's men reached the fog-covered river to find the bridges cut loose from the southern bank and the majority of the boats on the far shore. First Lieutenant Chester K. Leach of Company H, 2nd Vermont, wrote, "...we could not find the bridge for some time and when we did find it, it was not there.... You can guess something how we felt." A few severely wounded members of the rear guard were left in a barn a half a mile back from the ford. The remainder of Major Dudley's Vermonters crossed in abandoned pontoon boats.[25]

Sedgwick informed Hooker at 5:00 A.M., "The bridges at Banks' Ford [Scott's Ford] are swung, and in the process of being taken up. The troops are much exhausted. The dispatch countermanding my movement over the river was received after the troops had crossed." Again, at 7:00 A.M., Sedgwick notified his commander, "I re-crossed to the north bank of the Rappahannock last night, and am in camp about a mile from the ford. The bridges have been taken up."[26]

Julian Scott's oil painting of the *Vermont Division [Brigade] at Chancellorsville.* Seventeen-year-old Scott served as drummer/bugler with Company E 3rd Vermont, Second Division, Sixth Corps. The picture depicts Howe's Division withdrawing through the pre-dawn darkness of May 5, 1863, to Scott's Ford. A year earlier, Julian Scott earned the Medal of Honor at Lee's Mill (Dam No. 1) for re-crossing the Warwick River twice to help wounded Vermonters (Sotheby's).

Sedgwick's position was fairly strong. Brigadier General Howe explained, "After the repulse [Early's] the position of the Sixth Corps, in my judgment, was less liable to serious attack than it had been at any time before since the Sixth Corps crossed the Rappahannock; and I saw no occasion or necessity for crossing the river." Howe's view of the situation was a bit narrow and his remarks were jaded by his contempt for Sedgwick, but on his front the position was strong, favored by the high ground overlooking the ford.[27]

The Sixth Corps had been isolated and vulnerable to attack. Sedgwick recognized that the situation could quickly prove lethal if his corps were to remain hemmed in on the bank of the Rappahannock. A coordinated attack launched at him by Lee could have very well meant the destruction of his corps. To hold his position for as long as he did with no sign of reinforcements and only two narrow bridges as a contingency plan was in itself a commendable feat. The failure of Hooker to elaborate on his intentions left the Sixth Corps commander with no options. As the situation unfolded, Sedgwick's main objective became the preservation of his command.

Overall, the pursuing Confederates took several hundred prisoners during Sedgwick's withdrawal. Groups of Federals became disoriented in the dark and gave up or simply wandered into the hands of the enemy. Colonel Charles H. Tompkins, Sedgwick's chief of artillery, illustrated this when he wrote, "I became lost and found myself riding along in the dark next to a line of Confederate troops. Remaining calm I waited for the right moment and quietly sauntered away back into friendly lines."[28]

Other members of the Sixth Corps were not so lucky. The Sixth Corps reported a total of 1,471 soldiers as missing during the whole Chancellorsville Campaign, and almost two-thirds of the missing were counted on May 4. Some of the reported missing near Scott's Ford were not captured by the Confederates during the withdrawal, but had been killed or wounded during the fighting, and when Sedgwick contracted his lines, were left where they had fallen. Captured Yankees were marched to the rail lines and the following day steamed south.

There were anxious and chaotic moments for the Sixth Corps, especially with the Light Division on Sedgwick's far right. But there was no grand skedaddle on behalf of the Sixth Corps as they withdrew across the Rappahannock. The majority of the five regiments comprising Sedgwick's Light Division were surprised on the night of May 4 and retreated to the river in a panic. The notion that the entire Sixth Corps retreated in confusion was incorrectly heralded throughout the South. The *Richmond Enquirer* later exaggerated the scene, stating, "It may be fitly called, we think, the 'rout at Banks' Ford.'"[29]

Pursuing Confederates picked up large numbers of Federal knapsacks, which led many to surmise Sedgwick's corps had dropped everything and fled in a panic. But, prior to the fighting numerous Sixth Corps regiments were ordered to unsling knapsacks and stack them as part of impromptu entrenchments. Owing to darkness and the ebb and flow of battle, many of these knapsacks were never recovered by the Federals. Captain John E. Cooke accurately wrote of the situation, "General Sedgwick retreated rapidly but in good order to Banks' Ford [Scott's Ford], where a pontoon had been fortunately laid, and enabled him to cross his men." General Lee also made no mention of a disorderly retreat: "General Sedgwick had made good his escape and removed his bridges ... and our rear no longer threatened."[30]

Having crossed the Rappahannock, Sedgwick's regiments went into camp scattered about in the vicinity of the crossing. Private Henry Houghton of the 3rd Vermont wrote, "the next morning as soon as we started our fires to get our breakfast, the smoke revealed our whereabouts and the Rebs began to send their compliments in the shape of shell: we soon concluded from it was not quite breakfast time, and we fell back out of range." The bulk of the Sixth Corps established camp about one mile north from Scott's Ford on the Falmouth Road. A strong picket line was established as Union artillery covered likely crossing points. Samuel E. Pingree of the 3rd Vermont wrote, "I have not sleeped [sic] for over sixty hours and I cannot write now — This is the report of the 6th Army Corps — we have no connection with the main army."[31]

The Confederates controlled the riverbank from the far side, preventing the pontoon boats from promptly being removed. A short distance from Scott's Ford, detached companies from the 2nd Rhode Island, 139th Pennsylvania, and 98th Pennsylvania, under the guidance of members of the 15th New York Engineers, moved toward the riverbank to remove the boats. At sunset, volunteers raced down the bank to the boats dragging with them long tow ropes. The ropes were quickly secured to the bows of the boats. From the protection of the wood line, detachments of Federal infantry pulled the boats to cover, provoking fire from Confederate pickets.[32]

Early this same morning, downriver, Gibbon withdrew his Second Corps troops from Fredericksburg to the northern bank. Barksdale, having discovered the withdrawal, advanced his skirmishers and exchanged a few shots with the Federals' rear guard. Gibbon's men hindered the Confederate pursuit by removing the planks from the small bridges spanning the mill race to the rear of Fredericksburg. The 19th Massachusetts fired a last volley just before the ropes of the Federals' pontoons were cut and the bridge swung to the far side. Throughout this campaign, Gibbon's two brigades totaled 110 casualties, with eight killed, ninety wounded, and twelve missing.[33]

Just before midnight May 4, Hooker assembled his corps commanders for a council of war. This meeting was to consider whether the Army of the Potomac should move to the offensive or withdraw across the Rappahannock. At the time of this gathering Sedgwick precariously maintained his position, boxed in on the banks of the Rappahannock River. Stoneman was obviously operating much too far away to attend. Major General Slocum, commanding the Twelfth Corps on Hooker's far left flank, arrived after the council had broken up.

Following some deliberation, Hooker left the room. The attending corps commanders were to put the matter to a vote. Meade, Reynolds, and Howard voted to advance, and Sickles and Couch to withdraw. The army commander said nothing about plans to re-cross the Rappahannock in order to reinforce the Sixth Corps' position around Scott's Ford. Upon returning, Hooker disregarded the desires of the majority of his corps commanders and announced the course of action he actually had decided on well prior to the corps commanders' council of war. Hooker stated, "He would take it upon himself, the responsibility of withdrawing his army." Meade, who knew Slocum also wanted to advance, would later recount, "Four out of six of his corps commanders were positive and emphatic in their opposition to the withdrawal, and he did it contrary to their advice." Hooker's chief topographical engineer, Major General Warren, was also in favor of an advance and advocated "an attack in force." As the corps commanders were departing, Major General Reynolds exclaimed, "What was the use of calling us together at this time of night when he intended to retreat anyhow?"[34]

The opportunity for General Lee to strike Sedgwick's corps a fatal blow had slipped away. Lee left Early's division and Barksdale's brigade holding the heights to the rear of the city of Fredericksburg. Thunder rumbled and lightning crackled across the sky as McLaws and Anderson's divisions were marched back to Hooker's front. Lee's rain-soaked and battle-weary infantry trudged back into their old positions in the Chancellorsville area. Much fatigued, Lee's men were in no shape to pressure Hooker's well-fortified Yankees. Upon arrival at Chancellorsville, Lee found Hooker's infantry in the same strong defensive position with both flanks resting on the Rappahannock.

Through the daylight hours of the 5th, preparations were made for Hooker's force to withdraw across the river. In the afternoon Sedgwick received this dispatch from Hooker: "You are charged with the duty of guarding the river. General Gibbon's command is temporarily placed at your disposal for this purpose. The probabilities now are that all the forces on the south bank will retire across the river tonight. You will make your dispositions accordingly."[35]

At Chancellorsville, Lee's troops settled into their old positions. Regardless of his troops' wearied condition, the Confederate commander was still aiming to strike the Federals a death blow. Lee felt if he did not attack, he would be affording the Federals the options of either moving to the offensive or withdrawing to fight another day. The destruction of the Army of the Potomac was Lee's primary objective.

The much-fatigued General Lee became furious when news arrived of the Federals' escape. Brigadier General William Dorsey Pender brought him the news: "Hooker's gone. His works are empty." Lee responded crossly, "Why General Pender! That is what you young men always do. You allow these people to get away. I tell you what to do, but you don't do it." Pender dared not speak. Angrily, Lee closed, "Go after them and damage them all you can." Lee later reported, "Preparations were made to assail the enemy's works at daylight on the 6th, but, on upon advancing our skirmishers, it was found that under the cover of the storm and darkness of the night they had retreated across the river."[36]

Hooker's retreat might very well have been a fortunate turn of events for Lee as attacking the Army of the Potomac's entrenched defensive position near Chancellorsville could have proven a costly mistake. Confederate artillery battalion commander Lieutenant Colonel E.P. Alexander recounted the situation with relief:

> Hooker's entire army, some 90,000 infantry, were in the Wilderness, backed against the Rapidan [Rappahannock], & had had nearly three days to fortify a short front, from the river above to the river below. And, in the dense forest of small wood, a timber slashing in front of a line of breastworks could in a few hours make a position absolutely impregnable from assault.... And how I thanked God when in the morning the enemy were gone![37]

Hooker's forces, led by his artillery, began an orderly crossing of the Rappahannock at 7:15 P.M. on May 5. In the dark and under the protection of Federal guns high on the northern bank, Hooker was able to get much of his army across before Lee knew the Federal crossing had begun. The Federal force completed their retreat just after daylight of May 6. Hooker's bewildered troops slowly marched back toward their old camp grounds around Falmouth. Colonel Charles Wainwright recalled, "All appeared to feel that our retreat was a disgrace and none could understand it."[38]

The morning of the 6th was opened by a furious exchange between Alexander's Confederate artillery and Union guns positioned near Banks's Ford. While endeavoring to dig gun emplacements, Alexander's artillerists came under an annoying fire from two rifled Union batteries across the river. At a range of eight hundred yards Alexander answered the Federal shelling with counterbattery fire. In the open, from the front of his gun pits, Alexander commenced firing with seven guns, including a twenty-four pounder Napoleon. From within the gun pits, six additional Confederate guns soon joined the artillery duel. In a short time, two more rifled Federal batteries, made up of ten ten-pounder Parrotts, opened from across the river on Alexander's far right. Federal cannonfire proved accurate and poured shell on the Confederate gunners. Alexander reported, "The duel was kept up for half an hour briskly, when, finding the enemy too well sheltered in their pits to be run off." During these closing shots of the campaign, Alexander lost three ammunition chests and had a wheel shot off one of his guns before withdrawing his cannon out of range.[39]

Hooker addressed a message to General Lee requesting he be allowed to send ambulances and medical attendants across the river to aid and expedite the removal of Union casualties. After some delay, Lee responded:

> The reason that prevented me from complying with your request with reference to your wounded no longer existing, I have the honor to inform you that you can extend to them such attention as they may require. All persons whom it may be necessary to send within my lines for this purpose will remain until the wounded are finally disposed of. The burial of your dead has already been provided for.[40]

On the afternoon of May 8, twenty-six Union medical officers were ordered to report to Scott's Ford with their instruments. Five wagon loads of medical supplies accompanied the surgeons. Headquarters' instructions read, "They will report there to Asst. Surgeon M.F. Asche U.S.A. and will be sent thence under a flag of truce across the river to take care of the wounded, who are now within the lines of the enemy — It is important that there be no delay." Over four hundred wagons of the Union Ambulance Corps eventually lined the dirt roads leading down to United States Mine Ford and Scott's Ford.[41]

Several hundred wagon trips were made across the Rappahannock on a Union pontoon bridge built at United States Mine Ford. Confederate medical supplies were in short supply for the wounded, and numerous wagons containing beef, brandy, whiskey, and delicacies were forwarded through the lines by the Federals. Yankee wounded near Chancellorsville were hauled back across this ford in wagons. Sedgwick's wounded were

Alfred Waud's post-campaign sketch shows captured Confederate flags and prisoners being marched back to the Army of the Potomac's headquarters at Falmouth, Virginia (Library of Congress).

collected off of Salem Ridge and brought to Scott's Ford and Fredericksburg, where bridges had also been reconstructed. It would take two weeks for the Federals to retrieve all their suffering wounded from within Lee's lines.[42]

While the Army of the Potomac gathered their wounded, Lee's troops displayed many individual acts of respect honoring fallen enemy soldiers. The Confederates had buried most of the Federal dead. Lieutenant Forrester L. Taylor of the 23rd New Jersey remembered, "The body of poor [Lieutenant Charles] Sibley was buried within the Southern lines; H. Company of an Alabama regiment sending over his cap and shoulder straps, with a letter stating that he had been given a soldier's burial. This was done by flag of truce, after we crossed the Rappahannock River, on May 5, 1863."[43]

The bulk of the Sixth Corps remained encamped on the Falmouth Road through May 7. In the pouring rain of Friday morning May 8, Sedgwick's muddy corps, minus nearly 5,000 casualties, began marching the nine miles back to their old camps in the vicinity of White Oak Church. All Sixth Corps regimental standards were present, along with all 54 cannon that had accompanied the corps. Sedgwick reported the Sixth Corps captured "5 battle-flags, 15 pieces of artillery — 9 of which were brought off, the others falling into the hands of the enemy upon the subsequent reoccupation of Fredericksburg by his forces — 1,400 prisoners, including many officers of rank." Shortly after the campaign, Sedgwick's provost marshal, Major Thomas W. Hyde, presented the Confederate battle flags to Major General Hooker.[44]

CHAPTER 13

"While Such a Spirit Prevails"

Specifics concerning the outcome of the Chancellorsville Campaign were slow to arrive at the White House. Just after 4:30 P.M. on May 6, President Abraham Lincoln was informed of Hooker's retreat. The limited details provided to Lincoln left the Commander in Chief in great despair. One observer noted, "He walked up and down the room, hands clasped behind his back. 'My God, my God,' he exclaimed as he paced back and forth. 'What will the country say? What will the country say?'" The condition of Hooker's army was of great concern to Lincoln as all he really knew was that the Army of the Potomac had fallen back across the Rappahannock River. Late in the afternoon Lincoln and the Army's general-in-chief, Henry Halleck, hastily departed on a fact-finding mission to Hooker's headquarters at Falmouth.[1]

An exact recounting of Lincoln's meeting with Hooker does not exist. Lincoln came away from the meeting aware that the Army of the Potomac had been soundly defeated, but also understood Hooker's force remained remarkably in good shape. The roads and weather were improving, making the time right for active campaigning. The Army of the Potomac was made ready for action. A circular originating from Hooker's headquarters, dated May 6, 1863, was immediately sent out to corps commanders: "The Major General commanding directs that you have your command well in hand, arms inspected, ammunition dry, and everything in readiness for action by tomorrow P.M."[2]

President Lincoln was more than anxious to launch another offensive. On his return trip to Washington, Lincoln sent a dispatch to Hooker. The Commander in Chief urged Hooker to move to the offensive. Lincoln wrote, "The recent movement of your army is ended without affecting its objective, except, perhaps, some important breakings of the enemy's communications. What next? If possible, I would be very glad of another movement early enough to give us some benefit from the fact of the enemy's communication being broken [by Stoneman's cavalry]; but neither for this reason or any other do I wish anything done in desperation or rashness." In reality, Stoneman had not seriously injured Lee's communication line with Richmond. [3]

Major General Halleck remained behind at Falmouth in order to gain a fuller understanding of Hooker's check and subsequent retreat. After returning to Washington, Halleck met with Lincoln and the secretary of war, Edwin M. Stanton. The meeting at the War Department did not bode well for Major General Hooker. According to Halleck, the majority of Hooker's officer corps believed there was no real reason for the Army of the Potomac to have retreated. Halleck concluded that, "...both the check at Chancellorsville and the retreat were inexcusable, and that Hooker must not be entrusted with the conduct of another battle." The army's general-in-chief did not like Major General Hooker. The two had been at odds since before the war over business dealings. Lincoln most likely knew Halleck's recounting of events of the Chancellorsville Campaign would be tainted by his dislike for Hooker and probably did not expect a totally objective report.[4]

As biased as Halleck's report was, several of his findings were accurate. Stanton, who also was not a big supporter of Joe Hooker, had little to say in the army commander's defense. During his meeting with the President, Halleck also conveyed a message expressed by Hooker during one of their meetings at Falmouth. The essence of Hooker's statement according to Halleck claimed, "he [Hooker] had never sought the command, he could resign it without embarrassment, and would be only too happy if, in the new arrangement, he could have the command of his old division and so keep in active service."[5]

Naturally, Halleck's report proved disturbing to the President. Lincoln was not sure if Hooker was the main cause of the Chancellorsville defeat or not. Lincoln, Stanton, and Halleck speculated on Hooker's ability to command an entire army. Hooker's removal was openly discussed, but Lincoln understood the political reality and any action involving Hooker depended upon the existence of agreeable circumstances. Politically, the army commander's immediate removal would jeopardize relations between the President and Hooker's influential supporters. Salmon P. Chase and the Radical Republicans championed Hooker as the commander of the Army of the Potomac. This faction of Lincoln's Republican Party wielded substantial political clout and the chief executive feared a rupture with Chase and his followers. He also worried that the Democrats were continually on the lookout for weak spots in the administration's war policy. In Lincoln's eyes, the verdict on Hooker was still out, thus Hooker would remain commander of the Army of the Potomac. The real pending issue for Lincoln was not Hooker, but how the United States' largest and most powerful army, the Army of the Potomac, was going to bring battle to Lee's army.[6]

For several days following Hooker's defeat, citizens in the North heard scant news regarding the result of the offensive launched by the Army of the Potomac. Throughout the campaign, Hooker's Bureau of Information reduced the number of news reports leaving the battle area. The intelligence measures put in place by the bureau chief, Colonel G.H. Sharpe, had proven effective. The curtailed flow of information north left many people speculating on Hooker's move across the Rappahannock. Northern newspapers, starved for details, printed articles entitled, "The Results In Our Favor, But Indecisive," "General Lee Said To Be Calling For Reinforcements," and "Terrible Losses of the Enemy." These speculative newspaper reports and misinformation tempered the people's disappointment that was soon to follow.[7]

On May 6, 1863, Hooker issued General Order No. 49 publicly congratulating his army for their efforts. Hooker wrote, "The men are to be commended on the achievements of the past seven days...." The circulation of Hooker's congratulatory statement praising the Army of the Potomac misled many and left citizens unsure of the campaign's results. A *New York World* editorial commented on Hooker's carefully chosen words, "Whoever knows the facts of the last two weeks will shudder as he reads this order. Whoever does not, let him credit it and believe that his ignorance is bliss."[8]

Once accurate news of Hooker's defeat finally broke, Northern citizens were greatly disheartened. Many Union supporters began to speculate on the idea that maybe Lee's army was truly unconquerable. Discouraged Northerners were not sure if the war could ever be won, while others pondered the idea that maybe it was time for the Union to seek a peaceful resolution to the rebellion. This vacillation among war-weary Northern citizens strengthened the Peace Democrats' (Copperheads') political platform of armistice without reunion of the states. The trickle of unsubstantiated reports traveling back north had also fueled wild rumors, including tales of the arrest of various general officers in the Army of the Potomac, even of Hooker himself. The telegraphic dispatches departing from the Union camps remained vague and inaccurate. Sadly for United States citizens, some of the most accurate dispatches received by the newspapers were the lengthy Union casualty lists.

In an attempt to spread encouragement, the War Department sent out a bulletin to Federal army commanders and governors of all the Northern states:

> The President and General-in-Chief have just returned from the Army of the Potomac. The principal operation of General Hooker failed, but there has been no serious disaster to the organization and efficiency of the army. It is now occupying its former position on the Rappahannock, having re-crossed the river without any loss in the movement. Not more than one third of General Hooker's force was engaged. General Stoneman's operations have been a brilliant success. A part of his force advanced to within 2 miles of Richmond, and the enemy's communications have been cut in every direction. The Army of the Potomac will speedily resume offensive operations.[9]

The soldiers in the Army of the Potomac viewed Hooker's retreat as only a setback, and not as a crushing defeat. Once again, though, the soldiers' confidence within the Army of the Potomac had been shaken by the poor performance displayed by their army commander. The retreat also had heightened soldiers' concerns regarding the competency of the high command in Washington. This consternation was evident, but remarkably it had a limited effect on soldiers as the Army of the Potomac's fighting spirit remained strong. Private Wilbur Fisk of the 2nd Vermont remembered, "Positively, the army is in just as good fighting spirit today as they were the day we left our old camp." Chaplain David T. Morrill of the 26th New Jersey wrote to a hometown paper, "The army is disappointed, but not so dispirited as when repulsed at Fredericksburg before." Another recorded observation written after the Union defeat stated, "The general gloom and sickness at heart that followed the first and second Bull Run, the defeat of McClellan before Richmond and the battle of Fredericksburg, did not manifest themselves in anything like the same degree." Among the volunteer soldiers of the Army of the Potomac there was no talk of compromise with the South, as there remained an indomitable desire to crush the rebellion by force in order to preserve their beloved Union.[10]

Throughout the Confederacy, Southern loyalists were elated with the news of Lee's great victory. The *Richmond Whig* announced Lee's triumph as "A Glorious Confederate Victory." It began to appear that Lee's Army of Northern Virginia was truly invincible. The South's economy was in shambles as inflation soared. The Army of Northern Virginia's victory at Chancellorsville was just what Jefferson Davis needed to boost the spirits of his fellow countrymen. Although Lincoln's Emancipation Proclamation issued on January 1, 1863, had altered the war's focus, the hopes for diplomatic recognition by European powers were somewhat revitalized, strengthening the Confederacy's conviction to create an independent nation. President Davis and General Lee immediately began preparations to employ an earlier contrived plan that would shift the terrible War Between the States onto Northern territory.[11]

In his official battle report, General Lee highly commended many officers for their efforts during the Chancellorsville Campaign. In regard to Major General Early's conduct on the heights behind Fredericksburg, Lee wrote, "Major General Early performed the important and responsible duty entrusted to him in a manner which reflected credit upon himself and his command."[12]

Early's performance at Second Fredericksburg is at times criticized. Some of Early's critics focus on the fact that he retreated south down the Telegraph Road rather than west, toward Lee's position at Chancellorsville. Early never had the luxury to decide in which direction to fall back. Sedgwick's rapid attack split the Confederate line and left Early with no choice but to retire south along the Telegraph Road. The continuous pressure from Howe's Federals combined with the hilly terrain also influenced the direction of travel of Early's force.

Other analysts believe Early's troop dispositions were poor as he positioned too much of his force on his right, well below the city of Fredericksburg. Early held a larger percentage of his contingent stretching from Deep Run toward Hamilton's Crossing, but it is important to consider the fact that he was outnumbered and at all times had to his immediate front a Federal force as large or larger than his entire division. Although outnumbered nearly two to one, Early's first performance as a major general proved solid.[13]

Understandably, Lee held high praise for Brigadier General Cadmus M. Wilcox. Lee reported, "Wilcox is entitled to special praise for the judgement and bravery displayed in impeding the advance of General Sedgwick toward Chancellorsville, and for the gallant and successful stand at Salem Church." Wilcox's use of favorable terrain and his textbook delaying tactics were masterfully employed. Lee's verbal accolades for Wilcox's Salem Church performance were short lived. Following the campaign, the commander of the Army of Northern Virginia bypassed Wilcox for promotion to major general in favor of advancing William Dorsey Pender and Henry Heth, who were both junior to Wilcox in time-in-grade. Promotion to major general would eventually be realized by the thirty-nine-year-old Wilcox on August 3, 1863.[14]

Lee's victory was wonderful news for the South, but there remained the sobering fact that the Chancellorsville Campaign brought about no definitive result affecting an end to the war. The Army of Northern Virginia reported about 13,000 casualties, which equaled approximately 21 percent of Lee's fighting force. In comparison, the Army of the Potomac lost 17,000 men or approximately 13 percent of its manpower. Lee could only hope his victory at Chancellorsville would create sufficient disquiet within the North as to erode the Union's resolve to pursue the war. Lee would later comment on the campaign, "At Chancellorsville we gained another victory; our people were wild with delight—I, on the contrary, was more depressed than after Fredericksburg; our loss was severe, and again we had gained not an inch of ground and the enemy could not be pursued."[15]

Although the Army of Northern Virginia did receive a nominal number of recruits following the Chancellorsville victory, the problem of replacing battle losses and desertions hindered all Confederate armies until war's end. The one soldier Lee would never be able to replace was his most celebrated and aggressive corps commander, Stonewall Jackson. After smashing into Hooker's right flank at Chancellorsville, Jackson was wounded by friendly fire as he returned from a night reconnaissance of the battlefront. Tragically for the South, on Sunday, May 10, 1863, Thomas J. "Stonewall" Jackson died of pneumonia brought on by the wounds he had received at Chancellorsville. The following day Jefferson Davis wrote Lee, "A great national calamity has befallen us."[16]

Back at the Army of the Potomac's headquarters near Falmouth, Hooker became so concerned over his recent performance that he aggressively began blaming various corps commanders for the Chancellorsville defeat. In an effort to deflect attention from his own tactical timidity, Hooker singled out several subordinates for their shortcomings and refused to take responsibility for the failure. Hooker's finger pointing was very destructive to the Army of the Potomac's morale and ultimately proved ruinous for his own tenure as an army commander. A despondent Hooker acknowledged to Major General Meade after the campaign "that he was ready to turn over to me the Army of the Potomac; that he had enough of it, and almost wished he had never been born."[17]

There was no actual need for Hooker to launch a damage control campaign in an attempt to vindicate himself. His army had absorbed the Chancellorsville defeat and remained ready for immediate action. The combat readiness of the Army of the Potomac immediately following Chancellorsville directly reflected the outstanding job Hooker had done prior to the campaign of reorganizing, equipping, and boosting the morale of the Army of the Potomac. Hooker became caught up in a world of denial and self doubt instead of focusing on his army's primary mission of bringing Lee to battle.[18]

Hooker still retained the support of President Lincoln, the authority that had personally placed him in command of the Army of the Potomac in the first place. Nonetheless, Hooker continued alienating himself by pursuing his faultfinding crusade. Following the campaign, just after Lincoln and Halleck's visit to Hooker's headquarters, Major General Meade wrote home to his wife, explaining Lincoln's opinion of the Union defeat. Lincoln had told Meade "that the result was in his judgement most unfortunate; that he did not blame anyone—he believed everyone had done all in his power; and that the disaster was one that could not be helped." Understandably, Lincoln was aiming to bolster army morale, but he also obviously was not looking to place blame or cashier anyone. Lincoln wanted the Army of the Potomac to engage Lee's army as soon as possible. At this stage of the war, the removal of Hooker was the last thing the President desired.[19]

At all costs, Lincoln wanted to avoid giving the impression to political rivals, the nation, and the world that the Army of the Potomac was again in turmoil. Switching army commanders immediately following the Chancellorsville defeat might very well have rejuvenated England or France's interests in recognizing the Confederacy as a sovereign nation. At the time, an army of intervention from Spain, England, and France was active in Mexico. In October 1863, France went further and placed a puppet regime in Mexico under Archduke Maximilian. Most European monarchies were more than anxious for the United States of America's experiment in democracy to fail. Hooker's egocentric view of affairs clouded his perception of the big picture as he became consumed with protecting his own reputation. Burdened with insecurities regarding his poor performance at Chancellorsville, Hooker searched for scapegoats to deflect criticisms he believed would come his way.[20]

Immediately following the campaign various officers naturally sided with the commander of the Army of the Potomac to secure or preserve rank. Political wrangling for rank or position was nothing new, and no Civil War army was exempt from its intrigues. Alfred Pleasonton owed his recent promotion to command the Army of the Potomac's Cavalry Corps to Hooker, and the new cavalry chief had nothing critical to say about his commander. Major General Dan Butterfield, considered by several Regular Army officers as false, treacherous, and cowardly, naturally desired to deflect any criticism away from Hooker's headquarters, especially anything that might present his own performance as chief of staff suspect.[21]

During the last days of the campaign Major General Dan Sickles strongly denounced Hooker and questioned his ability to command. None of his statements appear to have been made while in the presence of the army commander, but Sickles obviously did not approve of Hooker's campaign performance. It did not take long for Dan Sickles' political shrewdness to become apparent. The career politician and former commander of the "Old Hooker Division" knew well of Hooker's military influence as well as his political connections. Sickles had little to say about Hooker's command decisions during the Chancellorsville Campaign and became a strong supporter of "Fighting Joe."[22]

Gouverneur K. Warren, chief topographer on Hooker's staff, played the political game and held off criticizing his commander's decisions. On the other hand, Warren had few kind words for Sedgwick's performance during the Chancellorsville Campaign. Warren told Hooker, in confidence, that he found it difficult to prod the Sixth Corps commander into action on the morning of May 3, 1863. Warren also said had he not been there Sedgwick might not have moved. Warren had been angling for the position of chief engineer of the Army of the Potomac, and reneged on saying anything about Hooker's idleness during the campaign. Hooker had earlier promised Warren the position of chief engineer of the Army of the Potomac "if it could be arranged." Warren played his cards right and on May 12, 1863, Hooker's Special Order No. 28 announced his promotion to chief engineer of the Army of the Potomac.[23]

Warren's support for Hooker waned as the war rolled on. Hooker angered Warren after the army commander breached their confidence by making public Warren's negative statements regarding Sedgwick's Chancellorsville Campaign performance. In a letter dated May 26, 1877, Warren, free form military repercussions, retracted his statement about Sedgwick not attacking had he not been present. Warren also admitted that Hooker's attempt to blame Sedgwick for the Chancellorsville defeat was "one of the meanest of the mean things which this mean lot of men [Hooker and friends] ever attempted."[24]

Immediately following the Chancellorsville Campaign, Hooker's duplicity and flagrant disloyalty toward many others under his command sundered his officer corps into factions and turned the majority against him. Totally discouraged by his commander's conduct, the Army of the Potomac's second in command, Major General Couch, promptly asked to be relieved and refused to serve any longer under Hooker. In an effort to escape Hooker's attempts to saddle him with blame, Major General Stoneman sought medical leave, which ended his career with the Army of the Potomac. Major General Slocum unsuccessfully attempted to unite all the corps commanders in an effort to take action and have Hooker removed.[25]

Hooker's critical post-campaign commentary was nothing new for "Fighting Joe." President Lincoln had, prior to the Chancellorsville Campaign, chastised Hooker for similar behavior previously directed at the former commander of the Army of the Potomac, Major General Ambrose Burnside. In a now famous letter explaining why he settled on Hooker to command the Army of the Potomac, Lincoln urged the new army commander to avoid reproachful remarks. Lincoln wrote, "I much fear that the spirit, which you have aided to infuse into the army, of criticizing their commander and withholding confidence from him, will now turn upon you. I shall assist you as far as I can to put it down. Neither you nor Napoleon, if he were alive again, could get any good out of an army while such a spirit prevails in it." Following the Chancellorsville Campaign, Hooker quickly resorted to his habit of criticizing others. His behavior naturally nurtured the same destructive spirit within the Army of the Potomac's officer corps that Lincoln had so feared.[26]

President Lincoln concluded that no serious disaster resulted from the defeat of the Army of the Potomac during the Chancellorsville Campaign. Lincoln understood Hooker and his army had been roughed up, but he also realized that the army commander had not committed his entire army to battle. It can only be imagined that the Commander in Chief chaffed to vent his disappointment that Hooker had not heeded his pre-campaign advice of "in your next fight, put in all your men." Immediately following the campaign, the President's concern was to find out how Hooker intended to bring Lee's army to battle. Hooker failed to recognize Lincoln's view of on the situation and remained anxious regarding his past campaign performance.[27]

In Washington, Lincoln received visits from many officers of the Army of the Potomac who were disturbed by Hooker's behavior. Other Union officers wrote letters to the President, condemning Hooker's actions and requested his removal. Hooker visited Washington on May 13, 1863, and spoke with the President. Lincoln told Major

General Hooker, "I have some painful entimations [*sic*] that some of your corps and division commanders are not giving you their entire confidence."[28]

Lincoln comprehended the contentious environment brewing within the Army of the Potomac. He understood Hooker as the creator of the venomous atmosphere. To determine in advance whether a field commander will be up to the task at hand is usually difficult and much depends on blind luck. Lincoln believed Hooker to be an aggressive officer and continued to hold faith in Fighting Joe's ability to command the Army of the Potomac. Lincoln told the visiting Major General Reynolds, "I am not disposed to throw away a gun because it missed fire once." During Reynolds' meeting with the President, several prospective replacements for Hooker were discussed, including Major General Sedgwick and Reynolds himself. Reynolds maintained his belief that the high command in Washington would not allow him a free hand to command the army, and rejected the President's idea. Later, when Sedgwick heard of the discussion he simply explained, "Why, Meade is the proper one to command this army."[29]

Following Chancellorsville, Major General Sedgwick had certainly not been exempt from Hooker's incriminations. Sedgwick's actions during the campaign became a main target of condemnation for the commander of the Army of the Potomac. Sedgwick quickly realized trouble was coming his way. Confident with his campaign performance, the Sixth Corps commander held his tongue and refrained from recrimination. To his sister, Sedgwick wrote, "I have received nothing but congratulations for the splendid conduct of my corps except the General, and he dare not come out boldly and accuse me or my corps of any want of skill in handling or bad behavior on the part of the men. I will not attempt to say where the fault lay. It will someday be exposed."[30]

Among subordinate officers, Hooker accused Sedgwick of "being slow and afraid to fight; also of disobeying orders directly." Sedgwick's pursuit of the enemy was cautious, which slowed his movements. However, the circumstances occurring on his front warranted this caution. Sedgwick's actions during the campaign did not cost the Army of the Potomac their chance at victory. When considering the reasons the Army of the Potomac lost the Chancellorsville Campaign, Hooker's complete inaction and subsequent retreat makes Sedgwick's deliberateness of action pale in significance by comparison. Responding to Hooker's comment that Sedgwick was afraid to fight, Adjutant of the Sixth Corps Colonel Martin T. McMahon angrily remarked, "Any man who says that the failure could in any degree whatever be attributed to Sedgwick, insults every soldier in his command and dishonors the memory of the dead."[31]

Hooker aggressively criticized Sedgwick's command decisions. He understood the Sixth Corps' circumstances offered the best evidence of his own reluctance to engage Lee's army. For Hooker to remain idle at Chancellorsville with the bulk of his army while the Sixth Corps fought on May 3–4, was truly blameworthy. Hooker could have sent Sedgwick reinforcements, moved to the offense, or simply made a reconnaissance in force at Chancellorsville to help the Sixth Corps and influence the outcome of the campaign. Instead, he did not act, and entrenched, abandoning the Sixth Corps to their fate. Consumed with the idea of withdrawing, Hooker wasted another grand opportunity on the 5th of May, by remaining inactive. Lee's greatly fatigued foot soldiers would have been hard pressed to withstand any attack by the Federals as they wearily dragged themselves back into position on Hooker's front.[32]

Hooker presumed his own performance would become suspect if Sedgwick's actions, along with the actions of other corps commanders, were not portrayed as lacking. Throughout the campaign, Sedgwick adhered the best he could to Hooker's orders, even though at times they were outdated and inappropriate for the current situation on the Sixth Corps' battlefront. In retrospect, Hooker's accusations appear more applicable to the commander of the Army of the Potomac himself, than to Sedgwick. Sedgwick, along with many officers of the Army of the Potomac, had lost all confidence in Hooker to command an army. John Gibbon recognized Hooker's anxious behavior indicative of someone searching for a scapegoat. Shortly after the campaign, the Sixth Corps commander went to see Hooker. Sedgwick angrily told his former West Point classmate "that the general's reports were a pack of lies, and that the Army of the Potomac was tragically reduced to petty bickering and personality clashes."[33]

Ten months after the Chancellorsville Campaign, on February 25, 1864, the Joint Congressional Committee on the Conduct of War commenced an investigation of Hooker's defeat. Congressional inquiries were common as all army commanders would undergo such an investigation except Ulysses S. Grant. During the fourteen-month inquiry, the political body interviewed numerous officers in an attempt to find cause for the Chancellorsville defeat. Radical Republicans dominated the board conducting the investigation. Ohio Senator Benjamin Franklin Wade, chairman of the committee, was a Radical Republican as were the majority of the six sitting members.[34]

Lincoln's Secretary of the Treasury Salmon P. Chase was a Radical Republican and held much influence amongst the Joint Congressional Committee members. The ambitious Chase had been scheming for the 1864 Republican nomination for president and had earlier championed "Fighting Joe Hooker" for command of the Army of the Potomac. Chase honestly believed Hooker was the soldier who ultimately would lead the Army of the Potomac to victory and restore the Union. It was obvious to the Radical Republicans that the army commander responsible for ending the rebellion would wield powerful political clout in post-bellum Washington. Chase's vested interest in Hooker stemmed from his belief that Fighting Joe's political naiveté and overall lack of political ambition made him an ideal pawn for Chase to use to promote his party's national ascendancy and capture the presidency. During the Chancellorsville investigation, the partisanship of the political committee quickly became apparent as Radical Republicans searched for officers to blame in an attempt to vindicate their compatriot, Joe Hooker.[35]

In his testimony, Hooker stated, "He [Sedgwick] was a perfectly brave man, and a good one; but when it came to maneuvering troops, or judging positions for them, in my judgment, he was not able or expert." Throughout the investigation, Hooker craftily explained his actions and talked of plans to move either to the offensive or to reinforce Sedgwick, if the Sixth Corps remained on the south side of the Rappahannock. The problem with this scheme is that by the time Hooker verbalized his plans to reinforce the Sixth Corps, Sedgwick's situation was untenable. The same applies to

Hooker's remarks about expecting to move to the offensive on May 5 or sending Sedgwick reinforcements. Sedgwick needed Hooker to act on May 3 in order to deny Lee the opportunity of deciding when and where to fight. Hooker's inertia negated his own plans. To escape censure, the army commander talked up his strategy, infusing it with new life after the campaign.[36]

It is obvious that during the campaign, Hooker had become weak-kneed. He remained idle behind his fortifications instead of using his superior manpower to carry out his original plan to give Lee battle. Hooker hoped the Army of Northern Virginia would either fall back south of the Rappahannock to a point along the North Anna River or else waste itself by attacking his entrenched army at Chancellorsville. When asked why he did not attack after the enemy had weakened his forces on his immediate front, Hooker stated, "I had been fully convinced of the futility of attacking fortified positions, and I was determined not to sacrifice my men needlessly, though it should be at the expense of my reputation as a fighting officer." Hooker waxed eloquently against needlessly sacrificing his men by attacking fortified positions. However, he was fast to lay the blame for his defeat on Sedgwick for not recklessly attacking the all but impregnable earthworks at Marye's Heights.[37]

Before Hooker's wishful thinking could materialize, he decided to withdraw his army across the Rappahannock. After noon May 3, the bulk of the Army of the Potomac near Chancellorsville was well entrenched and ready to receive an attack by Lee's army. Hooker simply opted out, although there was no real pressure from the Army of Northern Virginia forcing him to withdraw. He resorted to the excuse that he was compelled to retire due to the exhaustion of the eight days' rations initially issued to his army at the start of the campaign. If rations were a real issue, then what would have happened if Lee had fallen back from his position behind Fredericksburg? The army's supply depot at Aquia Creek was the largest constructed up to that time in the war. Food and supplies sat stacked in large piles awaiting distribution. Railroad lines had been extended to Falmouth. The army's chief of construction and transportation, Brigadier General Herman Haupt, was ready to spring rail lines over the Rappahannock when instructed.[38]

The issue of additional rations could have been accomplished simply on the army commander's order. The existence of ample rations was evident immediately following the campaign when thousands of rations of fresh bread, beef, and coffee were hauled across the Rappahannock and distributed to wounded soldiers. In February 1864, Hooker himself explained in a letter to a friend that during the campaign there were "one and a half million rations afloat in the Potomac." Hooker's excuse about having to retire from Chancellorsville due a shortage of rations fails to hold up under examination.[39]

Throughout the Joint Congressional Committee's investigation, Sedgwick remained resolute in his belief that he had done all he could during the Chancellorsville Campaign. Sedgwick would not retreat from Hooker's allegations. While testifying, the Sixth Corps commander admirably defended his actions to the committee by presenting the situation on his front and by displaying the confusing and often belated orders issued by Hooker. The committee asked Sedgwick, "If General Hooker had but

20,000 men oppose to him, and he had 80,000 men with him, how do you account for it that he did not make an attack, and why should he withdraw?" Sedgwick replied, "I believed if he had ordered an advance they could have gone right through. I can offer no explanation why he did not attack, and I cannot tell you why he withdrew."[40]

Throughout the hearings many Union officers were required to testify before the committee. Chief Engineer of the Army of the Potomac Major General Warren, who had observed both fronts during the campaign, was asked, "What would have been the effect of an attack by General Sedgwick in conjunction with the main army on the enemy's lines?" Warren answered:

> I think we ought to have destroyed Lee's Army. But it would depend a great deal upon how hard the other part [Hooker's] of the army fought, for General Sedgwick, with his 20,000 men, was in great danger of being destroyed if he became isolated ... If he [Sedgwick] had got over there, and the other part had fought as they ought to have done, I think we should have pretty nearly destroyed General Lee's army ... I do not believe that if General Sedgwick had done all that he could, and there had not been harder fighting at the other end of the line, we could have succeeded.[41]

The committee also asked Warren, "...what would have been the effect if General Hooker had ordered an attack, while General Sedgwick was fighting?" Warren accurately responded, "I think it very probable we would have succeeded."[42]

Two of the Sixth Corps officers chosen to testify obviously backed Major General Hooker. Brigadier General Howe had an ongoing dispute with the Sixth Corps commander ever since Sedgwick had let it be known that he felt Howe had mishandled his Second Division behind Lee's Hill on May 3, 1863. It was clear from the start that Howe was not going say anything positive about his corps commander's campaign performance. The other was Colonel Thomas D. Johns, commander of the 7th Massachusetts. Johns was an acquaintance of Hooker from their pre-war days as soldiers and citizens living in California. Johns certainly was not about to say anything derogatory about Hooker, especially while he commanded a regiment from Hooker's home state.[43]

The Congressional Joint Committee on the Conduct of War came up with four causes for the failure of the Army of the Potomac during the Chancellorsville campaign. The political body listed their findings as: the stampede of Major General Howard's Eleventh Corps, the injury to Major General Hooker, and the failure of Major General Stoneman's cavalry to perform their assigned tasks. Remarkably, Major General Sedgwick was also faulted for supposedly not carrying out his orders to fall upon the rear of Lee's forces.

Not having acknowledged Hooker's inactivity substantiates the partisanship of the Congressional Committee. A concerted effort was made to exonerate the army commander. The fact that Sedgwick was a long-time Democrat did not help the Sixth Corps commander's cause. None of the corps commanders faulted were officially sanctioned by the military as a result of the committee's findings. After strongly defending his actions during the campaign, Sedgwick retained the support of the majority military leaders. A renowned Hooker biographer remarked on the committee's findings, "The conclusions were formulated well in advance of the hearing and the only questions asked were posed to substantiate them." Brigadier General Abner Doubleday described the investigation conducted by the Joint Congressional Committee on the Conduct of War as "a farce, and necessarily unreliable." Doubleday, like the majority of participants, realized that as long as Hooker and other high-ranking officers retained their rank, "it was absurd to suppose their subordinates would testify against them. Any officer that did so would have soon found his military career brought to a close."[44]

As in any battlefield defeat, a litany of failures impacted the Chancellorsville loss, but none of the failures or mistakes committed by the corps commanders of the Army of the Potomac compare to Major General Hooker's total lack of aggressiveness and his inactivity. The responsibility for the defeat of the Army of the Potomac during the Chancellorsville Campaign rests directly with Major General Hooker. Fighting Joe Hooker's poor performance gave a much more competent army commander the opportunities needed to exercise his will over the battlefield. Hooker's decision to withdraw his army when he did was a grave error. Hooker compounded this error by attempting to dodge responsibility for the defeat and by setting out on a crusade to blame the corps commanders under his command. His lackluster performance might never have been so negatively viewed if the army commander had not placed himself at odds with fellow army officers. After the Chancellorsville defeat he failed to unite his corps commanders in an effort to defeat Lee. Hooker ruefully maintained the attitude of a victim and took to his grave the belief that he was faultless regarding the Chancellorsville defeat.

There are two paramount reasons pertaining to Hooker's defeat that should never be overlooked. These factors were the brilliant battlefield performance of General Robert E. Lee and the strength of conviction to their cause held by the soldiers making up the ranks of the Army of Northern Virginia. Many historians recognize the Chancellorsville Campaign as "Lee's Masterpiece," and there is no doubt the commander of the Army of Northern Virginia performed well. Lee wisely took advantage of every opportunity Hooker provided him. Although outmanned approximately two to one, Lee aggressively responded to the changing battlefield situation, proving the strategy of a strong offense is often the best defense. Throughout the war, Lee's attack posture prolonged the life of the Confederacy by reducing opportunities for the larger and better equipped Union war machine to contain and besiege Southern forces.[45]

Regarding the performance of the soldiers in the ranks of the Army of Northern Virginia, Lee himself summed it up best in a letter to Major General John B. Hood. Several weeks after the Chancellorsville Campaign, the commander of the Army of Northern Virginia wrote, "There never were such men in an army before. They will go anywhere and do anything if properly led." While defending against Hooker's invasion, the soldiers in Lee's army demonstrated remarkable mobility and a fighting tenacity, which justifiably earned them worldwide military acclaim.[46]

Lieutenant Colonel William F. Fox, author of *Regimental Losses in the Civil War*, believed, "To properly understand the relative importance of the various movements on the battlefield, the student must know the loss of life at the different points of the line. He will then see where the points of contact really were; where the pressure was the greatest; where the scenes of valor and heroism occurred." Lee's medical director,

Dr. Lafayette Gould, originally reported the casualties of the Army of Northern Virginia during the Chancellorsville Campaign in the official records. With the counts available to Gould, his tabulation showed an underestimated total of 10,281 casualties. Estimates that are more accurate place Lee's total losses in killed, wounded, and missing at 12,764 men. Units from Longstreet's First Corps accounted for 3,598 men killed, wounded or missing. Jackson's Second Corps lost 8,865 soldiers. Confederate artillery losses totaled roughly 169 cannoneers. Stuart's two cavalry brigades lost somewhere in the neighborhood of 154 troopers.[47]

The losses in killed, wounded, and missing to Confederate units in contact with the Sixth Corps can be totaled as follows. Early's division lost 1,474 soldiers. Barksdale's and Wilcox's combined brigade losses were 1,127 men. Confederate artillery units fighting Sedgwick lost an estimated 100 cannoneers. McLaws and Anderson's divisions saw action both at Chancellorsville and on Sedgwick's front. While engaged with the Sixth Corps, McLaws' lost 324 men at Salem Church. Wright's brigade of Anderson's division lost 89 the following day in the fight for Scott's Ford, bringing the combined total number of Confederate casualties sustained solely while in contact with the Sixth Corps to 3,014.[48]

Federal infantry losses in killed and wounded during the Chancellorsville Campaign reveal a great deal about Hooker's defeat. The statistics regarding Federal losses undoubtedly support President Lincoln's remark made before Hooker assumed command of the Army of the Potomac, "No general yet found can face the arithmetic." Lincoln was referring to overall availability of manpower, both North and South. Hooker's unwillingness to engage Lee's army proved the President correct.[49]

Fighting independently, Sedgwick's Sixth Corps loss was heaviest, with 4,610 troops killed, wounded, or missing during Hooker's offensive. There was desperate fighting conducted by the Federals near Chancellorsville, especially on the evening of May 2 and the early morning of May 3, but the percentage of Union casualties was low considering the number of troops commanded by Hooker. Sickles' Third Corps lost heavily, with 4,119 in killed, wounded, and missing. The Twelfth Corps lost 2,824 men and the Eleventh Corps lost approximately 2,412 soldiers. The Second Corps lost 1,925; Gibbon's division at Fredericksburg accounted for 110 of these casualties. Hooker never really committed to combat two infantry corps under his direct command. The Fifth Corps was not engaged after May 1 and only counted a total loss of 700 soldiers for the entire campaign. The First Corps saw no fighting near Chancellorsville and counted only 299 men killed, wounded, or missing, and 172 of those First Corps casualties were lost at Fitzhugh's Crossing, while engaged on Sedgwick's front. Stoneman returned from his ill-starred cavalry raid minus 150 of his Union horse soldiers. Throughout the Chancellorsville Campaign, the Army of Northern Virginia inflicted a total loss of approximately 17,287 casualties on the Army of the Potomac.[50]

Following the Chancellorsville Campaign, many accusations circulated that Major General Hooker's poor performance was due to the use of alcohol. There are no substantiated reports that Hooker had been drinking during the campaign. Investigations turned up many officers who testified he had not been drinking. Describing a meeting he had with Hooker, Major General Couch stated, "Hooker was not drunk at the time, nor at any other time during the campaign or battle, although perhaps it would have been better had he continued in his habit of consuming considerable quantities of alcohol."[51]

Much of the scuttlebutt within the Union ranks claimed that Hooker had been drinking. Officers and enlisted men belonging to units at which Hooker had directed blame openly spoke negatively about Hooker and advanced the notion that he was drunk. In his history of the 121st New York, Isaac O. Best claimed that Hooker had been drinking during the Chancellorsville Campaign. After Hooker's harsh criticisms of the Sixth Corps, Best held little, if any, respect for Hooker. Best's unsubstantiated claims regarding Hooker's drinking supposedly originated from a bugler assigned to army headquarters. It was common knowledge throughout the army that Hooker "communed with John Barley-corn and was said to be a three-bottle man." Washington Roebling, an aide on Hooker's staff, must not have been on good terms with his superior officer as he claimed the army commander "drank to excess to celebrate the unhindered crossing of the Rapidan and consequently slept in a deep stupor until almost 10 A.M. the next morning, when orders for the day's march were finally issued." The army commander's reputation as a hard drinker certainly worked against him and helped kindle stories concerning his alcohol consumption during the campaign.[52]

As standard practice, Hooker was given brandy by Dr. Jonathan Letterman as a stimulant after the solid shot knocked him from the Chancellor's porch. The dosage administered and the whereabouts of the remainder of the bottle is not recorded. Accounts of Hooker's drinking cannot be verified and appear fabricated by his detractors. Official inquiries conducted by Washington cleared Hooker of the accusations that he had been drinking during the campaign.[53]

There is a report of a conversation Hooker had in early June 1863 with Brigadier General Abner Doubleday. While the Army of the Potomac marched toward Gettysburg, Doubleday asked Hooker, "What was the matter with you at Chancellorsville? Some say you were injured by a shell, and others say you were drunk; now tell us what it was." Hooker answered, frankly and good naturedly, "Doubleday, I was not hurt by a shell, and I was not drunk. For once I lost confidence in Joe Hooker, and that is all there is to it." The fact that Hooker's route of travel varied from that of Doubleday's command for most of the long march to Gettysburg places the validity of this conversation in question. The description of the exchange between Doubleday and Hooker did not surface until forty years after the event. However, this does not prove the exchange never occurred sometime before the battle of Gettysburg. Mounted general officers often moved about quite freely and covered great distances during or prior to prolonged marches. The remark is definitely out of character for the vainglorious Major General Hooker, but it certainly appears to explain his second-rate performance at Chancellorsville.[54]

Epilogue

On the morning of June 3, 1863, Lee's army, refitted and reorganized into three corps, began withdrawing from the Fredericksburg area. Lee left his Third Corps behind on the heights overlooking Fredericksburg to keep Hooker guessing. Commanded by Major General Ambrose P. Hill, Lee's Third Corps was the largest corps in the Army of Northern Virginia.[1]

Hooker's reluctance to tangle with Lee again began to appear when he responded to the movements of the Army of Northern Virginia. As Lee commenced moving north, Hooker desired to attack his rear guard still positioned at Fredericksburg. Hooker initiated his plan on the morning of June 5th by ordering Sedgwick to make a forced crossing of the Rappahannock at Deep Creek (Franklin's Crossing) and develop the enemy's strength.[2]

Sedgwick selected Howe's Second Division to make the initial crossing. After a heavy cannonade, the 5th Vermont and several companies of the 26th New Jersey of Howe's Second Brigade established a foothold on the opposite side of the river. Remaining regiments of the Vermont Brigade crossed in boats to secure the Sixth Corps' bridgehead. The 1st Company Massachusetts Sharpshooters (Andrews) of the Second Division, Second Corps also crossed over to keep Confederate sharpshooters busy. The construction of a pontoon bridge was soon complete. Throughout the day, the Vermonters skirmished with elements of Anderson's division until darkness.[3]

The following morning, increased pressure applied by Major General Hill forced Howe to send over his Third Brigade under Colonel Daniel Bidwell. Bidwell had replaced Brigadier General Neill who was still recovering from a wound received a month ago at Scott's Ford. The First New Jersey Brigade, under Colonel Penrose, also crossed and relieved Colonel Grant's battle-weary Vermont Brigade. Sedgwick's men captured between one hundred and fifty to two hundred prisoners, while losing ten killed and fifty wounded before the Sixth Corps received orders to withdraw on the morning of June 13. Hostilities ceased and an unofficial truce evolved between picket outposts along the Rappahannock as contending armies awaited developments.[4]

Hooker's reconnaissance was unnecessary. Neither attacking the rear guard of Lee's Army nor determining the size of the enemy force left at Fredericksburg fulfilled his instructions. Hooker was well aware Lee's main body was marching north. His mission was to stay between Lee and Washington in order to give the Army of Northern Virginia battle whenever practicable. Lincoln and Halleck worked to convince Hooker of the shortcomings of his efforts. Lincoln clearly recognized the strength of the Confederate entrenchments behind Fredericksburg. He believed the Army of the Potomac's advantage in manpower would be negated by the natural strength of the entrenched Confederate position. The main concerns of Lincoln and Halleck were the whereabouts and direction of travel of Lee's main body. Lincoln felt Hooker's plan would place the Army of the Potomac in jeopardy of being "entangled upon the river, like an ox jumped half over a fence and liable to be torn by dogs front and rear, without a fair chance to gore one way or kick the other."[5]

On June 9, Hooker displayed trepidation toward bringing on a general engagement with Lee when he presented Lincoln with a plan to disengage from the Army of Northern Virginia and advance on Richmond. Lincoln wanted Hooker to attack Lee's maneuvering army. Lincoln responded by cipher and reminded Hooker, "I think Lee's Army, and not Richmond, is your true objective point." Hooker missed the important fact that territorial victories for the Union were not as important as destroying field armies of the Confederacy. Hooker's provost marshal general, Marsena H. Patrick, observed at the time. "He [Hooker] acts like a man without a plan and is entirely at a loss what to do, or how to match the enemy, or counteract his movements.... He know that Lee is his master [and] is afraid to meet him in battle."[6]

Finally abandoning his plans to advance on Richmond, Hooker focused on shadowing the Army of Northern Virginia on their march north. To determine the extent of Lee's movements, Hooker sent out a reconnaissance in force consisting of Pleasonton's Cavalry Corps, Brigadier General David Russell's brigade from the First Division Sixth Corps, Brigadier General Adelbert Ames' brigade from the First Division Eleventh Corps, and six artillery batteries. Pleasonton surprised Major General J.E.B. Stuart's cavalry encamped at Brandy Station, Virginia, initiating the biggest cavalry fight of the war. Stuart held the field in the end, but Hooker discovered that Lee was maneuvering his army to begin an invasion of the North.

Hooker displayed a degree of skill in handling his army, while countering Lee's movements. He placed the Army of the Potomac between Lee and Washington in order that it might strike a blow. Washington was anxious for the Army of the Potomac to attack. The anxiety-ridden Hooker felt the high command in Washington, namely Major General Halleck, was interfering with the operation of the Army of the Potomac. Lincoln tried, to no avail, to assuage Hooker by explaining that Halleck was not working against him. Lincoln was anxious for action, but recognized the fact that Hooker was beginning to falter as the stress of another major engagement loomed. The army commander's politician friends in Washington were not idle. Salmon P. Chase wrote the President in support of Major General Hooker.[7]

Lincoln ordered Hooker to no longer report directly to him, but to Major General Halleck. More importantly Hooker was instructed to respond to orders issued by the army's general-in-chief. Shortly before the Battle of Gettysburg, on June 28, 1863,

Hooker requested the garrison at Harper's Ferry, West Virginia, be attached to the Army of the Potomac. Major General Halleck refused and a much-troubled Major General Hooker requested to be relieved. Lincoln relieved Hooker from command of the Army of the Potomac and replaced him with the Fifth Army Corps commander, Major General George G. Meade. The Army of the Potomac's collision with the Army of Northern Virginia at Gettysburg, Pennsylvania, was the result of Hooker's counter movements while tracking Lee's movements north. Hooker's actions would later be praised, when he won the thanks of the United States Congress.[8]

With the strain of army command removed, the unburdened Hooker was sent west to command the Twentieth Corps, assigned to Major General William T. Sherman's Army of the Cumberland. Hooker's Twentieth Corps was formed by combining divisions from Howard's Eleventh Corps and Slocum's Twelfth Corps, along with a newly formed division under Fighting Joe's good friend Dan Butterfield. This meant Major General Henry Slocum, who had temporarily commanded Hooker's flanking force at Chancellorsville, was once again placed under Hooker's command. Upon hearing the news, Slocum refused to serve under Hooker and immediately submitted his resignation to the War Department. Lincoln turned down Slocum's resignation, and arrangements for Slocum to independently command a division at Nashville, Tennessee, were devised.[9]

Hooker performed well at the corps command level. However, Major General Sherman held Hooker in great disdain. The origins of the bad blood between the two predated the outbreak of the Rebellion. Sherman had strong misgivings about Hooker's ability to lead an entire army. Two weeks before the start of the Chancellorsville Campaign, Sherman had written home forecasting the future with some amount of accuracy, "I know Hooker well and tremble to think of his handling 100,000 men in the presence of Lee. I don't think Lee will attack Hooker in position because he will doubt if it will pay, but let Hooker once advance or move laterally and I fear for the result."[10]

Following the battlefield death of Major General James B. McPherson, Sherman passed Hooker over for command of the Army of the Tennessee. Sherman instead selected an officer with less time in grade than Hooker. Remarkably the officer chosen was Major General O.O. Howard, the former commander of the Eleventh Corps whose command had been stampeded by Stonewall Jackson's men during the Chancellorsville Campaign. Howard's promotion to army command outraged Hooker, who promptly asked to be relieved in "an army in which rank and service are ignored." Major General Hooker then accepted a position in the Northern Department until his retirement from the Regular Army in 1868.[11]

In the months following the Chancellorsville Campaign, Major General John Sedgwick continued to perform well while in command of the Sixth Corps. Events placed the majority of the Sixth Corps in reserve during the Gettysburg Campaign. In November 1863 Sedgwick gallantly led his corps at Rappahannock Station, capturing 1,700 prisoners and eight battle flags. After heavy fighting in the Wilderness, Sedgwick became the third and final Federal corps commander to be slain in combat. On May 9, 1864, at Spotsylvania Courthouse, Sedgwick was positioning a battery directly to the rear of the entrenched 14th New Jersey. Sedgwick's adjutant, Martin T. McMahon remembered the scene:

> A man who had been separated from his regiment passed directly in front of the general, and at the same moment a sharp-shooter's bullet passed with a long shrill whistle very close, and the soldier, who was then just in front of the general, dodged to the ground. The general touched him gently with his foot, and said, "Why, my man, I am ashamed of you, dodging that way," and repeated the remark, "They couldn't hit an elephant at this distance." The man rose and saluted and said good-naturedly, "General, I dodged a shell once, and if I hadn't, it would have taken my head off. I believe in dodging." The general laughed and replied, "All right, my man; go to your place." For a third time the same shrill whistle, closing with a dull, heavy stroke, interrupted our talk; as I was about to resume, the general's face slowly turned toward me, the blood spurting from his left cheek under the eye in a steady stream. He fell in my direction.

The fifty-year-old corps commander died instantly. The command of the Sixth Corps was given to the Sixth Corps' First Division commander, Major General Horatio Gouverneur Wright.[12]

Throughout the two years following Chancellorsville, the Greek Cross badge of the Sixth Corps would be illustriously displayed on numerous bloody battlefields. The corps earned a fighting reputation and performed exceptionally well on crucial battlegrounds in the eastern theater of war. All Union commanders knew of their marching and fighting ability, and many specifically requested their presence at fiercely contested points of the line. In 1898, Lieutenant Colonel Fox extolled, "Over all these scenes the Greek Cross waved proudly on the banners of the corps, while its veteran legions wrought deeds which linked that badge with an unfading glory and renown."[13]

The independent actions of the Sixth Corps at Second Fredericksburg and Salem Church and Scott's Ford proved to be a memorable chapter in the military annals of Major General Sedgwick's Sixth Corps. Those engagements marked the beginning of an illustrious battle record for the men fighting under the banners of the Sixth Corps. George T. Stevens of the 77th New York provided a glimpse into how members of his corps viewed their Greek Cross badge after having carried it into battle for the first time at Second Fredericksburg. Stevens wrote, "It had been baptized in blood, and amid wonderful achievements of heroism, every member of the noble corps felt an exulting pride in his relation to it, and regarded his badge as a mark of great honor."[14]

Although the Chancellorsville Campaign ended in defeat for the Army of the Potomac, the reputation of Sedgwick and his Sixth Corps was strengthened as most of the military establishment recognized their courageous efforts and the difficult, if not impossible, situation in which they were placed during Hooker's offensive. Following the Chancellorsville defeat, the *esprit de corps* of Sedgwick's corps soared to new heights as members of the Sixth Corps bonded through the realization that they had met Robert E. Lee's army in battle and performed gallantly. Major Hyde of Sedgwick's staff accurately captured his corps' attitude when he wrote, "This was glory enough for our young hearts and we began to be eager for the time when we could meet the enemy again."[15]

The soldiers of the Army of the Potomac's Sixth Corps deserve much acclaim for their efforts while attempting to defeat the Army of Northern Virginia on May 3–4, 1863. Perhaps one of the best tributes given to the Sixth Corps relating to the Chancellorsville Campaign came a few days after the fighting. A Confederate picket posted along the Rappahannock was bantering with Union pickets across the river. The defiant Rebel declared that none of the Union army could ever cross this river again except, "the fellows who took those heights."[16]

The Organization of the Armies, Spring 1863

*Legend: (K)= Killed; (MW)= Mortal Wound; (W)= Wounded; * = West Point Graduate; -t = On temporary assignment*

The Army of the Potomac

Army Commander	Joseph Hooker*	Major General
Chief of Staff	Daniel Butterfield	Major General
Provost Guard	Marsena R. Patrick*	Brigadier General
Chief of Engineers	Gouverneur K. Warren*	Major General
First Corps	John F. Reynolds*	Major General
1st Division	James S. Wadsworth	Brigadier General
2nd Division	John C. Robinson*	Brigadier General
3rd Division	Abner Doubleday*	Brigadier General
Second Corps	Darius N. Couch*	Major General
1st Division	Winfield S. Hancock*	Major General
2nd Division	John Gibbon*	Brigadier General
3rd Division	William H. French*	Major General
Third Corps	Daniel E. Sickles	Major General
1st Division	David B. Birney	Brigadier General
2nd Division	Hiram G. Berry (K)	Major General
3rd Division	Amiel W. Wipple* (MW)	Major General
Fifth Corps	George G. Meade*	Major General
1st Division	Charles Griffin*	Brigadier General
2nd Division	George Sykes*	Major General
3rd Division	Andrew A. Humphreys	Brigadier General
Sixth Corps	John Sedgwick*	Major General
1st Division	William T. H. Brooks*	Brigadier General
2nd Division	Albion P. Howe*	Brigadier General

3rd Division	John Newton*	Major General
Light Division	Hiram Burnham (W)	Colonel
Eleventh Corps	Oliver O. Howard*	Major General
1st Division	Charles Deven Jr. (W)	Brigadier General
2nd Division	Adolph von Steinwehr	Brigadier General
3rd Division	Carl Schurz	Major General
Twelfth Corps	Henry W. Slocum*	Major General
1st Division	Alpheus S. Williams	Brigadier General
2nd Division	John W. Geary	Brigadier General
Cavalry Corps	George Stoneman*	Major General
1st Division	Alfred Pleasonton*	Brigadier General
2nd Division	William W. Averell*	Brigadier General
3rd Division	David McMurtrie Gregg*	Brigadier General
Reserve Brigade	John Buford*	Brigadier General
Chief of Artillery	Henry J. Hunt*	Brigadier General
General Artillery Reserve	Robert O. Tyler*	Brigadier General
Artillery Reserve, Horse Artillery	James Robertson	Captain
Pieces of Artillery — 441		

Army's approximate strength		**Casualties**	
Infantry	111,000	Killed	1,606
Cavalry	11,500	Wounded	9,762
Artillery	8,000	Missing	5,919
Special troops	3,000	Total	17,287
Total	133,500		

Captured flags — 15
Lost Flags — 17
Captured guns — 8
Lost guns — 14

The Sixth Army Corps

Corps Commander	John Sedgwick*	Major General
Staff:		
Chief of Staff / Assistant Adjutant	Martin T. McMahon	Lieutenant Colonel
Chief of Artillery	Charles H. Tompkins	Colonel
Provost Marshal	Thomas W. Hyde	Major
Medical Director	Charles O'Leary	Surgeon
Chief Quartermaster	C.W. Tolles	Lieutenant Colonel
First Division	William T. H. Brooks*	Brigadier General
1st Brigade	Henry W. Brown (W)	Colonel
1st New Jersey	Mark W. Collet (K)	Colonel

2nd New Jersey	Samuel L. Buck (W)	Colonel
3rd New Jersey	J.W.H. Stickney	Major
15th New Jersey	William H. Penrose	Colonel
23rd New Jersey	E.B. Grubb	Colonel

K-66, W-359, M-86 = 511

2nd Brigade	Joseph J. Bartlett	Brigadier General
5th Maine	Clark S. Edwards	Colonel
16th New York	Joel J. Seaver	Colonel
27th New York	Alexander D. Adams	Colonel
121st New York	Emory Upton*	Colonel
96th Pennsylvania	William H. Lessig	Major

K-101, W-368, M-143 = 612

3rd Brigade	David A. Russell*	Brigadier General
18th New York	George R. Meyers	Colonel
32nd New York	Francis E. Pinto	Colonel
49th Pennsylvania	Thomas M. Hulings	Lieutenant Colonel
95th Pennsylvania	Gustavaus W. Town (K)	Colonel
119th Pennsylvania	Peter C. Elkmaker	Colonel

K-35, W-197, M-136 = 368

Second Division	Albion P. Howe*	Brigadier General
2nd Brigade	Lewis A. Grant	Colonel
2nd Vermont	James H. Walbridge	Colonel
3rd Vermont	Thomas O. Seaver	Colonel
4th Vermont	Charles B. Stoughton	Colonel
5th Vermont	John R. Lewis	Lieutenant Colonel
6th Vermont	Elisha L. Barney	Colonel
26th New Jersey	Andrew J. Morrison	Colonel

K-39, W-295, M-97 = 431

3rd Brigade	Thomas H. Neill*	Brigadier General
7th Maine	Seldon Connor	Lieutenant Colonel
21st New Jersey	Gilliam Van Houten (MW)	Colonel
20th New York	Ernst Von Vegesack	Colonel
33rd New York	Robert F. Taylor	Colonel
49th New York	Daniel B. Bidwell	Colonel
77th New York	Winsor B. French	Lieutenant Colonel

K-52, W-349, M-404 = 805

Third Division	John Newton*	Major General
1st Brigade	Alexander Shaler	Colonel
65th New York	Joseph E. Hamblin	Lieutenant Colonel

67th New York	Nelson Cross	Colonel
122nd New York	Silas Titus	Colonel
23rd Pennsylvania	John Ely	Colonel
82nd Pennsylvania	Isaac C. Bassett	Major

K-7, W-86, M-67 = 160

2nd Brigade	William H. Browne (W)	Colonel
7th Massachusetts	Thomas D. Johns (W)	Colonel
10th Massachusetts	Joseph B. Parsons	Colonel
37th Massachusetts	Oliver Edwards	Colonel
36th New York	James J. Walsh	Lieutenant Colonel
2nd Rhode Island	Horatio Rogers Jr.	Colonel

K-42, W-278, Missing-22, = 342

3rd Brigade	Frank Wheaton	Brigadier General
62nd New York	Theodore B. Hamilton	Lieutenant Colonel
93rd Pennsylvania	John S. Long	Captain
98th Pennsylvania	John F. Ballier (W)	Colonel
102nd Pennsylvania	Joseph M. Kinkead	Colonel
139th Pennsylvania	Frederick H. Collier	Colonel

K-48, W-237, M-200 = 485

Light Division	Hiram Burnham (W)	Colonel
6th Maine	Benjamin F. Harris	Lieutenant Colonel
5th Wisconsin	Thomas S. Allen	Colonel
61st Pennsylvania	George C. Spear (K)	Colonel
43rd New York	Benjamin F. Baker	Colonel
31st New York	Frank Jones	Colonel

K-94, W-404, M-310 = 808

Artillery	Charles H. Tompkins	Colonel
First Division (Brooks)	John A. Tomkins	Major
Massachusetts Light, Battery A.	W.H. McCartney	Captain
New Jersey Light, Battery A.	Agustus A. Parsons	Lieutenant
1st Maryland Light, Battery A.	J.H. Rigby	Captain
2nd United States, Battery D.	E.B. Williston	Lieutenant

K-2, W-5, M-5 = 12

Second Division (Howe)	J. Watts De Peyster	Major
1st New York Battery	Andrew Cowan	Captain
5th United States, Battery F.	Leonard Martin	Lieutenant

K-8, W-1 = 9

Third Division (Newton)	Jeremiah McCarthy	Captain
1st Pennsylvania, Battery C., D.	Jeremiah McCarthy	Captain

2nd United States, Battery G.　　John H. Butler　　　　　Lieutenant
K-1, W-4, M-4 = 9

Light Division (Burnham)
New York Light, 3rd Battery　　William A. Harn　　　　Lieutenant

Sixth Corps Strength　　　　　　　　　　　　　*Casualties*

Aggregate present	23,667	Killed	487
Pieces of Artillery	54	Wounded	2,638
		Missing	1,471
		Total	4,596

Captured Flags — 3
Lost Flags — 0
Captured Guns — 10 - 2 = 8
Lost Guns — 0

The Army of Northern Virginia

Army Commander	Robert E. Lee*	General
First Corps	James Longstreet*-t	Lieutenant General
Pickett's Division	George E. Pickett*-t	Major General
Garnett's Brigade	Robert B. Garnett*-t	Brigadier General
Kemper's Brigade	James L. Kemper -t	Brigadier General
Armistead's Brigade	Lewis A. Armistead -t	Brigadier General
Hood's Division	John B. Hood*-t	Major General
Law's Brigade	Evander M. Law -t	Brigadier General
Robertson's Brigade	Jerome B. Robertson -t	Brigadier General
Anderson's Brigade	George T. Anderson -t	Brigadier General
Benning's Brigade	Henry L. Benning -t	Brigadier General
McLaws's Division	Lafayette McLaws*	Major General
Wofford's Brigade	William T. Wofford	Brigadier General
Semmes's Brigade	Paul J. Semmes	Brigadier General
Kershaw's Brigade	Joseph B. Kershaw	Brigadier General
Barksdale's Brigade	William Barksdale	Brigadier General
Artillery Battalion	Henry C. Cabell	Colonel
Anderson's Division	Richard H. Anderson*	Major General
Wilcox's Brigade	Cadmus M. Wilcox*	Brigadier General
Wright's Brigade	Ambrose R. Wright	Brigadier General
Mahone's Brigade	William Mahone	Brigadier General
Posey's Brigade	Carnot Posey	Brigadier General
Perry's Brigade	Edward A. Perry	Brigadier General
Artillery Battalion	Robert A. Hardaway	Major

Artillery Reserve

Alexander's Battalion	Edward P. Alexander*	Colonel
Walton's Battalion	James B. Walton	Lieutenant Colonel
Second Corps	Thomas J. Jackson* (MW)	Lieutenant General

Light Division

	Ambrose P. Hill* (W)	Brigadier General
Heth's Brigade	Henry Heth* (W)	Brigadier General
Thomas's Brigade	Edward L. Thomas	Brigadier General
Lane's Brigade	James H. Lane	Brigadier General
McGowan's Brigade	Samuel McGowan (W)	Brigadier General
Archer's Brigade	James J. Archer	Brigadier General
Pender's Brigade	William D. Pender*	Brigadier General
Artillery Battalion	Reuben L. Walker	Colonel

Daniel H. Hill's Division

	Robert E. Rhodes	Brigadier General
Rhodes's Brigade	Edward A. O'Neal	Colonel
Colquitt's Brigade	Alfred H. Colquitt	Brigadier General
Ramseur's Brigade	Stephen D. Ramseur*	Brigadier General
Doles's Brigade	George Doles	Brigadier General
Iverson's Brigade	Alfred Iverson	Brigadier General
Artillery Battalion	Thomas H. Carter	Lieutenant Colonel

Early's Division

	Jubal A. Early*	Major General
Lawton's Brigade	John B. Gordon	Colonel
Hoke's Brigade	Robert F. Hoke (W)	Brigadier General
Smith's Brigade	William Smith	Brigadier General
Hays's Brigade	Harry T. Hays	Brigadier General
Artillery Battalion	Richard S. Andrews	Colonel

Trimble's Division

	Raleigh E. Colston	Brigadier General
Paxton's Brigade	Elisha F. Paxton (K)	Brigadier General
Jones's Brigade	John R. Jones	Brigadier General
Colston's Brigade	Edward T. H. Warren (W)	Colonel
Nicholls's Brigade	Francis R. T. Nicholls* (W)	Brigadier General
Artillery Battalion	Hilary P. Jones	Lieutenant Colonel
Artillery Reserve	Stapleton Crutchfield (W)	Colonel
Brown's Battalion	John T. Brown	Colonel
McIntosh's Battalion	David G. McIntosh	Major

Reserve Artillery

	William N. Pendleton*	Brigadier General
Sumter Battalion	Allen S. Cutts	Lieutenant Colonel
Nelson's Battalion	William Nelson	Lieutenant Colonel

Cavalry Division

	James E.B. Stuart*	Major General
Second Brigade	Fitzhugh Lee*	Brigadier General
Third Brigade	William H. F. Lee	Brigadier General
Horse Artillery	Robert F. Beckham	Major

Army's Approximate Troop		*Casualties*	
Strength	61,000	Killed	1,649
Pieces of Artillery	232	Wounded	9,106
		Casualties	
Captured Flags	17	Missing	1,708
Lost Flags	15	Total	12,463
Captured Guns	14		
Lost Guns	8		

Appendix B

Emblems of Valor

FLAGS OF THE SIXTH CORPS adorned with the Greek Cross were prescribed on March 21, 1863. Sixth Corps divisional flags were square with a colored Greek Cross designating the division as follows: first division (red cross on blue background), second division (white cross on blue background), and third division (blue cross on white background). The remaining six corps badges of the Army of the Potomac were color designated in this same manner. The badge of the First Corps was a lozenge, that of the Second a shamrock, of the Third a diamond, of the Fifth a Maltese Cross, of the Eleventh a crescent, and of the Twelfth a star.

The corps emblem of the Sixth Corps changed on April 19, 1864, from a Greek Cross to a St. Andrew's Cross. The St. Andrew's Cross is a Greek Cross tilted to the "X" position. Many original members of the Sixth Corps continued to wear the Greek cross design for their corps badge, while later recruits wore the St. Andrew's Cross. The only surviving Sixth Corps division flag adorning the original Greek Cross is a third division flag located in the museum at the United States Military Academy at West Point. Several original Sixth Corps flags bearing the St. Andrews' Cross, along with an 1875 reproduction adorned with the St. Andrew's Cross, can also be found at West Point. Two flags of Sixth Corps adorning the St. Andrew's Cross are displayed at Pamplin Park.

The Sixth Corps' flag change was in order to prevent confusion between the Sixth Corps insignia and the Nineteenth Corps' emblem. These two corps and the Eighth Corps would see combat together in the Army of the Shenandoah, under Major General Philip Sheridan. The corps emblem change did not go over too well with many original Sixth Corps members, who continued to wear the Greek Cross insignia on their jackets and kepis until the end of the war.

As ordered by Major General Hooker, all corps headquarters flags were to be of the swallowtail design or forked shape. Each headquarters flag was dark blue with a white cross *pomm'e* design with a red number designating the corps. Sedgwick's white cross *pomm'e* in the center of the blue field was marked with a red number six. Original Sixth Corps headquarters flags are on display at the Gettysburg National Museum and the State of Vermont's capital building, located in Montpelier.[1]

MAJOR GENERAL JUBAL A. EARLY'S headquarters flag was fashioned of a white rectangular field bearing a Confederate battle flag (Naval Jack) in the upper left hand corner. This design, known as the Stainless Banner, was adopted as the National Colors of the Confederate States of America in May 1863. This flag is often referred to as the "Jackson Flag" as it was the design draped over Thomas J. "Stonewall" Jackson's casket. The Stainless Banner replaced the original National Colors of the Confederacy, the Stars and Bars, because many felt it was too close in design to the National Colors of the United States of America. The well-known Confederate Battle Flag (Naval Jack) was never sanctioned as a national flag of the Confederacy. The Stainless Banner remained as the Confederacy's National Colors until the final days of the war. Its similarity to the white flag of truce prompted the Confederate government to adopt their third and final official national flag, the Appomattox flag. Major General Early carried the Stainless Banner as his headquarters flag until the end of the war.[2]

APPENDIX C

Deeds of Valor

THE CONGRESSIONAL MEDAL OF HONOR was created by the Congress of the United States on December 21, 1861. This medal superseded George Washington's Badge of Military Merit (the original Purple Heart), which was authorized in 1782. Thirty-eight soldiers of the Army of the Potomac won the Medal of Honor for their actions during the Chancellorsville Campaign. Breakdown follows: Sixth Corps = fourteen, Third Corps = seven, Twelfth Corps = six, Second Corps = three, First Corps = two, Fifth Corps = two, Cavalry Corps = two, Eleventh Corps = one, Light Artillery = one. William G. Tracy of the 122nd New York, Sixth Corps, was on detached duty as an aide-de-camp on the staff of Major General Henry Slocum and won the medal fighting with the Twelfth Corps on May 2, 1863, near Chancellorsville Crossroads.

The Medal of Honor was issued to 1527 soldiers and sailors who participated in the American Civil War. Through the active work of organizations like the Masons and the Grand Army of the Republic, the majority of recipients were awarded the medal during a thirty-year time period following the close of the war. Adhering to the established guidelines of the time, commanding officers provided Congress with documentation verifying the deed of valor. Witnesses also filed affidavits corroborating the action in question. Active G.A.R. members and politically connected veterans were able to foster approval for many of their applicants. Most all recipients were truly deserving of the award, but the well known political influence and the high number of American Civil War recipients has somewhat tarnished the significance of the award issued during this time. The majority of all Civil War Medal of Honor recipients had survived to tell of their heroic deed. Only twenty-five Civil War recipients received the award posthumously. Notable also is the fact that at the time there were no other Federal military awards in existence, i.e. Bronze Star, Silver Star, etc. The Pyramid of Honor was created during the First World War. The criterion to receive the award has since been refined, making the Medal of Honor the highest possible honor given to members of the United States military.[6]

* * *

THE CONFEDERATE ROLL OF HONOR was created on October 13, 1862, by General Order No. 93. The Confederate government had difficulties in procuring metal to produce the proposed medals. In addition to a medal, each recipient's name was to be read aloud in front of his regiment during dress-parade. A list of the names would also be published in at least one major newspaper in each state of the Confederacy. Individual companies voted to select one man from amongst their ranks who conspicuously displayed courage during a victorious engagement. Two hundred and ninety privates and non-commissioned officers were added to the Confederate Roll of Honor during the Chancellorsville Campaign.[7]

APPENDIX D

Trophies of Battle

FIVE CONFEDERATE BATTLE FLAGS were claimed to have been captured by the Sixth Army Corps during the Chancellorsville Campaign. Various reports document the loss of regimental standards belonging to the 18th Mississippi, 21st Mississippi, and 58th Virginia. No record was found concerning the remaining two Confederate standards in question. Many Confederate regimental flags were adorned with the stars and bars or other designs with no writing or identifying marks, making the owner's identification impossible. Numerous Confederate regiments not only carried a regimental standard, but often State Militia banners. If there were two additional flags captured, they may not have been regimental standards, but any of several types of flags on a Civil War battlefield such as company flags, battalion flags, battery flags or unit guidons. Other flags belonging to larger organizations, possibly on the field but not likely to have been captured by the Sixth Corps are infantry corps flags, divisional flags, or various departmental flags such as Chief of Engineers flag or Quartermaster flag.

* * *

CONFEDERATE CANNON captured by the Sixth Corps during the assault on Marye's Heights and Lee's Hill, May 3, 1863. Brigadier General Pendleton reported eight guns captured, while Chief of Ordnance Lieutenant Colonel G.B. Baldwin reported ten. An interpolation from numerous sources finds ten captured, two recovered.

Walton's Battalion (Washington Artillery) First Corps

Squire's 1st Company = two three-inch ordnance rifles. Captured — Marye's Heights.

Richardson's 2nd Company = one twelve-pounder Napoleon. Captured — Telegraph Road.

Miller's 3rd Company = one twelve-pounder Napoleon. Captured — Marye's Heights.

Eshleman's 4th Company = two twelve-pounder Howitzers. Captured — Marye's Heights.

Alexander's Battalion (First Corps Reserve).

Parker's Virginia Battery, Brown = two ten-pounder Parrott rifles. Captured — Willis Hill.

Cutts' Battalion (General Artillery Reserve).

Patterson's Sumter, Battery B. = one twelve-pounder Napoleon and one twelve-pounder Howitzer. Captured — Telegraph Road. Both guns were later recaptured by Early's troops.

The Washington Artillery, under Colonel Walton, had a total of twelve guns in their battalion. Captain Squire's 1st Company consisted of two three-inch rifles and both were captured on Marye's Heights. Lee's chief of artillery, Brigadier General Pendleton, mistakenly reported only one three-inch ordnance rifle as captured, when actually Squire's 1st Company lost two.

Lieutenant Norcom lost two Howitzers of Eshleman's 4th Company in the gun pits on the far left of Marye's Heights. This section was originally positioned in gun pits along side the Orange Plank Road, but prior to the attack was ordered, by Pendleton, to shift several hundred yards to a position on the far left of Marye's Heights. Pendleton shifted these guns in order to counter Gibbon's Federals advancing west of Fredericksburg toward the canal. Pendleton assumed that the shift of Norcom's guns would leave Miller's two guns positioned along side the Orange Plank Road. Unbeknownst to Pendleton, the shifting of Norcom's guns left only one of Miller's guns in battery along the Orange Plank Road, which greatly weakened Confederate defenses on the roadways leading up the heights.

Miller's 3rd Company of the Washington Artillery reported both its guns in position on Marye's Heights. One was positioned along side the Orange Plank Road, while Miller's second gun appears to have been positioned higher on the heights. Both were captured. During the engagement, two guns of Richardson's company were reported to have been under repair at Chesterfield depot, Lee's Artillery Headquarters. Pendleton reported Captain Richardson commanding four guns along the Telegraph Road on May 3, 1863. Richardson lost one of his four guns behind Lee's Hill during Howe's assault. The four guns behind Lee's Hill, under Richardson, had to consist of two from Richardson's company and two from Eshleman's company.

Lieutenant John Thompson Brown, of Parker's Virginia Battery, also lost two guns on Willis Hill. Two guns under Captain George B. Patterson, Cutts' Battalion (General Artillery Reserve) also were temporarily seized on Lee's Hill by the Federals, and later abandoned. This accounts for Pendleton's artillery losses on May 3, 1863.[5]

APPENDIX E

Campaign Aftermath

THE SIXTH CORPS LIGHT DIVISION was disbanded on May 11, 1863.

General Order No. 21 Headquarters Sixth Corps,

May 11, 1863.

In consequence of the discharge from service of the two years and nine months regiments, it becomes necessary to break up one of the brigade [division] organizations of the corps. The following assignments are, therefore, ordered: The 43rd New York Volunteers and 61st Pennsylvania Volunteers to report to Brigadier General Howe. The 31st New York Volunteers and 6th Maine Volunteers and 5th Wisconsin Volunteers to report to Brigadier General Brooks. Harn's [3rd New York] independent battery to report to Brigadier General Newton. The general commanding the corps regrets exceedingly the necessity which compels him to break up the Light Brigade [Light Division]. Its services during the recent operations entitle it to a permanent existence, and its gallant leader, Colonel Burnham, to its permanent command. But the necessity of filling up the older brigades in the divisions compels the assignment herein ordered. The General commanding thanks the officers and men of the Light Brigade [Light Division] for their faithful and distinguished services, and assures them that, although they cease to exist as a separate organization, they have nevertheless won a permanent place in the history of the Army of the Potomac.

By command of Major-General Sedgwick.

M. T. McMahon,

Assistant Adjutant-General.[3]

* * *

In March 1863, Hooker had placed a Regular Army officer, Captain Cyrus B. Comstock, in overall charge of balloon operations. Throughout the Chancellorsville Campaign, conflicts arose between Chief Balloonist Professor Thaddeus S.C. Lowe, a volunteer, and Lieutenant Comstock. During the prior two years of fighting, Lowe's balloon detachment had been assigned and re-assigned to three departments within the Army of the Potomac. They were originally with the Signal Corps, then transferred to the Quartermaster Corps, and re-assigned by Hooker to the Engineer Corps on April 7, 1863. Appropriation of equipment, transportation of balloon outfittings, and administration problems plagued balloon operations during its existence. Discouraged by Hooker's management and Comstock's promotion, Professor Lowe resigned from the army on May 8, 1863. In June 1863, while en route to Gettysburg, Pennsylvania, the aeronautic train was ordered back to Washington and disbanded.[4]

Chancellorsville Campaign Timeline, April 13–May 8, 1863

April 13: Major General George Stoneman departs Falmouth, Virginia, leading six brigades of Federal cavalry. Stoneman holes up for almost two weeks at Warrenton Junction as heavy rains swell the Rappahannock River.

April 26: Hooker initiates Infantry operations. The Army of the Potomac's First and Sixth Corps cross the Rappahannock River and make a demonstration against Lee's entrenchments at Fredericksburg.

April 27, dawn: The Army of the Potomac's Fifth, Eleventh, and Twelfth Corps begin their march up the Rappahannock River to flank Lee's position at Fredericksburg.

April 28: Two divisions of Major General Couch's Corps move from Falmouth to the vicinity of United States Mine Ford. Sickle's Third Corps move to a position between the Sixth and the First Corps' crossing points.

April 28: Stoneman receives supplemental orders from Hooker. He is instructed to divide his cavalry force and attack specific targets before reuniting along the Pamunkey River, northeast of Richmond, Virginia.

April 29: The Army of the Potomac's flanking column crosses the Rappahannock River at Kelly's Ford. Hooker's infantry force divides into two columns and advance south toward Chancellorsville.

April 29: Stoneman's cavalry force crosses Rappahannock River at Kelly's Ford.

April 29, 3:00 P.M.: Howard's Eleventh Corps and Slocum's Twelfth Corps cross Rapidan River at Germanna Ford.

April 29, 5:00 P.M.: Meade's Fifth Corps cross Rapidan River at Ely's Ford.

April 30: A Fifth Corps Division under Sykes uncovers United States Mine Ford in order for Second Corps troops to join Hooker's flanking movement.

April 30, 1:30 P.M.: Major General Anderson establishes his three Confederate brigades across the Turnpike at a position near the Tabernacle Church.

April 30, 2:00 P.M.: The two columns of Hooker's flanking force begin to reunite in the vicinity of Chancellorsville.

April 30: Lee receives intelligence reports from J.E.B. Stuart's cavalry shadowing Hooker's flanking columns.

April 30, 2:00 P.M.: Sickles' Third Corps begin marching up river to join Hooker's flanking force.

April 30—May 1: Lee splits his army to counter Hooker's movements. Jubal Early is left to defend Fredericksburg defenses, while the balance of Lee's army moves to Chancellorsville.

May 1, noon: Hooker suspends advance and pulls his troops back to establish a defensive position at Chancellorsville Crossroads.

May 1, 4:20 P.M.: Hooker's troops at Chancellorsville have completed their pull back and have established a strong defensive position.

May 1, near midnight: Lee receives intelligence that Hooker's right flank is in the air. Lee and Jackson formulate a flank attack aimed at Hooker's right.

May 2, 7:30 A.M.: Three and a half hours later than Jackson's originally planned start time, Jackson's flanking column sets out. Throughout the day, Jackson marches his corps around the Army of the Potomac's right flank. Lee applies pressure on Hooker's front.

May 2, 9:30 P.M.: Hooker sends dispatch to Major General Howard suggesting he examine his right flank in order to be prepared for a possible flank attack.

May 2, 1:30 P.M.: Elements of Sickles' Third Corps attack the trailing units of Jackson's column. Throughout the afternoon, Confederate forces on Lee's front fight off Sickles' force, enabling Jackson's column to continue.

May 2, 5:15 P.M.: Jackson attacks and routs the Army of the Potomac's unprepared Eleventh Corps.

May 2, 7:00 P.M.: 8th Pennsylvania Cavalry accidentally collides with Confederate infantry along the Turnpike.

May 2, 9:30 P.M.: Thomas J. "Stonewall" Jackson is accidentally shot by his own troops while reconnoitering battlefront. Stuart is placed in command of Jackson's troops.

May 3, 9:00 A.M.: Hooker injured.

May 3, daybreak—10:00 A.M.: Lee and Stuart launch fierce assaults on Hooker's front and reunite their forces near Chancellorsville. Hooker orders his force around Chancellorsville to pull back to the north.

May 3, 10:35 A.M.: Sixth Corps attack Confederate entrenchments behind Fredericksburg.

May 3, noon: Lee prevented from continuing attacks on Hooker, when he receives word from Early that the Union Sixth Corps have captured the heights behind Fredericksburg. Lee dispatches McLaws to reinforce Early near Fredericksburg.

May 3, 4:30 P.M.: Sixth Corps attack at Salem Church and is turned back by Confederate troops under McLaws and Wilcox.

May 4, noon: Lee arrives at Salem Church with additional reinforcements.

May 4, 5:30 P.M.: Lee attacks Union Sixth Corps near Scott's Ford. Early's Division is roughly handled by Second Division of the Sixth Corps.

May 4, 6:45 P.M.: Sixth Corps begins withdrawing to Scott's Ford.

May 5, 2:00 A.M.: Sixth Corps commences withdrawal across the Rappahannock River at Scott's Ford.

May 5, 11:00 A.M.: Hooker has Butterfield wire President Lincoln to inform him of the defeat and begins his blame game.

May 5, 7:15 P.M.: Under the cover of heavy rainstorms, Hooker begins withdrawal across the Rappahannock River.

May 6, daybreak: Confederates discover the Army of the Potomac positioned near Chancellorsville have withdrawn across the Rappahannock.

May 6, 1:00 P.M.: Butterfield informs Lincoln that the Army of the Potomac has re-crossed the Rappahannock River and is returning to its old camps.

May 8: Stoneman's troopers enter Federal lines at Gloucester, Virginia, on the York River after venturing within two miles of Richmond.

Chapter Notes

Abbreviations: B&L: Battles and Leaders of the Civil War. Vol. III, The Tide Shifts; C.W.R.T.: Civil War Roundtable; F.S.N.M.P.: Fredericksburg & Spotsylvania National Military Park; M.O.L.L.U.S.: Military Order of the Loyal Legion of the United States; OR: United States Department of War, The War of the Rebellion: A Compilation of the official Records of the Union and Confederate Armies, 128 vols; N.A.: National Archives; P.M.H.S.M.: Papers of the Military Historical Society of Massachusetts; S.H.S.P.: Southern Historical Society Papers. Richmond, Virginia. 52 vols. 1876–1959; U.S.M.A.: United States Military Academy; U.S.A.M.H.I.: United States Army Military History Institute. Carlisle, Pennsylvania.

Preface

1. Mark G. Penrose, *Red: White: and Blue Badge: A History of the 93rd Regiment Pennsylvania Veteran Volunteers "Lebanon Infantry,"* 207.
2. Thomas Hyde, *Following the Greek Cross: Memories of the Sixth Army Corps,* 135–136; Catton, Bruce, *The Army Of The Potomac: A Stillness At Appomattox,* 280.
3. General Order No. 10 Headquarters of the Army of the Potomac, March 7, 1865, *OR* 46: I, 865–878.
4. Samuel P. Bates, *The Battle of Chancellorsville,* 207–210.

Epigraph

1. Sedgwick report, *OR,* 25: I, 562.

1. "No Advance Beyond Chancellorsville..."

1. Walter H. Hebert, *Fighting Joe Hooker,* 183.
2. Hassler, *Commanders of the Army of the Potomac,* 134.
3. Bigelow, *The Campaign of Chancellorsville,* 185.
4. Warren report, *OR,* 25: I, 193.
5. Jennings Cropper Wise, *The Long Arm of Lee: The History of the artillery of the Army of Northern Virginia,* 442–443.
6. Johnson & Buel, eds., *B&L,* Vol. III, 238; Wise, *The Long Arm of Lee: The History of the Artillery of the Army of Northern Virginia.* 442. Jones' brigade and Captain R. Preston Chew's battery were on detached duty in western Virginia. Brigadier General Robert Ransom's division, First Corps, was on duty in the Carolinas. John B. Hood and George Pickett's divisions were on duty at Southside, Virginia. The commander of the Army of Northern Virginia had not been in the best physical condition during the Chancellorsville Campaign. A month earlier, Lee unknowingly suffered a heart attack. Diagnosed at the time as rheumatism, Lee's heart condition did not hinder his ability to effectively command the Army of Northern Virginia. See Charles B. Flood, *Lee: The Last Years,* 31.
7. Thomas Cutrer & Michael T. Parish, eds., *Brothers in Gray: The Civil War Letters of the Piearson Family,* 178.
8. Stoneman report, *OR,* 25: I, 1066–1077; *Joint Committee on the Conduct of War,* Vol. IV, 113–114.
9. Stoneman to Hooker, *OR, 25:* II, 221.
10. Abner Doubleday, *Chancellorsville and Gettysburg,* 4; General Order 48, *OR,* 25: II, 316.
11. *OR,* 25: II, 250, 225–226, 262.
12. Clarence E. Mccartney, *Lincoln and His Generals,* 147.
13. William Child, M.D., *History of the Fifth New Hampshire Volunteers,* 175, 179.

14. Ed Malles, ed. *Bridge Building in Wartime: Memoir of the 50th New York Volunteer Engineers,* 138. Major James Horace Lacy served the Confederacy in Southwestern Virginia.

15. For Hooker's preliminary movements see Bigelow, *The Campaign of Chancellorsville,* 184–187; Edward T. Bates, *Chancellorsville,* 46–52.

16. Lee report, *OR,* 25: I, 796.

17. Ingalls to Megis, *OR,* 25: II, 544, enclosures A–H; LeDuc report, *OR,* 25: II, 555–557. Following Chancellorsville adjustments were made to the standard packing list to lighten the load, and the ammunition issue per man was lowered to forty rounds, "forty dead men."

18. Benham report, *OR,* 25: I, 215; Malles, ed. *Bridge Building in Wartime,* 386.

19. Bigelow, *The Campaign of Chancellorsville,* 187–188.

20. Stuart report, *OR,* 25: I, 1046; H.B. McClellan, *The Life and Campaigns of Major General J.E.B. Stuart,* 209–215.

21. Bates, *Chancellorsville,* 46–47; Bigelow, *The Campaign of Chancellorsville,* 201–202.

22. Slocum, Howard reports, *OR,* 25: I, 627–631, 669–673.

23. Amos M. Judson, *History of the Eighty-Third Pennsylvania Volunteers,* 112.

24. Lee to Anderson, *OR,* 25: II, 759.

25. Theodore A. Dodge address December 13, 1886, in *P.M.H.S.M.* Vol. 3, 195.

26. Lee to Davis, *OR,* 25: II, 761; James Longstreet, *From Manassas to Appomattox,* 326.

27. Lee, Anderson reports, *OR,* 25: I, 796, 849.

28. Bigelow, *The Campaign of Chancellorsville,* 209–215; Emory M. Thomas, *Robert E. Lee,* 280.

29. Bates, *Chancellorsville,* 49.

30. Mathew F. Steele, *American Campaigns,* 347; Warner, *Generals in Blue,* 13.

31. *Joint Committee on the Conduct of War,* Vol. IV, 140; For more on Stoneman's raid see Edward G. Longrace, *Mounted Raids of the Civil War,* 148–174.

32. *OR,* 25: II, 304.

2. "May God Help Us and Give Us Victory"

1. Frank Lemont to mother, April 14, 1863. White Oak Church still stands today and is located six miles east of Falmouth, Virginia, on White Oak Road.

2. Emil & Ruth Rosenblatt, eds., *Hard Marching Everyday: The Civil War Letters of Private Wilbur Fisk,* 75.

3. Rosenblatt, eds., *Hard Marching Everyday,* 75.

4. John Hyde, ed. *The Civil War Letters of Thomas Hyde,* 70.

5. Edward Stackpole, *The Fredericksburg Campaign: Drama On The Rappahannock,* 148.

6. Tompkins report, *OR,* 25: I, 563.

7. Wainwright report, *OR,* 25: I, 257.

8. Hunt report, *OR,* 25: I, 247; C.A. Stevens, *Berdan's Sharpshooters in the Army of the Potomac,* 245; *Vermont Riflemen in the War for the Union, 1861–1865,*

85. Widow Gray's property bordered White Oak Run, in the Vicinity of Pollock's mill.

9. Wainwright Cushing, *War Papers,* Maine M.O.L.L.U.S., "*Charge of the Light Division at Marye's Heights, May 3, 1863,*" Vol. III, 355.

10. Warner, *Generals in Blue,* 385.

11. Stephan Minot Weld, *War Diary of Stephan Minot Weld,* 187–190.

12. *Ibid;* Ed Malles, ed. *Bridge Building in Wartime: Colonel Wesley Brainerd's Memoir of the 50th New York Volunteer Engineers,* 141.

13. Rosenblatt, eds., *Hard Marching Everyday,* 76; Slade, *That Sterling Soldier: The Life of David A. Russell,* 123.

14. Russell report, *OR,* 25: I, 591. For more information on Confederate officers in the Army of Northern Virginia, See works by John Esten Cooke.

15. David W. Judd, *The Story of The Thirty-Third New York Volunteers,* 281; Martin T. MaMahon, *M.O.L.L.U.S.,* New York Commandery, May 3, 1893, 164–167.

16. Richard Elliot Winslow, *General John Sedgwick: The Story of a Union Corps Commander,* 64.

17. Jubal A. Early, *Autobiographical Sketch and Narrative of the War Between the States,* 194.

18. For an excellent description of pontoon bridge building see: Malles, ed., *Bridge Building in Wartime: Colonel Wesley Brainerd's Memoir of the 50th New York Volunteer Engineers,* 278–280.

19. Brooks report, *OR,* 25: I, 566; Francis A. O'Reilly, *The Fredericksburg Campaign "Stonewall" Jackson at Fredericksburg: The Battle of Prospect Hill December 13, 1863,* 16.

20. Private Urbanus Dart Jr. to son, May 7, 1863.

21. Alan T. Nolan, *The Iron Brigade: A Military History,* 211.

22. Meredith, Bragg reports, *OR,* 25: I, 266–267, 271–272.

23. Weld, *Diary and Letters of Stephan Minot Weld,* 186.

24. Alan T. Nolan, *The Iron Brigade,* 212; Meredith report, *OR,* 25: I, 268; Elon Brown to parents, May 18, 1863.

25. Alan T. Nolan & S. Eggleston, eds., *Giants in Their Tall Black Hats: Essays on the Iron Brigade,* 93.

26. Terry L. Jones, *Lee's Tigers,* 150; Reynolds report, *OR,* 25: I, 253.

27. Beardslee report, *OR,* 25: I, 229.

28. Russell, Benham, Reynolds reports, *OR,* 25: I, 591, 208–209, 253.

29. Hunt report, *OR,* 25: I, 247.

30. Robert Johnson & Clarence Buel, eds., *B&L,* Vol. III, 203.

31. Edward J. Stackpole, *Chancellorsville: Lee's Greatest Battle,* 135.

32. Ralph Happel, *Salem Church Embattled,* 22.

33. George T. Stevens, *Three Years in the Sixth Corps,* 190; Alanson A. Haines, *History of the Fifteenth Regiment New Jersey Volunteers,* 50.

34. Thomas Hyde, *Following the Greek Cross: Memoirs of the Sixth Corps,* 121.

35. O'Reilly, *The Fredericksburg Campaign "Stonewall" Jackson at Fredericksburg: The Battle Of Prospect Hill December13, 1862,* 23; Robert H. Rhodes,

ed., *All For The Union: The Civil War Diary and Letters of Elisha Hunt Rhodes,* 105.

36. John L.G. Wood to Nancy Harvey, May 10, 1863.

3. Make a Demonstration

1. Augustus Buel, *The Cannoneer,* 51; O.B. Curtis, *History of the Twenty-fourth Michigan of the Iron Brigade,* 127.

2. Samuel Pingree, 3rd Vermont, diary entry April 30, 1863; George W. Bicknell, *History of the Fifth Maine Regiment,* 213; Haines, *History of the Fifteenth Regiment New Jersey Volunteers,* 49.

3. Butterfield to Sedgwick, *OR,* 25: II, 312.

4. Hooker's headquarters to Sedgwick, *OR,* 25: II, 306.

5. Butterfield to Sedgwick, *OR,* 25: II, 307; Walter H. Hebert, *Fighting Joe Hooker,* 194; Butterfield to Hooker, *OR,* 25: II, 333.

6. Sickles report, *OR,* 25: I, 385.

7. Lowe to Sedgwick, *OR,* 25: II, 324.

8. Hunt to Hooker, *OR,* 25: II, 230; Hunt report, *OR,* 25: I, 248; Bigelow, *The Campaign of Chancellorsville,* 266–267. A total of 404 pieces of artillery accompanied the Army of the Potomac during the Chancellorsville Campaign.

9. Hunt report, *OR,* 25: I, 248.

10. Reynolds, Benham reports, *OR,* 25: I, 253–254, 213.

11. Alan A. Siegal, *For the Glory of the Union: Myth, Reality, and Media in Civil War New Jersey,* 160.

12. Burke Davis, *Gray Fox: Robert E. Lee and the Civil War,* 184.

13. William Swinton, *Campaigns of the Army of the Potomac,* 277; Bigelow, *The Campaign of Chancellorsville,* 232; Lee to McLaws and Jackson, *OR,* 25: II, 762.

14. Jubal A. Early, *Lieutenant General Jubal A. Early: Narrative of the War Between the States.* Introduction by Gary Gallagher, ii; Henry Kyd Douglas, *I Rode with Stonewall,* 33. Captain John Esten Cooke lawyer/writer. Among his written works, *The Life of Stonewall Jackson* (1863) and *Life of Robert E. Lee* (1871).

15. Ralph L. Eckert, *John Brown Gordon: Soldier. Southerner. American,* 36–39.

16. A.S. Pendleton letter, April 26, 1863, in *Papers of the Military Historical Society of Massachusetts,* Vol. III, 244. See Griffith's *Battle Tactics of the Civil* War. *Psychological Power of Fortifications,* 127–135; D. H. Mahan, *A Complete Treatise on Field Fortifications,* 1836, reprinted New York: Green Land Press, 1968.

17. Barksdale report, *OR,* 25: I, 835.

18. Pendleton report, *OR,* 25: I, 814.

19. Jay Luvas & Harold W. Nelson, *The U.S. Army War College Guide to the Battlefields of Chancellorsville and Fredericksburg,* 137; Charles H. Banes, *History of the Philadelphia Brigade,* 159.

20. Bates, *The Battle of Chancellorsville,* 54.

21. Bicknell, *History of the Fifth Maine Regiment,* 215.

22. Lowe to Sedgwick, *OR,* 25: II, 336.

23. Lowe to Sedgwick, *OR,* 25: II, 324, 340.

24. Hooker circular, *OR,* 25: II, 324, 326; Smith, *History of the 19th Maine Volunteers,* 48. Meade's notorious temper led his soldiers to dub him, "A damn old snapping turtle."

25. Hooker to Butterfield, *OR,* 25: II, 328; Bigelow, *The Campaign of Chancellorsville,* 222; John E. Cooke, *Life of Robert E. Lee,* 251; Theodore A. Dodge address December 13, 1886, in *P.M.H.S.M.* Vol. 3, 194.

26. Hooker to Butterfield, *OR,* 25: II, 326, 328; Bigelow, *The Campaign of Chancellorsville,* 166–167.

27. Lowe to Sedgwick *OR, 25:* II 341.

28. Butterfield to Hooker, *OR,* 25: II, 326.

29. Hooker to Sedgwick, *OR,* 25: II, 338, 343.

30. Sedgwick report, *OR,* 25: I, 558.

31. Sedgwick to Hooker, *OR,* 25: II, 343.

32. Reynolds report, *OR,* 25: I, 227.

4. "The Enemy Is Fleeing..."

1. Allen Nevins, ed., *Diary of Battle: The Personal Journals of Charles S. Wainwright,* 190.

2. Reynolds report, *OR,* 25: I, 259; *OR,* 25: I, 172–191.

3. Elon Francis Brown, diary, 1863.

4. Sedgwick report, *OR,* 25: I, 558.

5. Hall to Sedgwick, *OR,* 25: II, 362.

6. Bigelow, *The Campaign of Chancellorsville,* 330–331; *OR,* 25: II, 352, 363.

7. Lowe to Butterfield, *OR,* 25: II, 353.

8. *Ibid,* 392; George Contant, *Path of Blood: The True Story of the 33rd New York Volunteers,* 298. The members of the 20th New York who refused to cross were incarcerated at Fort Jefferson in the Dry Tortugas off Key West, Florida. The second week of May would end the time in service for many Federal troops including the 27th, 18th, 31st, and 32nd New York regiments of the Sixth Corps.

9. Allen to Butterfield, *OR,* 25: II, 362.

10. Hooker to Lincoln, *OR,* 25: II, 628.

11. Rosenblatt, eds., *Hard Marching Everyday: The Civil War Letters of Private Wilbur Fisk,* 76; Alanson A. Hanes, *History of the Fifteenth New Jersey Volunteers,* 50.

12. Butterfield to Hooker, *OR,* 25: II, 355.

13. Lee, Early, Pendleton reports, *OR,* 25: I, 800, 1001, 812–813; Douglas Southall Freeman, *Lee's Lieutenants: A Study in Command,* 60.

14. Early, *Lieutenant General Jubal A. Early: Narrative of the War Between the States,* 202; Pendleton report, *OR,* 25: I, 812.

15. Pendleton report, *OR,* 25: I, 812.

16. Lowe to Butterfield, *OR,* 25: II, 354.

17. Lowe to Butterfield, *OR,* Non-Battle reports, Series III, Vol. III, 315.

18. John J. Nicolay and John Hay, *Abraham Lincoln: A History,* abridged and edited by Paul M. Angle, 76; Hooker to Peck, *OR,* 25: II, 241.

19. Butterfield to Sedgwick, *OR,* 25: II, 225; Signal Station F. report, *OR,* 25: II, 267–268.

20. Burke Davis, *JEB Stuart: The Last Cavalier,* 288. For more on Jackson's flank attack see, A. Hamlin's *The Attack of Stonewall Jackson at Chancellorsville,*

introduction by F. O'Reilly; Johnson & Buel, *B&L*, Vol. III, 203–214.

21. Bigelow, *The Campaign of Chancellorsville*, 291–319; Abner Doubleday, *Chancellorsville and Gettysburg*, 33–34.

22. Early, *Jubal A. Early: Narrative of the War Between the States*, 203.

23. Freeman, *Lee's Lieutenants*, 611; Boatner, *The Civil War Dictionary*, 154.

24. Hooker's headquarters to Sedgwick, *OR*, 25: I, 363.

25. Hooker's headquarters to Sedgwick, *OR*, 25: I, 363.

26. Sedgwick report, *OR*, 25: I, 558.

27. Krick, *Parker's Virginia Battery C.S.A.*, 137.

28. James M. Treichler memoir, Co. H, 96th Pennsylvania.

29. Sedgwick to Butterfield, *OR*, 25: II, 364; Butterfield to Sedgwick, *OR*, 25: II, 365.

30. Haines, *History of the Fifteenth Regiment New Jersey Volunteers*, 50.

5. *"Between Us We Will Use Him Up"*

1. Reynolds report, *OR*, 25: I, 254.

2. Hooker's Headquarters to Sedgwick, *OR*, 25: II, 365.

3. James F. Huntington address November 2, 1897, in *P.M.H.S.M.* Vol. 3, 184.

4. John Bigelow, *P.M.H.S.M.* Vol. 3, *The Battles of Marye's Heights and Salem Church*, 240.

5. Deborah Hamblin, *Brevet Major General Joseph Eldridge Hamblin*, 30–31.

6. Charles H. Brewster, *When This Cruel War is Over: The Civil War Letters of Charles Harvey Brewster*, 224.

7. Johnson & Buel, *B&L*, Vol. III, 225–227.

8. Bigelow, *The Campaign of Chancellorsville*, 335.

9. Gibbon testimony, *Joint Committee on the Conduct of War*, Vol. IV, 87–88.

10. Neill report, *OR*, 25: I, 609.

11. Butterfield to Hooker, *OR*, 25: II, 383, 385; Brooks report, *OR*, 25: I, 567.

12. Bigelow, *The Chancellorsville Campaign*, 382.

13. Tompkins report, *OR*, 25: I, 563, 567.

14. Warren report, *OR*, 25: I, 201.

15. Jubal Early, *Lieutenant General Jubal A. Early*, 206; Wise, *The Long Arm of Lee*, 519–520.

16. Bartlett report, *OR*, 25: I, 580; Best, *History of the 121st New York State Infantry*, 61–62.

17. Bicknell, *History of the Fifth Maine Regiment*, 219.

18. Early, *Lieutenant General Jubal A. Early*, 206.

19. Butterfield to Hooker, *OR*, 25: II, 383, 385; Benham report, *OR*, 25: I, 215.

20. *OR*, 25: II, 383; Freeman, *Lee's Lieutenants*, 613.

21. Cowan report, *OR*, 25: I, 613.

22. George W. Peck, *Revised Rosters of Vermont Volunteers*, 726–727.

23. Benham report, *OR*, 25: I, 215.

24. Winslow, *General John Sedgwick*, 72.

25. Lowe to Sedgwick and Butterfield, *OR*, 25: II, 284.

26. Butterfield to Hooker, *OR*, 25: II, 286.

6. *Forward Into Battery*

1. Laflin report, *OR*, 25: I, 352–353.

2. John Gibbon, *Personal Recollections of the Civil War*, 113; Gibbon report, *OR*, 25: I, 350–351.

3. Beverly, Laflin reports, *OR*, 25: I, 357, 352–353; Gibbon, *Personal Recollections of the Civil War*.

4. John D. Smith, *The History of the Nineteenth Regiment of Maine Volunteer Infantry 1861–1865*, 52; Pullen, *The Twentieth Maine*, 73–76.

5. Wilcox report, *OR*, 25: I, 854–857.

6. Barksdale report, *OR*, 25: I, 839.

7. Terry L. Jones, *Lee's Tigers: The Louisiana Infantry in the Army of Northern Virginia*, 151.

8. Benjamin G. Humphreys, "Recollections of Fredericksburg, 1863," *The Land We Love*, 3:6, October 1867, 448.

9. Pendleton report, *OR*, 25: I, 814; Krick, *Parker's Virginia Battery*, 138–141.

10. Robert K. Krick, *Parker's Virginia Battery C.S.A.*, 135; Jennings C. Wise, *The Long Arm Of Lee: The History of the Artillery in the Army of Northern Virginia*, 454. Captain A.B. Rhett's attendance record may have been scrutinized more so than other officers of his rank due to political backlash stemming from his family's well known dislike of Jefferson Davis. Robert Barnwell Rhett had long been a vocal critic of President Davis. Editor of the Charleston, South Carolina, *Mercury*, R.B. Rhett Jr. once referred to Davis as "this little head of a great country." Steven A. Channing. *Confederate Ordeal: The Southern Home Front*, from The Civil War Series (Time Life Books, 1984), 53; Robert Barnwell Rhett, *Fire-eater Remembers: The Confederate Memoir of Robert Barnwell Rhett*, ed. William C. Davis.

11. Carlton report, *OR*, 25: I, 845.

12. George Contant, *Path of Blood: The True Story of the 33rd New York Volunteers*, 304.

13. Cabell, Carlton reports, *OR*, 25: I, 843, 846.

14. Barksdale report, *OR*, 25: I, 840; Terry L. Jones, *Lee's Tigers*, 151.

15. Wilcox report, *OR*, 25: I, 854–857.

16. Penick report, *OR*, 25: I, 884.

17. Pendleton report, *OR*, 25: I, 814; Krick, *Parker's Virginia Battery*, 139.

18. Oliver Wendell Holmes, *Touched With Fire*, 92

19. Noah Trudeau, *Bloody Roads South: The Wilderness to Cold Harbor, May–June, 1864*, 306–307.

20. Robert Garth Scott, ed., *Fallen Leaves: The Civil War Letters of Major Henry Livermore Abbott*, 174.

21. Holcombe, *History of the First Minnesota Volunteer Infantry*, 295–296; Laflin report, *OR*, 25: I, 352. In Colonial times, crushed oyster shells were routinely applied to steep sloping dirt roads in an effort to improve traction. This accounts for the name of the dirt way, Oyster Shell Road, northwest of Fredericksburg, leading up to Dr. Taylor's house (Fall Hill).

22. Penick report, *OR,* 25: I, 884.
23. Rhodes, *All For The Union,* 105.
24. *Adjutant General Report of Rhode Island, 1861–1865.*
25. Carlton Feltch diary entry May 3, 1863.
26. Rogers report, *OR,* 25: I, 615.
27. Francis A. Walker, *General John Gibbon in the II Corps,* New York M.O.L.L.U.S., 304–305.
28. Butterfield to Sedgwick, *OR,* 25: II, 384.
29. Cushing report, *OR,* 25: I, 220.
30. Bigelow, *The Campaign of Chancellorsville,* 345.
31. Bigelow, *The Campaign of Chancellorsville,* 362–363.
32. Johnson & Buel, eds., *B&L,* Vol. III, 167.
33. Hebert, *Fighting Joe Hooker,* 213.
34. Couch report, *OR,* 25: I, 306.
35. Wheaton report, *OR,* 25: I, 617.
36. Wheaton report, *OR,* 25: I, 617; Hyde, *Following the Greek Cross,* 123–124.
37. Martin T. MaMahon, *Proceedings of the Reunion Society of Vermont Officers, 1864–1884,* 340. Sedgwick named his horse "Cornwall" in honor of his hometown Cornwall Hollow, Connecticut.
38. Butterfield to Hooker, *OR,* 25: II, 387; Orin Rugg to parents, May 9, 1863.
39. French report, *OR,* 25: I, 611.

7. Second Fredericksburg

1. Comstock to Sedgwick, *OR,* 25: II, 387–388; Sedgwick report, *OR,* 25: I, 559.
2. James H. Mundy, *No Rich Man's Sons,* 110.
3. Bigelow, *The Campaign of Chancellorsville,* 390; Robert W. Wells, *Wisconsin in the Civil War,* 55.
4. Pendleton report, *OR,* 25: I, 815.
5. Robert W. Wells, *Wisconsin in the Civil War,* 55; A.T. Brewer, *History of the Sixty-First Pennsylvania Volunteers,* 53.
6. Richard Elliott Winslow, III, *General John Sedgwick: The Story of A Union Corps Commander,* 73.
7. Thomas Hyde, *Following the Greek Cross,* 128.
8. Tompkins' report, *OR,* 25: II, 564; William Deloss Love, *Wisconsin in the Rebellion,* 355.
9. Butterfield to Sedgwick, *OR,* 25: II, 391.
10. Howe report, *OR,* 25: I, 599.
11. Howe's order of battle in Neill, Grant reports, *OR,* 25: I, 603, 609.
12. Butterfield to Hooker, *OR,* 25: II, 389. Accounts conflict regarding the exact time Sedgwick's main assault began. Many claim it began closer to 11:00 than 10:30 A.M. The signal for Burnham's battle line to advance was the sight of the assaulting columns advancing up the roadways. It may have been that the battle line to the left of the columns on the roadways had not been fully deployed as the columns on the roads began advancing. Any delay would have hindered coordination of the assault and varied participants' or observers' chronicling of the event. See: Judd, *The Story of the Thirty-Third New York State Volunteers,* 294–295; Best, *History of the 121st New York State Infantry,* 62; Maier, *Rough and Regular: A History of Philadelphia's 119 Regiment of Pennsylvania Volunteer Infantry, The Gray Reserves,* 41.
13. John J. Pullen, *The Twentieth Maine: A Volunteers Regiment in the Civil War,* 49.
14. Johnson & Buel, *B&L,* Vol. III, 228; John Sedgwick, *Correspondence of John Sedgwick,* Vol. II, 119.
15. Winslow, *General John Sedgwick,* 73; Brewer, *History Sixty-First Regiment, Pennsylvania Volunteers, 1861–1865,* 54. The 61st Pennsylvania reported nineteen officers killed or mortally wounded throughout the war. This was the highest loss of officers in any infantry regiment. See Fox, *Regimental Losses,* 39.
16. Johnson & Buel, *B&L,* Vol. III, 229.
17. Mundy, *No Rich Man's Sons,* 111; Ben Thaxter to Elinor Comer, May 21, 1863.
18. Barksdale report, *OR,* 25: I, 840. The time placement of the appearance of the white flag varies. Several accounts state the flag was raised prior to 10:30 A.M., which incorrectly points to the flag being presented by Wheaton or Howe's men during their earlier probes towards the heights. According to Wheaton's official report his reconnoiter was stopped some 250 yards shy of the stone wall. His wounded were nowhere close to the entrenched Confederates, making it improbable that any Federals gathering wounded could near the works to get a look inside. Howe's probe was also stifled shortly after it began and took place off to the side and further away from the stone wall than Wheaton's. The white flag had to make a brief appearance amongst the chaos of Sedgwick's main assault of the heights.
19. *Southern Historical Society Papers,* Vol. 14, 416.
20. Charles A. Clark, *Campaigning With The Sixth Maine,* Iowa M.O.L.L.U.S., 47.
21. *Ibid.*
22. Bigelow, *The Campaign of Chancellorsville,* 391. Several accounts claim the white flag was intentionally used as a strategy to gain access to the Confederate earthworks. It may have appeared to some defenders that the Federals had used the white flag as a trick, but in actuality it appears to have been a happenstance caused by battlefield chaos.
23. Bigelow, *The Campaign of Chancellorsville,* 391.
24. Rosenblatt, eds., *Hard Marching Everyday: The Civil War Letters of Private Wilbur Fisk,* 78.
25. Paul G. Zeller, *The Second Vermont Volunteer Infantry, 1861–1865,* 128.
26. Alan A. Siegal, *For The Glory Of The Union: Myth, Reality, and the Media in the Civil War,* 165; George W. Parsons, *Put The Vermonters Ahead: The First Vermont Brigade in the Civil War,* 49; Beyer & Keydel, *Deeds of Valor,* 171.
27. Siegal, *For The Glory Of The Union,* 165; *The Rebellion Record,* Vol. VI, 282–283. Colonel Andrew J. Morrison was later convicted in a military court, but owing to his political connections his punishment was simply dismissal from the service.
28. Bigelow, *P.M.H.S.M.,* Vol. 3, *The Battle of Marye's Heights and Salem Church,* 256.
29. *America's Medal of Honor Recipients,* 897.
30. Noel Harrison, *A Walking Tour of Civil War Sites on the Campus of Mary Washington College,* 14.
31. Rosenblatt, eds., *Hard Marching Everyday,* 79; *The Rebellion Record,* Vol. VII, 282–283.
32. Grant, Carlton reports, *OR,* 25: I, 603, 846.

33. Jones, *Lee's Tigers*, 152.

34. Pendleton report, *OR*, 25: I, 815; *Civil War Regiments: A Journal of the American Civil War*, Vol. 5, No. 1, Richardson report, 117–119.

35. Neill report, *OR*, 25: I, 609.

36. *Civil War* Regiments, Vol. 5, No. 1, Owen Diary, 117; Johnson & Buel, *B&L*, Vol. III, 229; Winslow, *General John Sedgwick*, 75.

37. William Stowe to parents, May 15, 1863.

38. Neill report, *OR*, 25: I, 609; Fuller, *One of the Boys: Battles of the Seventy-Seventh New York State Foot Volunteers*, 12.

39. Jennings Cropper Wise, *The Long Arm of Lee: The History of the Artillery of the Army of Northern Virginia*, 522–523; Pendleton report, *OR*, 25: II, 815.

40. Zeller, *The Second Vermont Infantry Regiment, 1861–1865*, 134.

41. Cushing, *War Papers*, Maine M.O.L.L.U.S., Vol. III, "Charge of the Light Division At Marye's Heights, May 3, 1863," 341. W.F. Beyer & O. F. Keydel, eds., *Deeds of Valor*, 554–555; Johnson & Buel, eds., *B&L*, Vol. III, 229.

42. *Ibid*; Mundy, *No Rich Man's Sons*, 111. John A. Gray would be killed in action on November 7, 1863, at Rappahannock Station. Gray's gallant performance at Second Fredericksburg very well would have earned him the Medal of Honor following the war, but at the time it was uncommon to award the medal posthumously.

43. J.H. Stine, *History of the Army of the Potomac*, 373; R.J. Profit & Mitch Demars, eds., *America's Medal of Honor Recipients*, 782; Beyer & Keydel, eds., *Deeds of Valor*, 146.

44. Beyer & Keydel, eds., *Deeds of Valor*, 554–555; Johnson & Buel, eds., *B&L*, Vol. III, 229.

45. Beyer & Keydel, eds., *Deeds of Valor*, 150–151.

46. Abner Doubleday, *Chancellorsville and Gettysburg*, 59; Robert Tomes, *War with the South*, 129–130.

47. Johnson & Buel, *B&L*, Vol. III, 237; Hyde, *Civil War Letters of Thomas W. Hyde*, 73.

48. Fox, *Regimental Losses in the Civil War*, 128; Cushing, *War Papers*, Maine M.O.L.L.U.S., Vol. III, "Charge of the Light Division at Marye's Heights, May 3," 1863, 340.

49. Lee, Early, Barksdale reports, *OR*, 25: I, 801, 1001, 840.

50. *War Papers*, Maine M.O.L.L.U.S., Vol. III, 341.

51. Owen Diary, *Civil War Regiments*, Vol. 5, No. 1, 117; Krick, *Parker's Virginia Battery C.S.A.*, 141.

52. Hyde, *Following the Greek Cross*, 128. Potomac Creek Hospital was the U.S. Army's largest tent hospital established up to this time in the war. It contained its own quartermaster and commissary. Steam trains hauled freight cars full of hospital supplies and materiel from Washington to Alexandria, Virginia, which were forwarded down the Potomac River, without break in bulk, via barges to wharves at Aquia Creek and Uba Dam. For more on Potomac Creek Hospital see *United States Christian Commission for the Army and Navy. For the Year 1863*, 2nd Annual Report (Philadelphia: 1864); James Weber, *Northern Railroads in the Civil War* (New York), 1952.

53. Sedgwick report, *OR*, 25: I, 561–562.

8. *"A Force Yet to His Front"*

1. Wilcox report, *OR*, 25: I, 856.

2. Bicknell, *History of the Fifth Maine Regiment*, 219–220; Isaac O. Best, History of the 121st New York State Infantry, 62.

3. George Contant, *Path of Blood: The True Story of the 33rd New York Volunteers*, 310.

4. Cabell, Carlton, reports, *OR*, 25: I, 842, 846.

5. William M. Owen, *In Camp with the Washington Artillery*, 221.

6. Pendleton, Carlton reports, *OR*, 25: I, 815, 846.

7. Ingals to Butterfield, *OR*, 25: II, 391; Butterfield to Hooker, *OR*, 25: II, 392. For full report on fighting at Chancellorsville see Ernest B. Furgurson, *Chancellorsville: Souls of the Brave*, 221–253.

8. Warren to Hooker, *OR*, 25: II, 393.

9. Early, *Lieutenant General Jubal A. Early*, 211.

10. Ibid.

11. Burke Davis, *Gray Fox: Robert E. Lee and the Civil War*, 194; Warner, *Generals in Blue*, 430–431. Sedgwick had been promoted to major in the 1st Cavalry, and Lee was placed in command of that outfit upon his promotion to colonel in 1861.

12. Cooke, *Life of Robert E. Lee*, 255; Randolph H. McKim, *A Soldier's Recollections*, 130.

13. Robert Stiles, *Four Years Under Marse Robert*, 168–169.

14. Haines, *History of the Fifteenth Regiment New Jersey Volunteers*, 58; Penrose report, *OR*, 25: I, 572.

15. Furgurson, *Chancellorsville 1863:The Souls Of The Brave*, 267; Sewell C. Gray, May 3, 1863.

16. Ingalls to Butterfield, *P.M.H.S.M.*, Vol. III, 261; Peck to Butterfield, *OR*, 25: II, 345.

17. Siegal, *For the Glory of the Union*, 166.

18. *Ibid*.

19. McMahon to Butterfield, *OR*, 25: II, 392.

20. Howe, Pendleton reports, *OR*, 25: I, 600, 816.

21. Wilcox report, *OR*, 25: I, 856–857.

22. Chester A. Leach to wife, May 14, 1863; Rosenblatt, *Hard Marching Everyday*, 79; G.G. Benedict, *Vermont in the Civil War: A History of the part Taken by the Vermont Soldiers and Sailors in the War for the Union, 1861–5*, Vol. 1, 364.

23. Gibbon report *OR*, 25: I, 350–351.

24. Hall report, *OR*, 25: I, 359.

25. Hilary A. Herbert, *History of the Eighth Alabama Volunteer Regiment, C.S.A.*, 100.

26. Hyde, *Following the Greek Cross*, 129.

27. Paul G. Zeller, *The Second Vermont Volunteer Infantry Regiment, 1861–1865*, 134.

28. Benedict, *Vermont in the Civil War*, Vol. 1, 367; Rosenblatt, eds. *Hard Marching Everyday*, 81.

29. Warner, *Generals in Blue*, 239.

30. Hunt to Hooker, *OR*, 25: II, 381.

31. Walker, *The Second Army Corps*, 251.

32. Federal dispatches, *OR*, 25: II, 396–397.

33. Wilcox report, *OR*, 25: I, 858.

34. Penick report, *OR*, 25: I, 884; born in Pennsylvania, Collins graduated the United States Military Academy in 1859. A highly regarded soldier by J.E.B. Stuart and Fitzhugh Lee, Collins was killed in action at Todd's Tavern, May 7, 1864. E.P. Alexander said. "He was superb and admirable, both in person and

character, and universally popular" (Fortier, *15th Virginia Cavalry*, 66; Krick, *Lee's Colonels*, 96).

35. Wilcox report, *OR*, 25: I, 858.
36. *Ibid.*
37. Signal station to Hooker, *OR*, 25: II, 394.
38. Johnson & Buel, eds., *B&L*, Vol. III, 233.
39. Benham report, *OR*, 25: I, 213; *P.M.H.S.M.*, Vol. 3, 265.
40. Hunt report, *OR*, 25: I, 247.
41. Nevins, ed., *Diary of Battle: The Personal Journals of Charles S. Wainwright*, 199.

9. Salem Church

1. Wilcox report, *OR*, 25: I, 857; Ralph Happel, *Salem Church Embattled*, 39.
2. Wilcox, McLaws reports, *OR*, 25: I, 857, 827; Camille Baquet, *History of Kearney's First New Jersey Brigade*, 240; Ralph Happel, *Salem Church Embattled*, 40.
3. Wilcox report, *OR*, 25: I, 858.
4. Brooks report, *OR*, 25: I, 568; Baquet, *History of Kearney's First New Jersey Brigade*, 254.
5. McLaws report, *OR*, 25: I, 827.
6. Ibid.
7. Semmes report, *OR*, 25: I, 835.
8. Best, *History of the 121st New York State Infantry*, 69; Wilcox report, *OR*, 25: I, 858.
9. Baquet, *First New Jersey Brigade*, 243.
10. Bartlett report, *OR*, 25: I, 581.
11. John L.G. Wood to aunt, May 10, 1863.
12. Grubb report, *OR*, 25: I, 579.
13. Russell report, *OR*, 25: I, 592.
14. Beaver report, *OR*, 25: I, 586; Curtis, *From Bull Run to Chancellorsville*, 267; Profit & Keydel, eds., *America's Medal of Honor Recipients*, 786.
15. William McClellan to father May 10, 1863, as cited in Stephen W. Sears, *Chancellorsville*, 383.
16. John L.G. Wood to aunt, May 10, 1863.
17. Haines, *History of the Fifteenth Regiment New Jersey Volunteers*, 54; Penrose report, *OR*, 25: I, 572; Edmund Halsey diary, May 3, 1863.
18. John G. Barrett, *Yankee Rebel*, 102; Upton report, *OR*, 25: I, 589.
19. Jacob Haas to brother, May 12, 1863.
20. Wyckoff, *History of the 3rd South Carolina Infantry, 1861–1865*, 198.
21. Edwards, *War Paper*, Maine M.O.L.L.U.S., Vol. IV, *Personal Reminiscences of the 5th Maine*, 421.
22. Rogers report, *OR*, 25: I, 615; Harold R. Barker, *History of Rhode Island Combat Units in the Civil War*, 151.
23. Rogers report, *OR*, 25: I, 616.
24. Rhodes, *All for the Union*, 107–108; John R. Bartlett, *Memoirs of Rhode Island Officers in the Civil War*, 310–313; Semmes report, *OR*, 25: I, 836; Rogers report, *OR*, 25: I, 616.
25. Rogers report, *OR*, 25: I, 615.
26. Baquet, *History of the First New Jersey Volunteers, 1861–1865*, 276.
27. Fred H. West to sister, May 18, 1863. Command of the 51st Georgia devolved upon Major

Anthony following the wounding of Colonel William Slaughter and Lieutenant Colonel Edward Ball near Chancellorsville.

28. Semmes report, *OR*, 25: I, 835–836.
29. Bernard, *War Talks of Confederate Veterans*, 59.
30. McLaws report, *OR*, 25: I, 827.
31. Wheaton report, *OR*, 25: I, 619; Griffith, *Battle Tactics of the Civil War*, 74–75.
32. Wheaton report, *OR*, 25: I, 619; Butterfield to Hooker, *OR*, 25: II, 394.
33. Williston report, *OR*, 25: I, 598.
34. Fred H. West letter of May 18, 1863; Holt report, *OR*, 25: I, 838.
35. Profit, *America's Medal of Honor Recipients*, 723.
36. Ibid., 738. Years after the war, Daniel Wheeler married a girl from Fredericksburg, Virginia. This Vermonter received his Medal of Honor in 1892. Upon Wheeler's death, he was buried in the civilian section of the Fredericksburg City Cemetery. Wheeler's gravesite has never been honored with the placing of an official Medal of Honor plaque.
37. Howe report, *OR*, 25: I, 600; Doubleday, *Chancellorsville and Gettysburg*, 61. Not in his presence, Sixth Corps soldiers fondly referred to Sedgwick as "Uncle John" or "Johnny Sedgwick."
38. Wheaton report, *OR*, 25: I, 618; Zeller, *The Second Vermont Volunteer Infantry Regiment, 1861–1865*, 135–136.
39. John S. Sanders to parents, as cited in Gerrad A. Patterson, *From Blue to Gray: The Life of Confederate General Cadmus M. Wilcox*, 57.
40. G. Norton Galloway, *The Ninety-Fifth Pennsylvania Volunteers*, 74.
41. Beyer, ed., *Deeds of Valor*, 148.
42. William F. Fox, *Regimental Losses in the American Civil War 1861–1865, A Treatise on the Extent and Nature of the Mortuary Losses in the Union Regiments, with Full and Exhaustive Statistics Compiled from the Official Records on File in the State Military Bureaus and at Washington*, 229. In addition, the 102nd Pennsylvania in Wheaton's Third Brigade of Newton's Division, Sixth Corps lost their regimental mascot during the fighting at Salem Church. "Dog Jack" mingled into the fray and was captured. Six months later, "Dog Jack" was exchanged for a Confederate prison of war and rejoined his regiment. *Soldiers & Sailors National Military Museum and Memorial, Pittsburgh, Pennsylvania.*
43. Peter S. Michie, *The Life and Letters of Emory Upton: Colonel of the Fourth Regiment of Artillery, and Brevet Major-General, U.S. Army*, 81; Best, *History of the 121st New York State Infantry*, 72.
44. Baquet, *History of the First Brigade, New Jersey Volunteers, 1861–1865*, 248–250; Slade, *That Sterling Soldier: The Life of David A. Russell*, 127–128.
45. Warner, *Generals in Blue*, 47; Zeller, *The Second Vermont Volunteer Infantry Regiment, 1861–1865*, 142.
46. Wilcox report, *OR*, 25: I, 859.
47. Semmes report, *OR*, 25: I, 835; W.R. Stillwell to brother, May 29, 1863.

10. *"I Find Everything Snug Here"*

1. Early, *Lieutenant General Jubal A. Early,* 221; Cowan report, *OR,* 25: I, 613.
2. Lee to Early, *OR,* 25: II, 769.
3. Lee to McLaws, *OR,* 25: II, 770.
4. Noel Harrison, *Chancellorsville Battle Sites,* 162; Saunders, 171–172.
5. Martin T. McMahon, *United States Service Magazine,* V, 21.
6. Warren testimony, *Joint Committee on the Conduct of War,* Vol. IV, 48; Samuel P. Bates, *The Battle of Chancellorsville,* p. 151.
7. Warren to Sedgwick, *OR,* 25: I, 396.
8. Augustus C. Hamlin, *The Attack of Stonewall Jackson at Chancellorsville,* introduction by Frank O'Reilly, 164.
9. Rhodes, *All For The Union,* 107.
10. James M. Greiner, Janet L. Coryell, and James R. Smither, eds., *A Surgeon's Civil War: The Letters and Diary of Daniel M. Holt, M.D.,* 93–94.
11. *Ibid.,* 96, 100.
12. Sedgwick to Butterfield, *OR,* 25: II, 403.
13. Larry B. Maier, *Rough & Regular: A History of Philadelphia's 119th Regiment of Pennsylvania Volunteer Infantry, The Gray Reserves,* 58.
14. William W. Hassler, *A.P. Hill: Lee's Forgotten General,* 140–141; Anderson report, *OR,* 25: I, 852.
15. John B. Gordon, *Reminiscences of the Civil War,* 100–101.
16. Harrison, Chancellorsville Battle Sites, 188; Richard Snowden Andrews, *A Memoir,* 90.
17. George Contant, *Path of Blood: The True History of the 33rd New York Volunteers,* 335; Rosenblatt, eds., *Hard Marching Everyday: The Civil War Letters of Private Wilbur Fisk, 1861–1865,* 81.
18. Pharris Deloach Johnson, *Under the Southern Cross: Soldiers Life with Gordon Bradwell and the Army of Northern Virginia,* 112.
19. J.B. Gordon, *Reminiscences of the Civil War, 101.* Gordon rode this horse while presenting Lee's surrender at Appomattox Courthouse. For years after the war, Mrs. Fanny Gordon rode this steady animal at Confederate veteran reunions.
20. Jennings Cropper Wise, *The Long Arm of Lee: The History of the Artillery of the Army of Northern Virginia,* 530–531.
21. Butterfield to Hooker & Sedgwick, *OR,* 25: II, 406; Early, *Lieutenant General Jubal A. Early,* 225.
22. Hall report, *OR,* 25: I, 359.
23. Cushing report, *OR,* 25: I, 221. On February 12, 1863, the Phillips house accidentally caught fire after several Union cavalry officers attempted to ignite a Sibley cook stove in the attic. In May 1863, the large chimney and support beams of the building were all that remained.
24. Butterfield to Sedgwick, *OR,* 25: II, 404.
25. Butterfield to Hooker, *OR,* 25: II, 404.
26. Hooker to Sedgwick, *OR,* 25: II, 402; Butterfield to Sedgwick, *OR,* 25: II, 405.
27. Huey report, *OR,* 25: I, 784.
28. Denicke report, *OR,* 25: I, 235.

29. Sedgwick to Hooker, *OR,* 25: II, 405.
30. Sedgwick to Hooker, *OR,* 25: II 496.
31. Lowe to Sedgwick, *OR,* 409.
32. Hooker to Sedgwick, *OR,* 25: II, 407, 409–410.
33. Federal dispatches, *OR,* 25: II, 412.
34. Early, *Lieutenant General Jubal A. Early,* 226.
35. Profit, *America's Medal of Honor Recipients,* 845; Lieutenant Colonel Connor to father, May 10, 1863 as cited in Sears, *Chancellorsville,* 396.
36. Neill, Early reports, *OR,* 25: II, 610, 1003; Sedgwick to Hooker, *OR,* 25: II, 409; Early, *Lieutenant General Jubal A Early,* 226.
37. Bigelow, *The Campaign of Chancellorsville,* 406–407.
38. Porter A. Alexander, *Fighting for the Confederacy,* 213.
39. Hardaway report, *OR,* 25: I, 880.
40. MaMahon, *Proceeding of the Reunion Society of Vermont Officers,* 342.
41. Hooker to Sedgwick, *OR,* 25: II, 409; Benham report, *OR,* 25: I, 213–215; Sedgwick to Hooker, *OR,* 25: II, 410.
42. Jubal A. Early, *Autobiographical sketch and narrative of the War Between the States,* 227.
43. Pendleton report, *OR,* 25: I, 817; Wise, *The Long Arm of Lee,* 534.
44. William S. Tyler, ed., *Reminiscences of the Civil War,* 87.

11. *Battle for Scott's Ford*

1. Howe, Grant reports, *OR,* 25: I, 599–607.
2. Tompkins report, *OR,* 25: I, 565.
3. Barefoot, *General Robert F. Hoke: Lee's Modest Warrior,* 83; Walter Clark, ed., *Histories of the Several Regiments and Battalions from North Carolina in the Great War, 1861–1865,* 410; Henry E. Handerson, *Yankee in Gray: The Civil War Memoirs of Henry E. Handerson with a Selection of His Wartime Letters,* 75.
4. Hyde, *Following the Greek Cross,* 130–131; Hyde, *The Civil War Letters of Thomas W. Hyde,* 75.
5. Hyde, *Following the Greek Cross,* 133.
6. Grant report, *OR,* 25: I, 604.
7. Jeffery D. Marshall, ed., *A War of the People: Vermont Civil War Letters,* 171; Siegal, *For the Glory of the Union,* 169.
8. Rigby report, *OR,* 25: I, 597; Beyer & Keydel, eds., *Deeds of Valor,* 155.
9. Jones, *Lee's Tigers,* 155. On page 227 of his memoir Jubal Early mentioned Lee was not present for the May 4 attack. Lee was present for the attack, which made him the ranking Confederate officer on the field. See Jones, *Lee's Tigers,* 155; Freeman, *R. E. Lee,* Vol. 2, 554.
10. Urbanus Dart Jr., printed in *Brunswick Georgia News,* May, 4, 1963; William Redding , letter May 8, 1863.
11. Mark, *A History of the 93rd Regiment Pennsylvania Veteran Volunteers,* 240; Wheaton report, *OR,* 25: I, 619.
12. Henry E. Handerson, *Yankee in Gray,* 102; Erastus H. Scott to father, May 18, 1863.

13. William Stowe, letter May 10, 1863; Thomas Cutrer & Michael Parrish, eds., *Brothers in Gray,* 189.

14. Siegal, *For the Glory of the Union,* 170; Unidentified Vermonter's letter to parents, found in Pingree papers, Vermont Historical Society.

15. Benedict, *Vermont in the Civil War,* Vol. II, 371–372; Barney report, *OR,* 25: I, 608–609.

16. Early, *Lieutenant General Jubal A. Early,* 230.

17. Beyer & Keydel, eds., *Deeds of Valor,* 171.

18. Joseph C. Elliott, *Richard H. Anderson: Lee's Noble Soldier,* 68; Anderson report, *OR,* 25: I, 853.

19. Edwards, *War Papers,* Maine M.O.L.L.U.S., Vol. IV, *Personal Reminiscences of the 5th Maine Regiment,* 123.

20. Henry G. Hore to cousin, May 10, 1863; Brooks report, *OR,* 25: I, 568.

21. McLaws report, *OR,* 25: I, 828–829.

22. Bartlett, *Memoirs of Rhode Island Officers who were engaged in the Service of their Country During the Great Rebellion of the South,* 378.

23. William G. Piston, *Lee's Tarnished Lieutenant: James Longstreet and His Place in Southern History,* 39; Thomas, *Robert E. Lee,* 290.

24. Hardaway, McCarthy reports, *OR,* 25: I, 881, 848.

25. Jones, *Lee's Tigers,* 154; Profit, *America's Medal of Honor Recipients,* 141; *Revised Rosters of Vermont Volunteers in the War of the Rebellion, 1862,* 69. In May, 1864, Colonel Barney was killed during the Wilderness Campaign. His body was sent home to Vermont for burial. Colonel Leroy A. Stafford's captured sword was consigned to the grave atop Barney's coffin. George G. Benedict, *Vermont in the Civil War,* Vol. 1, 224.

26. Warner, *Generals in Gray,* 140.

27. Rosenblatt, eds., *Hard Marching Everyday,* 84.

28. Bigelow, *The Campaign of Chancellorsville,* 474–475; National Archives, RG 109, M-836-6.

29. *Civil War Regiments,* Vol. V, No. 1, Owen Diary, 11–120.

30. Boatner, *The Civil War Dictionary,* 270–271; Fox, *Regimental Losses,* 50–51.

31. *OR,* 25: I, 190; Rosenblatt, eds., *Hard Marching Everyday,* 83.

32. Samuel E. Pingree to father, May 9, 1863. There is a tendency to blend the battle of Salem Church, May 3, 1863, with the engagement that took place the following day near Scott's Ford. Many Federal participants held scant knowledge about the area's landmarks. Most likely, for simplicity of reporting, many Union soldiers including Sedgwick grouped together the fighting done on the afternoon of May 3, 1863 with the action on the afternoon of May 4, 1863 under the title of Salem Heights. Be that as it may, this often-used title is misleading owing to the fact that the fighting on May 4, 1863, took place over two miles away from Salem Church. More importantly, most combatants heavily engaged at Salem Church saw little or no action near Scott's Ford on May 4, 1863, and vice versa. Salem Church was a great victory for Lee's Army of Northern Virginia. The following day at Scott's Ford, Lee's men suffered a repulse prior to Sedgwick retiring. The attempt by modern historians to combine these two actions under the title of Salem Church confounds the historical record and

detracts from the efforts put forth by individual units engaged.

12. *"An Immediate Reply Is Indispensable…"*

1. Winslow, General John Sedgwick, 83.

2. Bigelow, *The Campaign of Chancellorsville,* 415; Rhodes, *All For the Union,* 107.

3. Grant, Seaver reports, *OR,* 25: I, 606–608.

4. Lee to McLaws, *OR,* 25: II, 860–861.

5. Hyde, *Following the Greek Cross,* 133.

6. Johnson & Buel, eds., *B&L,* Vol. III, 232.

7. Fairchild, C.B., *History of the 27th New York,* 171.

8. Mitchell, *Badge of Gallantry,* 173–174.

9. Wheaton report, *OR,* 25: I, 619. The 62nd New York (Anderson Zouaves) were named in honor of Major Robert Anderson of Fort Sumter fame.

10. Stevens, *Three Years in the Sixth Corps,* 205; Mundy, *No Rich Men's Sons,* 131.

11. Clark, *War Papers,* Iowa M.O.L.L.U.S., *Campaigning with the Sixth Maine,* 35–36; Beyer & Keydel, eds., *Deeds of Valor,* 152–153.

12. Kershaw report, *OR,* 25: I, 831.

13. Howe testimony, *Joint Committee on the Conduct of War,* Vol. IV, 21.

14. *Ibid.*

15. Benedict, *Vermont in the Civil War,* Vol. 1, 373.

16. Tyler to Butterfield, *OR,* 25: II, 418.

17. Sedgwick to Hooker, *OR,* 25: II, 412.

18. Doubleday, *Chancellorsville and Gettysburg,* 66–67; Sedgwick to Hooker, *OR,* 25: II, 418.

19. Hooker to Sedgwick, *OR,* 25: II, 418–419.

20. Penrose report, *OR,* 25: I, 574–575.

21. Stevens, *Three Years in the Sixth Corps,* 205; Benedict, *Vermont in the Civil War,* Vol. II, 373.

22. Benedict, *Vermont in the Civil War,* Vol. II, 373; Henry Houghton, *The Ordeal of the Civil War: A Recollection,* 32.

23. Hardaway report, *OR,* 25: II, 882; Alexander, *Fighting for the Confederacy,* 214.

24. Sedgwick to Hooker, *OR,* 25: II, 419.

25. Chester A. Leach to wife, May 9, 1863; Grant Seaver reports, *OR,* 25: I, 802.

26. Sedgwick to Hooker, *OR,* 25: II, 419.

27. Howe testimony, *Joint Committee on the Conduct of War,* Vol. IV, 21.

28. Bartlett, *Memoirs of Rhode Island Officers Who Were Engaged in the Service of Their Country During the Great Rebellion of the South,* 378.

29. *The Rebellion Record,* Vol. VI, 559.

30. Cooke, *Life of Robert E. Lee,* 250; Lee report, *OR,* 25: I, 802.

31. Henry Houghton, *The Ordeal of Civil War: A Recollection,* 32; Samuel Pingree to mother, May 5, 1863.

32. Wynkoop, Collier reports, *OR,* 25: I, 621, 625; Rhodes, *All For the Union,* 108.

33. Gibbon, Hall reports, *OR,* 25: I, 351, 359.

34. Hooker testimony, *Joint Committee on the Conduct of War,* Vol. IV, 134; Meade, *Life and Letters of George Gordon Meade,* Vol. I, 374; Bigelow, *The Cam-*

paign of Chancellorsville, 420. For more on Hooker's council of war see Addenda, *OR,* 25: I, 510–512.

35. Hooker to Sedgwick, 25: II, 419.

36. Lee report, *OR,* 25: I, 802; Clement E. Evens, *Confederate Military History,* Vol. III, 392.

37. Hooker to Butterfield, *OR,* 25: II, 328; Gallagher, ed. *Fighting for the Confederacy,* 92; Meade, *Life and Letters of George Gordon Meade,* Vol. I, 373.

38. Wainwright, *Diary of Battle,* 201.

39. Alexander report, *OR,* 25: I, 821–822.

40. Lee to Hooker, *OR,* 25: II, 447.

41. Henry Janes letter, May 8, 1863; Peck, *Revised Roster Vermont Volunteers During the War of the Rebellion 1861–66,* 726–727; Bates, *The Battle of Chancellorsville,* 206–207.

42. Holt, *A Surgeon's Civil War: The Letters & Diary of Daniel M. Holt, M.D.,* 97; *OR,* 25: II, 441.

43. Mitchell, *Badge of Gallantry,* 176; Haines, *History of the Fifteenth Regiment New Jersey Volunteers,* 60.

44. Sedgwick report, *OR,* 25: I, 561; *Maine Adjutant General's Report, 1861–1865,* Vol. I, 399.

13. *"While Such a Spirit Prevails"*

1. Shelby Foote, *The Civil War: A Narrative,* Vol. II, *Fredericksburg to Meridian,* 316.

2. Hooker circular, *OR,* 25: I, 435.

3. Bigelow, *The Campaign of Chancellorsville,* 436; Hebert, *Fighting Joe Hooker,* 226.

4. Charles F. Benjamin, *Hooker's Appointment and Removal, B&L,* 240–241.

5. *B&L,* 240–241.

6. *Ibid.*

7. Coddington, *The Gettysburg Campaign,* 49; *New York Times,* May 7, 1863.

8. James F. Huntington Address November 2, 1897, in *P.M.H.S.M.* Vol. 3, 191; *New York World,* May 6, 1863.

9. Bigelow, *The Campaign of Chancellorsville,* 438; *OR,* 25: II, 439.

10. Rosenblatt, eds., *Hard Marching Everyday,* 87; Siegal, *For Glory of the Union,* 175; James F. Rhodes, *History of the United States,* Vol. IV, 266.

11. *Richmond Whig,* May 5, 1863.

12. Lee report, *OR,* 25: I, 803.

13. Early, *Lieutenant General Jubal A. Early,* 219.

14. Lee report, *OR,* 25: I, 795; Gerard A. Patterson, *From Blue to Gray: The Life of Confederate General Cadmus M. Wilcox,* 58–59.

15. *Southern Historical Society Papers,* Vol. III, 153–154.

16. Davis to Lee, *OR,* 25: I, 791.

17. Meade, *Life and Letters of George Gordon Meade,* Vol. I, 373.

18. Stackpole, *Chancellorsville: Lee's Greatest Battle,* 2nd ed., 14–15.

19. Meade, *The Life and Letters of George Gordon Meade,* Vol. I, 372.

20. Boatner, *Civil War Dictionary,* 521.

21. Hebert, *Fighting Joe Hooker,* 227, 229.

22. Jordan, *"Happiness Is Not My Companion": The Life of General G. K. Warren,* 78.

23. *Ibid.,* 331.

24. Warren Papers as found in Jordan, *"Happiness Is Not My Companion,"* 331.

25. Carl Sandberg, *Abraham Lincoln: The War Years,* Vol. II, 98. Major General Winfield Scott Hancock assumed command of the Second Corps. Major General Couch was given command of the Department of the Susquehanna and commanded the Pennsylvania Militia during the Gettysburg campaign. In 1864, Couch was sent west to command a division of the Twenty-third Corps. Major General Stoneman became chief of the Cavalry Bureau in Washington, until he was sent west to command the Twenty-third Corps. He was captured on July 31, 1864.

26. Nicolay and Hay, *Abraham Lincoln: A History,* abridged and edited by Paul M. Angle, 174.

27. Augustus C. Hamlin, *The Attack of Stonewall Jackson at Chancellorsville,* introduction by Frank O'Reilly, i–xxi, 156–162; Johnson & Buel, *B&L,* Vol. III, 155.

28. T. Harry Williams, *Lincoln And His Generals,* 246–247; *OR,* 25: II, 479; Hebert, *Fighting Joe Hooker,* 229. A concise discussion of Hooker's performance is found in Edwin B. Coddington's *The Gettysburg Campaign: A Study in Command,* 26–46.

29. MaCartney *Lincoln and His Generals,* 163; Tag, *The Generals of Gettysburg,* 105.

30. Sedgwick, *Correspondence of John Sedgwick,* Vol. III, 109; Catton, *Glory Road,* Vol. 2, 214.

31. Wainwright, *Diary of Battle,* 213; MaMahon, *Address Delivered Before the Vermont Officer's Reunion Society,* 24.

32. Theodore A. Dodge, *The Romances of Chancellorsville,* read December 13, 1886, *P.M.H.S.M.,* Vol. 3, 201–202.

33. Catton, *Glory Road,* Vol. 2, 214; John Gibbon, *Personal Recollections of the Civil War,* 122; Meade, *Life and Letters of George Gordon Meade,* 373, 377, 379.

34. Hebert, *Fighting Joe Hooker,* 223.

35. *Ibid.,* 147. The political platform of the Radical Republicans was immediate emancipation and a punitive policy toward the South after surrender. Chase had lost the previous 1860 Republican nomination for president due to his Radical Republican stance.

36. Hooker testimony, *Joint Committee on the Conduct of War,* Vol. IV, 146.

37. Theodore A. Dodge Address December 13, 1886, in *P.M.H.S.M.,* Vol. 3, 200.

38. Butterfield to Hooker, *OR,* 25: II, 329, 365, 378, 400; Bigelow, *The Campaign of Chancellorsville,* 404; John Bigelow, *The Battles of Marye's Heights and Salem Church* in *P.M.H.S.M.,* Vol. 3, 291–292. Herman Haupt never accepted an officer's commission and served without pay or official rank until he left the service in September 1863. The Army of the Potomac received supplies via steam trains that hauled materiel from Washington, D.C., to Alexandria, Virginia. Supplies were then forwarded down the Potomac River, without break in bulk, via barges to wharves at Aquia Creek and Uba Dam.

39. Bates, *The Battle of Chancellorsville,* 206; *B&L,* 223.

40. Sedgwick testimony, *Joint Committee on the Conduct of War,* Vol. IV, 101.

41. Warren testimony, *Joint Committee on the Conduct of War,* Vol. IV, 47–49.

42. *Ibid.*

43. Thomas W., *Massachusetts in the Army and Navy, 1861–1865,* Vol. 1, 208, "7th Massachusetts Infantry."

44. Walter H. Hebert, *Fighting Joe Hooker,* 223, 227; Doubleday, *Chancellorsville and Gettysburg,* 32; Jordan, "Happiness Is Not My Companion," 331.

45. Stackpole, *Chancellorsville: Lee's Greatest Battle,* foreword by William C. Davis.

46. John Bell Hood, *Advance and Retreat,* 53.

47. Fox, *Regimental Losses in the Civil War,* 1, 550; *OR,* 25: I, 806–808; Johnson and Buel, *B&L,* Vol. III, 238.

48. Early report, *OR,* 25: I, 1002; Johnson & Buel, *B&L,* Vol. III, 237–238.

49. Gabor S. Boritt, *Lincoln and the Economics of the American Dream,* 273.

50. *OR,* 25: I, 172–191; Johnson & Buel, *B&L,* Vol. III, 237; Fox, *Regimental Losses in the Civil War,* 544.

51. Johnson & Buel, *B&L,* Vol. III, 170; Hebert, *Fighting Joe Hooker,* 225.

52. Isaac O. Best, *"Upton's Regulars": History of the 121st New York State Infantry,* 83; Warren W. Hassler Jr., *Commanders of the Army of the Potomac,* 130; Hebert, *Fighting Joe Hooker,* 65; Jordan, *"Happiness Is Not My Companion,"* 330–331.

53. Huntington address November 2, 1897, in *P.M.H.S.M,* Vol. 3, 187; Bigelow, *P.M.H.S.M.,* Vol. 3, 309. A new cocktail was invented after Chancellorsville, which became very popular in the bar rooms of Washington and New York. Its name was "Hooker's Retreat." Hebert, *Fighting Joe Hooker,* 230.

54. Major E. P. Halstead to W.F.H. Godson, April 19, 1903; Stine, *History of the Army of the Potomac,* 368; Catton, *Glory Road,* 211.

Epilogue

1. William Woods Hassler, *A.P. Hill: Lee's Forgotten General,* 143–145; Coddington, *The Gettysburg Campaign,* 11–25.

2. Coddington, *The Gettysburg Campaign,* 52.

3. Zeller, *The Second Vermont Volunteer Infantry Regiment, 1861–1865,* 143–144.

4. George Parsons, *Put The Vermonters Ahead: The First Vermont Brigade in the Civil War,* 57–58; Grant report, *OR,* 27: I, 678; Hassler, *A.P. Hill: Lee's Forgotten General,* 147.

5. Freeman, *Lee's Lieutenants.* Vol. II, 712; Coddington; *The Gettysburg Campaign,* 48–50.

6. Roger P. Basler, ed., *The Collected Works of Abraham Lincoln,* Vol. VI, 257; Stephan E. Ambrose,

Halleck: Lincoln's Chief of Staff, 133; Edwin B. Coddington, *The Gettysburg Campaign,* 84.

7. Williams, *Lincoln and His Generals,* 252–256; Albert B. Hart, *American Statesmen: Salmon Portland Chase,* 297. Chase was an effective secretary of state. He maintained national credit and raised tremendous amounts of money for the war effort.

8. Hebert, *Fighting Joe Hooker,* 269–270. West Virginia was admitted to the Union as a state on June 20, 1863. Major General George Sykes replaced Meade as commander of the Fifth Corps. After assuming command, Meade queried Halleck regarding a withdrawal of a portion of the Harper's Ferry garrison. Halleck left the decision to Meade's discretion and in a short time the majority of the garrison joined the Army of the Potomac.

9. Boatner, *Civil War Dictionary,* 765. Before the start of Sherman's Atlanta Campaign, Slocum was reassigned to the District of Vicksburg and soon after would take command of the Twentieth Corps.

10. Hebert, *Fighting Joe Hooker,* 257. Ulysses S. Grant commented that Sedgwick's loss to the army was greater than the loss of an entire division. See Porter, *Campaigning with Grant,* 90.

11. Warner, *Generals in Blue,* 235, 452.

12. *B&L,* Vol. III, 175. Prior to Sedgwick's death, Brigadier General Joseph King Fenno Mansfield and Major General John Fulton Reynolds died while in command of an army corps.

13. Fox, *Regimental Losses in the Civil War,* 79.

14. Stevens, *Three Years in the Sixth Corps,* 215.

15. Hyde, *Following the Greek Cross,* 135–136.

16. Tyler, *Recollections of the Civil War,* 91; Mundy, *No Rich Man's Sons,* 112.

Appendix A

1. Bigelow, *The Campaign of Chancellorsville,* 491–492; Whitney, *Civil War Flags,* Flag Research Center; Slade, *That Sterling Soldier: The Life of David A. Russell,* 133–134.

2. Crute, *Emblems of Southern Valor.*

3. *OR,* 25: II, 466.

4. Stansbury, *Aeronautics in the Union and Confederate Armies, 1861–1865.*

5. Pendleton report, *OR,* 25: I, 811–815; Owen, *In Camp and Battle with the Washington Artillery,* 117; Bigelow, *The Campaign of Chancellorsville,* 500; Krick, *Parker's Virginia Battery,* 442; National Archive day report found in Smith, *Chancellorsville 1863: Jackson's Lightning Strike,* 32–34.

6. Full citations in Profit, *United States of America Medal of Honor Recipients.*

7. *OR,* 25: I, 992, 1051; Bigelow, *The Campaign of Chancellorsville,* 495.

Bibliography

Unpublished Personal Accounts

Abbott, Peter M. 3rd Vermont, papers, (MSS-17, #002). Vermont Historical Society, Barre.

Beattie, Alexander. 3rd Vermont, letters. Manuscript Collection of the Shelburne Museum, Shelburne, Vermont.

Brooks, W.T. Papers. United States Army Military History Institute. Carlisle, Pennsylvania.

Brown, Elon Francis. 6th Wisconsin, diary, 1863. State Historical Society of Wisconsin, Madison.

Connor, Seldon. 7th Maine, letters. John Hay Library, Brown University, Providence, Rhode Island.

Dart, Urbanus Jr. 26th Georgia, letter May 7, 1863. Georgia Archives, Atlanta.

Dean, Elisha A. 7th Wisconsin, diary, 1863. State Historical Society of Wisconsin, Madison.

Feltch, Carlton. 3rd Vermont, diary. Fairbanks Museum, St. Johnsbury, Vermont.

French, John S. 5th Maine, letters May 5 and 10, 1863. Fifth Maine Community Center. Peaks Island, Maine.

French, Winsor B. 77th New York, letter May 6, 1863. Saratoga Springs Historical Society, Saratoga Springs, New York.

Gray, Sewel C., Co. A., 6th Marine, diary. Maine State Archive, Augusta.

Green, Marcus. Lieutenant Phillips' Georgia Legion. Kennesaw Mountain National Military Park, MF226 R24.

Haas, Jacob W. Co. G., 96th Pennsylvania, letter May 12, 1863. Fredericksburg & Spotsylvania National Military Park.

Halsey, Edmund D. 15th New Jersey. United States Army Military History Institute.

Hore, Harry G. May 10, 1863, letter. Fredericksburg & Spotsylvania National Military Park.

Howell, Edward Vernon, papers. Southern His-torical Collection, Wilson Library, the University of North Carolina at Chapel Hill.

Janes, Henry. Surgeon 3rd Vermont, letters 1862–1863. HCWRTCOLL-Gegory Coco Collection, United States Army Military History Institute.

Leach, Chester K. Company H., 2nd Vermont, letter of May 9, 1863. Special Collections, University of Vermont Library, Burlington.

Lemont, Frank L. Company E., 5th Maine, letter April 14, 1863, and May 5, 1863. University of Maine, Orono.

McMillan, Robert. 24th Georgia, Confederate Letters, Diaries, Memoirs, Georgia Archives, Atlanta.

Pingree, S.E. and S.M. Civil War letters, 1861–1864, in the Lyndon State College Collection: Pingree (Pingry)/Hunton/Stickney Family Papers (Doc. 382), Vermont Historical Society, Barre.

Redding, W.R. 13th Georgia, letter May 8, 1863. Southern Historical Collection, Wilson Library, The University of North Carolina at Chapel Hill.

Richardson, Sidney J. Letters, Drawer 71, Georgia Archives, Atlanta.

Rugg, Orin. Company G, 77th New York, Civil War letters. www.gunsites.com/77th/letters.html

Sale, John F. Co. H., 12th Virginia, letter. Vol. 3. Fredericksburg & Spotsylvania National Military Park.

Sanders, J.C.C. 11th Alabama. General Order May 12, 1863. Alabama Department of Archives and History, Montgomery.

Scott, Erastus H. Letter May 18, 1863. Special Collections, University of Vermont Library, Burlington.

Sixth Corps, Order and Letter Book of the

United States Army, Medical Department, Sixth Corps, Army of the Potomac, September 24, 1862, to March 13, 1865. Library of Congress, Washington, D.C.

Stillwell, W.R. 53rd Georgia. United Daughters of the Confederacy Bound Typescripts, Georgia Archives, Atlanta.

Stone, Edward P. 6th Vermont, letters. Vermont Historical Society, Barre.

Stowe, William. Company F., 2nd Vermont, letters. Vol. 47. Fredericksburg & Spotsylvania National Military Park.

Thaxter, Benjamin R.J. Sixth Maine. Fredericksburg & Spotsylvania National Military Park.

Toffey, John J. 21st New Jersey. Vol. 41. Fredericksburg & Spotsylvania National Military Park.

Treichler, James M. Co. H, 96th Pennsylvania, memoir. Vol. 41. Fredericksburg & Spotsylvania National Military Park.

Upton, Emory. Emory Upton Collection, Genesee County Department of History.

Walker, Nathan. Fifth Maine, letters. The Fifth Maine Community Center, Peaks Island, Maine.

West, Fred H. 51st Georgia, letter May 18, 1863. Vol. 47. Fredericksburg & Spotsylvania National Military Park.

Wood, John L.G. 53rd Georgia, letter May 10, 1863. Georgia Archives, Atlanta.

Published Primary Sources

Alexander, E.P. *Fighting for the Confederacy: Personal Recollections of General Edward Porter Alexander*. Gary W. Gallagher, ed. Chapel Hill: University of North Carolina Press, 1989.

Andrews, Richard Snowden. *A Memoir ...* Baltimore, 1910.

Ashe, R.Y. Adjutant 11th Alabama. Letter published in the *Birmingham Age-Herald*, Wednesday, September 24, 1890.

Banes, Charles H. *History of the Philadelphia Brigade: Sixty-Ninth, Seventy-First, Seventy-Second, and One Hundred and Sixth Pennsylvania Volunteers*. Philadelphia: J.B. Lippincott, 1876.

Baquet, Camille. *History of the First Brigade, New Jersey Volunteers, From 1861–1865*. Trenton: MacCrellish & Quigley, 1910.

Barrett, John G. *Yankee Rebel: The Civil War Journal of Edmund DeWitt Patterson*. Chapel Hill: University of North Carolina Press, 1966.

Bartlett, John R. *Memoirs of Rhode Island Officers Who Were Engaged in the Service of their Country During the Great Rebellion of the South*. Providence, 1867.

Bates, Samuel P. *The Battle of Chancellorsville*. Meadville, Pennsylvania: W.M. Rutter, 1892.

Benedict, G.G. *Vermont in the Civil War: A History of the Part taken by the Vermont Soldiers and Sailors in the War for the Union, 1861–65*. 2 vols. Burlington: Free Press Association, 1866.

Bennet, A.J. *The Story of the First Massachusetts Light Battery*. Boston, 1886.

Bernard, George S. *War Talks of Confederate Veterans*. Petersburg, Virginia: Fenn & Owen, 1892.

Best, Isaac O. *History of the 121st New York State Infantry*. Chicago: W.S. Conkey, 1921.

Beyer, W.F. and O. F. Keydel, eds. *Deeds of Valor: How America's Civil War Heroes Won the Congressional Medal of Honor*. Detroit, 1906.

Bicknell, George W. *History of the Fifth Maine Volunteers*. Portland: Hall L. Davis, 1871.

Bigelow, John. *The Campaign of Chancellorsville*. New Haven: Yale University Press, 1910.

_____. *Papers of the Military History Society of Massachusetts*. Vol. 3, *Campaigns in Virginia, Maryland, and Pennsylvania 1862–1863. The Battle of Marye's Heights and Salem Church*. Boston: Houghton, Mifflin, 1895.

Billings, John D. *Hard Tack and Coffee*. Boston: G.M. Smith, 1887.

Bowen, James L. *History of the Thirty-Seventh Regiment Massachusetts Volunteers*. Holyoke, 1884.

Brewer, A.T. *History of the Sixty-First Regiment, Pennsylvania Volunteers, 1861–1865*. Pittsburgh, 1911.

Brewster, Charles Harvey. *When this Cruel War is Over: The Civil War Letters of Charles Harvey Brewster*. David W. Blight, ed. Amherst: The University of Massachusetts Press, 1992.

Buringame, M., and J.R.T. Ettlinger, eds. *Inside Lincoln's White House: The Complete Civil War Diary of John Hay*. Carbondale: Southern Illinois University Press, 1997.

Caldwell, J.F.J. *The History of a Brigade of South Carolinians known as "Gregg's" and Subsequently as McGowan's Brigade*. Philadelphia: King and Baird, 1866.

Clark, Charles A. *War Sketches and Incidents. "Campaigning with the Sixth Maine."* A paper read before the Iowa Commandery, Military Order of the Loyal Legion of the United States. Des Moines: The Kenyon Press, 1897.

Clark, Walter. *Histories of the Several Regiments and Battalions from North Carolina in the Great War, 1861–1865*. Goldsboro, North Carolina: Nash Brothers, 1901.

Cooke, John Esten. *Life of Gen. Robert E. Lee*. New York: D. Appleton, 1871.

Curtis, O.B. *History of the Twenty-fourth Michigan of the Iron Brigade.* Detroit: Winn and Hammond, 1891.

Cushing, Wainwright. *War Papers.* Vol. III: *"Charge of the Light Division at Marye's Heights, May 3, 1863."* Military Order of the Loyal Legion of the United States. Portland, Maine, 1898–1908.

Cutrer, Thomas, and Michael Parrish, eds. *Brothers in Gray.* Baton Rouge: Louisiana State University Press, 1997.

De Peyster, J.W. *Decisive Battles of the Civil War or Slaveholders Rebellion.* New York: MacDonald, 1867.

Dodge, Theodore A. *The Campaign of Chancellorsville.* 2nd ed. Boston: Ticknor & Fields, 1881.

Doubleday, Abner. *Chancellorsville and Gettysburg.* New York: C. Scribner's Sons, 1882.

Douglas, Henry Kyd. *I Rode With Stonewall.* Chapel Hill: The University of North Carolina Press, 1940.

Dowdey, Clifford, and Louis H. Manarin, eds. *The Wartime Papers of R. E. Lee.* Boston: Little Brown. 1961.

Early, Jubal A. *Autobiographical sketch and narrative of the War Between the States.* Philadelphia: J.B. Lippincott, 1912.

Edwards, Clark. *War Papers.* Vol. IV: *Personal Reminiscences of the 5th Maine Regiment.* Military Order of the Loyal Legion of the United States. Portland, Maine, 1898.

Evans, Clement E, ed. *Confederate Military History.* 12 vols. Atlanta: Confederate Publishing Company, 1899.

Fairchild, C.B. *History of the 27th New York Volunteers.* New York: Carl & Mathews, 1892.

Fox, William F. *Regimental Losses in the Civil War 1861–1865.* Albany: Brandow, 1898.

Fuller, Edwin H. *Battles of the 77th New York State Foot Volunteers.* New York: privately published, 1901.

Galloway, G. Norton. *The Ninety-Fifth Pennsylvania Volunteers in the Sixth Corps.* Philadelphia, 1884.

Gibbon, John. *Personal Recollections of the Civil War.* New York: G.P. Putnam's Sons, 1928.

Gordon, John B. *Reminiscences of the Civil War.* New York: Scribner's and Son, 1903.

Greiner, James, Janet Coryell, and James Smither, eds. *A Surgeon's Civil War: The Letters & Diary of Daniel M. Holt.* Kent, Ohio: Kent State University Press, 1994.

Haight, Theron W. *War Papers.* Vol. I. *"Among the Pontoons at Fitzhugh's Crossing."* Wisconsin: Military Order of the Loyal Legion of the United States, 1891–1914.

Haines, Alanson A. *History of the Fifteenth Regiment, New Jersey Volunteers.* New York: Jenkins & Thomas, 1883.

Hamblin, Deborah. *Brevet Major General Joseph Eldridge Hamblin 1861–1865.* Boston, 1902.

Handerson, Henry E. *Yankee in Gray: The Civil War Memoirs of Henry E. Handerson.* Clyde Lottridge Cummer, ed. Cleveland: Press of Western Reserve University, 1962.

Headley, P.C. *Massachusetts in the Rebellion.* Walker, Fuller, and Company, 1866.

Herbert, Hilary A. *"History of the Eighth Alabama Volunteer Regiment, C.S.A."* Maurice S. Fortin, ed. *Alabama Historical Quarterly* 39 (1977): 5–125.

Higginson, Thomas W. *Massachusetts in the Army and Navy, 1861–1865.* Boston: Wright and Potter, 1896.

Holcombe, R.I. *History of the First Regiment Minnesota Volunteers Infantry.* Stillwater, Minnesota: Easton & Masterman, 1916.

Hood, John Bell. *Advance and Retreat, Personal Experiences in the United States and Confederate States Armies.* New Orleans: 1880.

Hotchkiss, Jed, and William Allen. *The Battlefields of Virginia: Chancellorsville.* New York: D. Van Nostrand, 1867.

Houghton, Henry. *The Ordeal of the Civil War: A Recollection.* Montpelier: Vermont Historical Society.

Huey, Pennock. *A True History of the Charge of the Eighth Pennsylvania Cavalry at Chancellorsville.* Philadelphia, 1883.

Hyde, John, ed. *Civil War Letters of Thomas W. Hyde.* Boston: 1933.

Hyde, Thomas W. *Following the Greek Cross: Memories of the Sixth Army Corps.* Boston: Houghton, Mifflin, 1894.

Johnson, Pharris Deloach, ed. *Under The Southern Cross: Soldier Life with Gordon Bradwell and the Army of Northern Virginia.* Macon, Georgia: Mercer University Press, 1999.

Johnson, Robert, and Clarence Buel, eds. *Battles and Leaders of the Civil War.* 4 vols. New York: Century, 1887–1888.

Jones, William, ed. *Southern Historical Society Papers.* 52 vols. 1877–1959. Rpt. Wilmington, North Carolina: Broadfoot, 1990–92.

Jordan, David M. *"Happiness Is Not My Companion": The Life of General G. K. Warren.* Indianapolis: Indiana University Press, 2001.

Lane, Mills, ed. *"Dear Mother Don't Grieve for Me...": Letters from Georgia Soldiers in the Civil War.* Savannah: Beehive Press, 1977.

Lee, Susan Pendleton. *Memoirs of William Nelson Pendleton.* Philadelphia: Lippincott, 1893.

Livermore, Thomas L. *Numbers and Losses in the Civil War in America 1861–65.* Boston: Houghton, Mifflin, 1901.

Longstreet, James. *From Manassas to Appomattox: Memoirs of the Civil War in America.* Philadelphia: L.B. Lippincott, 1896.

Love, William DeLoss. *Wisconsin in the War of the Rebellion.* Chicago, 1866.

Malles, Edward, ed. *Bridge Building in Wartime: Colonel Wesley Brainerd's Memoir of the 50th New York.* Knoxville: The University of Tennessee Press, 1997.

Maness, Lonie E. "Lee vs. Sedgwick." *Confederate Veteran, 1893–1932.* Vol. III.

Mark, Penrose G. *Red, White, and Blue Badge: A History of the 93rd Regiment Pennsylvania Veteran Volunteers.* Harrisburg: Aughinbaugh Press, 1911.

Marshall, Jeffery D., ed. *A War of the People: Vermont Civil War Letters.* Hanover, New Hampshire: University Press of New England, 1999.

McClure, Alexander K. *Recollections of Half a Century.* Massachusetts: The Salem Press Company, 1902.

McIntosh, David G. *The Campaign of Chancellorsville.* Richmond, Virginia, 1915.

McMahon, Martin T. *General John Sedgwick: An Address Delivered Before the Vermont Officer's Reunion Society at their Sixteenth Annual Meeting at Montpelier, Nov. 11, 1880.* Rutland: Tuttle, 1880.

_____. *Proceedings of the Reunion Society of Vermont Officers 1864–1868.* Burlington, Vermont: Burlington Free Press, 1885.

_____. "The Sixth Army Corps." *United States Service Magazine.* Vol. V. 1866.

Meade, George G. *The Life and Letters of George Gordon Meade.* 2 vols. New York: Scibners's, 1903.

McKim, Randolph H. *A Soldier's Recollections: Leaves From The Diary Of A Young Confederate.* New York: Longman's, Greens, and Company. 1911.

More, Frank, ed. *The Rebellion Record: A Diary of American Events with Documents, Narratives, Illustrative Incidents, Poetry, Etc.* New York: Putnam's, 1863.

Nevins, Allen, ed. *A Diary of Battle: The Personal Journals of Colonel Charles S. Wainwright, 1861–1865.* New York: Harcourt, Brace & World, 1962.

Newell, Joseph K. *"Ours": Annals of the 10th Regiment Massachusetts Volunteers in the Rebellion.* Springfield, Massachusetts: C.A. Nichols, 1875.

Newton, Martin Curtis. *From Bull Run to Chancellorsville: The Story of the 16th New York Infantry.* New York: G.P. Putnam's Sons, 1906.

Nicolay, John G., and John Hay. *Abraham Lincoln: A History.* Paul M. Angle, ed. Chicago: The University of Chicago Press, 1966.

Oden, John P. "The End of Oden's War: A Confederate Captain's Diary." Michael Barton, ed. *Alabama Historical Quarterly,* 1981.

Owen, William M. *In Camp with the Washington Artillery.* Boston: Ticknor, 1885.

_____. "William M. Owen Diary." *Civil War Regiments: A Journal of the American Civil War,* Vol. 5, No. 1. Campbell, California, 1993.

Peck, T.S. *Revised Roster of Vermont Volunteers During The War Of The Rebellion 1861–66.* Montpelier, Vermont: Watchman, 1892.

Rhodes, Robert H., ed. *All For The Union: The Civil War Letters and Diary of Elisha Hunt Rhodes.* New York: Orion, 1985.

Richardson, Charles. The Chancellorsville Campaign: Fredericksburg to Salem Church. New York: Neale, 1907.

Ripley, Wm. Y.W. *Vermont Riflemen in the War for the Union 1861–1865: A History of Company F., First United States Sharp Shooters.* Rutland: Tuttle, 1863.

Roe, Alfred S. *The Tenth Regiment Massachusetts Volunteer Infantry.* Springfield: Nichols, 1909.

Ropes, John C. *Papers of the Military Historical Society of Massachusetts.* 15 Vols. Boston: Military Historical Society of Massachusetts, 1913.

Rosenblatt, Emil, and Ruth Rosenblatt, eds. *Hard Marching Every Day: The Civil War Letters of Private Wilbur Fisk, 1861–1865. (Anti-Rebel.)* Lawrence: University Press of Kansas, 1983.

Scott, Robert G., ed. *Fallen Leaves: The Civil War Letters of Major Henry Livermore Abbott.* Kent, Ohio: Kent State University Press, 1991.

Sedgwick, John. *Correspondence of John Sedgwick, Major General.* 2 vols. New York: The Di Vinne Press, printed for Carl and Ellen Battelle Stoeckel, 1902–1903.

Smith, A.P. *Seventy-Sixth New York.* New York: Cortland, 1867.

Smith, John D. *The History of the Nineteenth Regiment of Maine Volunteers Infantry.* Minneapolis: Great Western Printing, 1909.

Southern Historical Society Papers. Richmond, Vol. 1–52, 1876–1959.

Stevens, George T. *Three Years in the Sixth Corps.* New York, 1866.

Stevens, John H. *Civil War Diary.* Gladys Stevens Stuart and Adelbert M. Jakeman, Jr., eds. Miller Books, 1997.

Stiles, Robert. *Four Years Under Marse Robert.* New York: Neale, 1910.

Stine, J.H. *History of the Army of the Potomac.* Philadelphia: J.B. Rogers, 1893.

Swinten, William. *Campaigns of the Army of the Potomac: The Story of the Grand Army.* New York: Charles Scribner's Sons, 1882.

Taylor, John C. *History of the 1st Connecticut Heavy Artillery and the Siege Trains Operating Against Richmond 1862–1865.* Hartford, Connecticut: Case, Lockwood, Brainard, 1893.

Tomes, Robert. *The War with the South: A History of the Late Rebellion.* 3 vols. New York, 1866.

Tyler, Mason Whiting. *Recollections of the Civil War; With Many Original Diary Entries and Letters Written from the Seat of War and with Annotated References.*

Welch, Emily Sedgwick. *John Sedgwick, Major-General: A Biographical Sketch.* New York: The Divine Press, 1899.

William S. Tyler, ed. New York: G.P. Putnam's Sons, 1912.

Uhler, George H. "The Sixth Corps at Chancellorsville." *National Tribune,* November 28, 1901.

_____. "With Sedgwick at Fredericksburg during the Battle of Chancellorsville." *National Tribune,* January 6, 1887.

Unknown soldier, Letter signed F. written on May 12, 1863, published in the *Eutaw Whig & Observer.*

Walker, Francis A. *General John Gibbon in the II Corps.* Military Order of the Loyal Legion of the United States, 1887.

_____. *Second Army Corps.* New York: Charles Scribner's Sons, 1887.

War Papers Read Before the Commandery of the State of Maine, Military Order of the Loyal Legion of the United States. 4 vols. Portland: 1898–1908.

Welch, Spencer G. *A Confederate Surgeon's Letters to his Wife.* New York: Neale, 1911.

Weld, Stephan M. *War Diary and Letters of Stephen Minot Weld, 1861–1865.* Cambridge: Riverside Press, 1912.

Whitman, William E., and Charles H. True. *Maine in the War for the Union: A History of the Part Borne by the Maine Troops in the Suppression of the American Rebellion.* Lewiston, Maine: Nelson Dingley Jr., 1865.

Secondary Sources

Barker, Harold R. *History of the Rhode Island Combat Units in the Civil War.* 1964.

Beers, Henry P. *Guide to the Archives of the Government of the Confederate States of America.* Washington, 1968.

Boatner III, Mark M. *Civil War Dictionary.* New York: David Mckay, 1959.

Boritt, Gabor S. *Lincoln and the Economics of the American Dream.* Memphis: Memphis State University Press, 1978.

Catton, Bruce. *The Army of the Potomac: Glory Road,* Vol. 2. New York: Doubleday, 1952.

Davis, Danny. "Return to Fredericksburg." *The American Civil War.* September 1992.

Eckert, Ralph Lowell. *John Brown Gordon: Soldier. Southerner. American.* Baton Rouge: Louisiana State University Press, 1989.

Elliott, Joseph C. *Lee's Noble Soldier: Lieutenant General Richard Heron Anderson.* Dayton, Ohio: Morningside, 1985.

Foote, Shelby. *The Civil War: A Narrative,* 3 vols. New York: Random House, 1963.

Fortier, John. *15th Virginia Cavalry,* Lynchburg: H.E. Howard, 1993.

Freeman, Douglas Southall. *Lee's Lieutenants: A Study in Command.* 4 vols. New York: Charles Scribner's Sons, 1944.

Furgurson, Ernest B. *Chancellorsville 1863: Souls of the Brave.* New York: Knopf, 1992.

Harrison, Noel G. *Chancellorsville Battlefield Sites.* Lynchburg: H.E. Howard, 1990.

Hart, Albert Bushnell. *American Statesmen: Salmon Portland Chase.* John T. Morse, Jr., ed. Boston: Houghton, Mifflin, 1899.

Hassler, Jr., Warren W. *Commanders of the Army of the Potomac.* Baton Rouge, 1962.

Herbert, Walter H. *Fighting Joe Hooker.* Indianapolis: Bobbs-Merrill, 1944.

Katcher, Philip. *The Army of Robert E. Lee.* London: Arms and Armor Press, 1994.

Krick, Robert K. *Lee's Colonels: A Biographical Register of Field Officers in the Army of Northern Virginia.* Dayton, Ohio: Morningside House, 1992.

_____. *Parker's Virginia Battery.* 2nd ed. revised. Berryville, Virginia: Virginia Book Company, 1975.

Macartney, Clarence E. *Lincoln and His Generals.* New York: Books For Libraries Press, 1925.

Major, Duncan K. *The Battle of Chancellorsville, May 3, 1863, The Retreat of the Federal Army, May 5, 1863, The Federal Left in the Campaign of Chancellorsville, Including the Second Battle of Fredericksburg, May 3, 1863; The Action at Salem Church, May 3, and 4, 1863.* Army War College, Session 1911–1912. United States Army Military History Institute, Carlisle, Pennsylvania.

McClellan, H.B. *The Life and Campaigns of J.E.B. Stuart.* Boston: Houghton Mifflin, 1886.

Michie, Peter Smith. The Life and Letters of Emory Upton. New York: D. Appleton, 1885. Rpt, New York: Arno Press, 1979.

Mundy, James H. *No Rich Man's Sons: The Sixth Maine Volunteer Infantry.* Scarborough, Maine: Harp Publications, 1994.

Naisawald, L. Van Loan. *Grape and Canister: The Story of the Field Artillery of the Army of the Potomac.* New York: Oxford University Press, 1960.

Nolan, Alan T. *The Iron Brigade.* New York: Macmillan, 1961.

Nolan, Alan T., and Sharon Eggleston Vipond. *Giants in Their Tall Black Hats: Essays on the Iron Brigade.* Bloomington: Indiana University Press, 1998.

Parsons, George W. *Put the Vermonters Ahead: The First Vermont Brigade.* Shippensburg, Pennsylvania: White Maine, 1995.

Patterson, Gerard A. *From Blue to Gray: The Life of Confederate General Cadmus M. Wilcox.* Mechanicsburg, Pennsylvania: Stackpole, 2001.

Proft, R.J., and Mitch Demars, eds. *United States of America's Congressional Medal of Honor Recipients: Complete Official Citations.* Minnesota: Highland Publishing, 1980.

Rhodes, James F. *History of the United States from the Compromise of 1850.*

Sands, George H. *Historical Ride. Memorandum for May 13th, 1911. "Movements leading up to the 2nd Battle of Fredericksburg, to include Capture of Marye's Hill and Battle of Salem Church."* Unites States Army Military Institute, Carlisle, Pennsylvania.

Siegal, John D. *For the Glory of the Union: Myth, Reality, and the Media in Civil War New Jersey.* New York: Fairleigh Dickinson University Press, 1939.

Slade, A.D. *That Sterling Soldier: The Life of David A Russell.* Dayton, Ohio: Morningside, 1995.

Smith, Gerald J. *"One of the Most Daring of Men": The Life of Confederate General William Tatum Wofford.* Journal of Confederate History Series, Vol. XVI. John McGlone, series ed. Murfreesboro, Tennessee: Southern Heritage Press, 1997.

Stackpole, General Edward J. *Chancellorsville: Lee's Greatest Battle.* Harrisburg, Pennsylvania: Stackpole Books, 1958.

Stansbury, Haydon. *Aeronautics in the Union and Confederate Armies 1861–1865.* 2 vols. Baltimore: The John Hopkins Press, 1941.

Steele, Mathew F. *American Campaigns.* Washington: U.S. Infantry Association, 1935.

Swinfen, David B. *Ruggle's Regiment: The 122nd New York Volunteers in the American Civil War.* Lebanon, New Hampshire: University Press of New England, 1982.

Thomas, Emory M. *Robert E. Lee.* New York: W. W. Norton, 1995.

_____. *The Confederacy as a Revolutionary Experience.* Englewood Cliffs, New Jersey: Prentice Hall, 1971.

Trudeau, Noah. *Bloody Roads South: The Wilderness to Cold Harbor, May–June, 1864.* New York: Faucett and Colunbine, 1989.

Ward, David A. "Of Battlefields and Feuds: The 96th Pennsylvania Volunteers." *Civil War Regiments: A Journal of the American Civil War.* Vol. 3. Campbell, California, 1993.

Warner, Ezra J. *Generals in Blue.* Baton Rouge: Louisiana State University Press, 1964.

_____ *Generals in Gray.* Baton Rouge: Louisiana State University Press, 1959.

Weber, James. *The Northern Railroads in the Civil War.* New York, 1952.

Williams, T. Harry. *Lincoln And His Generals.* New York: Vintage Books, 1952.

Winslow, Richard Elliott III. *General John Sedgwick: The Story of a Union Corps Commander.* Novato, California: Presidio Press, 1982.

Wise, Jennings Cropper. *The Long Arm of Lee or The History of the Artillery Arm of the Army of Northern Virginia.* 2 vols. Lynchburg, Virginia: J.P. Bell, 1915.

Public Documents

Annual Report, Adjutant General, State of New York, Albany, 1863–1900.

Annual Report of the Adjutant General of the State of Maine, Vol. I, 1862–1867.

Annual Report of the Adjutant General of the State of Massachusetts, 1862–1866.

Annual Report of the Adjutant General of Pennsylvania Transmitted in Pursuance of Law, For The Year 1866. Harrisburg, 1867.

Annual Report of the Adjutant General of the State of Wisconsin: For the Years Ending 1863–65.

National Archives, Pension Records, Washington D.C.

National Archives, War Record Groups 94, 107, 109, 393, 404. Washington D.C.

National Park Service, Washington D.C. "Troop Movement Maps, Chancellorsville."

National Park Service, Washington D.C. "Topography of Chancellorsville Battlefield."

Report of the Adjutant and Inspector General of the State of Vermont, 1864–1865.

United States Christian Commission for the Army and Navy. For the Year 1863. Second annual report. Philadelphia, 1864.

United States Congress. *Report of the Joint Committee on the Conduct of War,* Senate Documents, 37th Congress, 3d Session, Washington, 1863.

United States Department of War, *Official Army Register of the Volunteer Force of the United States Army for the Years 1862, 1863.* Washington, 1865.

United States Department of War, *The War of the Rebellion: A Compilation of the Official Records of the Union and Confederate Armies.* 128 vols., Washington, 1880–1901. Supplement. Wilmington, N.C.: Broadfoot Publishing, 1994.

Newspapers

Bangor [Maine] Daily Whig & Courier, May 1863.
Brunswick Georgia News, May 1963
Harper's Weekly, May 23, 1863.
Newark Daily Journal, May 1863.
New York Herald, May 1863
New York Times, May 1863.
New York Tribune, May 9, 1863.
Piscataquis Observer. Dover, Maine, May 1863.
Portland [Maine] Daily Advertiser, May 1863.
Richmond Enquirer, May 1863.
Richmond Whig, May 1863.

Index

*Numbers in **bold italics** indicate pages with photographs or illustrations.*